THE YOUTH

OF

MADAME DE LONGUEVILLE,

OR

NEW REVELATIONS

OF

COURT AND CONVENT IN THE SEVENTEENTH CENTURY.

FROM THE FRENCH OF VICTOR COUSIN.

BY F. W. RICORD.

NEW YORK:
D. APPLETON & CO., 346 & 348 BROADWAY,
AND 16 LITTLE BRITAIN, LONDON.
M DCCC LIV.

TO

ABRAM COLES, M.D.,

OF NEWARK, N. J.,

AS A TRIBUTE TO HIS MANY VIRTUES,

AND AS A SMALL RETURN FOR HIS MANY KINDNESSES,

This Volume

IS RESPECTFULLY AND AFFECTIONATELY INSCRIBED

BY HIS FRIEND,

THE TRANSLATOR.

CONTENTS.

INTRODUCTION.

CHAPTER I.

1619 to 1635.

CHAPTER II.

1635 to 1642.

CHAPTER III.

1642 to 1644.

CHAPTER IV.

1644 to 1649.

PREFACE.

Villefore has written the life of Madame de Longueville, and it is not our intention to re-write it. We have only wished to penetrate into the intimacy of a lofty spirit, that inspires us with an especial interest, by the aid of the most reliable documents that history can employ — confidential correspondences, in which hearts, opening themselves far from the eye of the public, involuntarily reveal characters, that is to say, the truest causes of human events. In order to procure such documents, we have delved, with the perseverance of passion, in libraries public and private, and have succeeded in laying hands upon a very great number of unpublished letters, which have elucidated for us many obscure points in the life of Mme. de Longueville, of that of Condé, her brother, of their most celebrated contemporaries, male and female.

In default, then, of every other merit, this production will at least have that of offering to the reader things hitherto unknown, or scarcely perceived: for example, the interior, for the first time opened, of that great convent of the Carmelites of the *Rue Saint Jacques*, which served as an asylum to so many wounded hearts, where Mlle. de Bourbon was, as it were, brought up, and wished, at fifteen years of age, to bury her beauty and her genius; the graceful pastimes of her youth at the Louvre, at the hôtel de Rambouillet, at Chantilly, at Ruel, at Liancourt; her charming friends, her brilliant and valiant adorers; the skilful and too little appreciated politics of her father; the military education, and also the first loves of Condé; above all, that pure and touching Mlle. Du Vigean, worthy object of the tenderness of a hero, whom we have in some sort found again, whom we dare to put by the side of Mlle. de La Vallière.

For more than fifteen years, in our hours of leisure, we have dreamed of a work the most foreign to our ordinary labors, which has attracted us, and attached us by its very contrast. The great men, and particularly the great writers, of the seventeenth century, are almost our contemporaries; but the women were then not less remarkable than the men, and scarcely any of them, except Mme. de Sévigné, Mme. de La Fayette, and a very few others, are known; whilst there were everywhere, at the court and in the *salons* of Paris, in the brilliant country-seats of the aristocracy, and in the austere retreats of religion, women of great spirit and great heart, who doubtless knew not how to write like professional authors, who nevertheless wrote much, because it was the mode of the times, who would not write in a mediocre manner, with the thoughts and sentiments on which they had been nourished. We have therefore amused ourselves in searching for, and we have succeeded in discovering a literature wholly feminine, three-quarters unknown, which does not seem to us unworthy of having a place by the side of the manly literature in possession of universal admiration. Hence the project of a gallery of illustrious females of the seventeenth century, upon the model of the illustrious men of Perrault. We have given the first page of such a history in JACQUELINE PAS-

CAL;[1] and this is probably the last. Age is coming on; the heavens are growing dark; and we owe ourselves to more serious thoughts, to a great cause which we have heretofore served with the ardor and the energy of youth, which to-day, compromised by some, betrayed by others, claims our last efforts, and our highest devotion.[2] Nevertheless, we shall not regret the moments that we have given to these studies, somewhat light, if they can increase the knowledge of, and a taste for the most admirable epoch of our history, of that powerful French society of the seventeenth century, which is the more admired the more it is seen under its different aspects; when France was a spectacle to the nations, and marched at the head of humanity, when philosophy was an honor, as well as poetry and the arts, the religious spirit and the military spirit; when Descartes divided public esteem with Corneille and Condé; when Mme. de Grignan studied him with a passionate vivacity; when Bossuet and Arnauld, Fenelon and Malebranche, openly declared themselves his dis ciples. So that, to speak truly, at that common focus of the great and the beautiful, our literary predilections and our

---

[1] Fourth Series of our works, *Literature*, vol. ii.

[2] It remains for us to collect from all our writings the scattered elements of a new Theodicea, especially founded upon an exact Psychology, fecundated by a legitimate induction, with the double purpose of defending the great faith of the human race against the detestable philosophy which Germany, in these last times, has sent into France, after having borrowed it from her, and of defending also true and good philosophy against a pusillanimous devotion, unworthy of Christianity, and condemned by the Church, which refuses to human reason the right and the power of elevating itself, even to God. It especially remains to us to put the last hand to that translation of Plato, which we would make the least perishable monument of our philosophic enterprise.

philosophic faith are tied to each other in an intimate manner, and reciprocally vivify each other.

But if the seventeenth century has more than ever our admiration, we guard ourselves from the too much accredited error that confounds that century with the reign of Louis XIV. Surely Louis XIV. is for us also a great king. He had, what is rarest in the world, grandeur in character; that is his immortal glory. Moreover, he was reserved, attentive, laborious, capable of a firm and persistent course; but, it must be said, he was profoundly selfish, and loved his person and his family much more than France. He was radically deceived in the only two enterprises that originated in his own will,—the revocation of the Edict of Nantes, and the wars of the Succession. He left France humiliated, enfeebled, discontented, and already full of the germs of revolutions; whilst Henry IV., Richelieu, and Mazarin had transmitted it to him covered with glory, powerful and preponderant abroad, tranquil and satisfied at home. Louis XIV. terminates the seventeenth century: he did not inspire it, and he is far from being its perfect representative. It was under Henry IV., under Louis XIII., and under Queen Anne, that were born, formed, and even developed, the great statesmen and the great warriors, as well as the greatest writers of either sex, those even, like Madame de Sévigné and Bossuet, whose career was most prolonged. The influence of Louis XIV. made itself felt sufficiently late. He took the reins of government only in 1661, and at first he followed his times, and did not control them; he truly appeared himself, only when he was no longer guided by Lyonne and Colbert, the last disciples of Richelieu and Mazarin. It was then that, governing almost alone and superior to all around him, he placed everywhere the impress of his taste, in politics, in religion, in manners, in arts, and in letters. He substituted in every way simplicity for *naïveté*, nobility for grandeur, dignity for force, elegance for grace: he effaced characters, and polished, as it were, the surface of souls; he eradicated great vices and great virtues; he put the purely literary, and consequently the somewhat inferior school of Racine and Boileau in the place of that great school of virtue, politics, and war, instituted by Corneille; as heirs to Descartes, Pascal, and Bossuet, he gave Massillon, Fontenelle, and Voltaire—the true children of the end of the seventeenth century. After Madame de Sévigné, that rival of Molière, formed, like him, from 1640 to 1660, appeared Mme. de Maintenon, the model of the common-place, with her agreeable small-talk, Mme. de Coylus, Mme. de Stael, and Mme. Lambert. Add to that, as we have already said, the wholly gratuitous revocation of the Edict of Nantes, when Protestants, subdued, but protected, rivalled in zeal the Catholics for the service of the state, and when their most illustrious families were by degrees converted; add especially, the deplorable wars undertaken by Louis XIV., with a ministry of court clerks and generals, in order to put the crown of Spain on the head of his grandson, when in exchange for his pretensions, and without drawing the sword, he might have given Belgium to France; and you have the end of a reign that little resembles its beginning; for the beginning comes from a wholly different genius—from that genius which inspired Henry IV., Richelieu, and Mazarin, dictated the Edict of Nantes, the treaty of Munster, and that of the Pyrenees, the Cid, Polyeucte, and Cinna, the Discours de la Methode, and the Provinciales, Don Juan, and the Misanthrope, and the most pathetic sermons of Bossuet. It is genius that we recall, and glorify everywhere in this work; because to our eyes it is the genius itself of France at the epoch of her true greatness.

If the public receives these studies somewhat favorably,

we shall offer to it their sequel; we will exhibit also Mme. de Longueville during the Fronde, and after her conversion, from 1649 to 1680. It is certainly not the least beautiful part of the seventeenth century.

V. Cousin.

December 15, 1852.

MADAME DE LONGUEVILLE.

INTRODUCTION.

The person of Madame de Longueville—Description of contemporaries—Authentic portraits—Her wit and style—Her character—Explanation of her conduct in the Fronde—Mademoiselle de La Vallière and Madame de Longueville.

THERE are three well-defined periods in the life of the Duchess de Longueville.[1]

Born in 1619, in the castle of Vincennes, during the captivity of her father, Henri de Bourbon, prince de Condé, whose imprisonment was shared by his young wife, that celebrated beauty, Charlotte Marguerite de Montmorency, we at first see Mademoiselle de Bourbon, growing in graces by the side of such a mother, dividing her time between the convent of the

---

[1] See the work of Villefore: *The Life of Madame the Duchess de Longueville*, in two parts. There are two somewhat different editions. The first, which we shall quote, is of 1738, without indication of place; the second of Amsterdam, 1739.

Carmelites and the hôtel de Rambouillet, nourishing her heart with pious emotions and romantic reading; going to a ball, but with an under-garment of hair-cloth; sharing the confidence of a hero, her brother, the Duke d'Enghien; sympathizing with him in his love of the beautiful Mademoiselle Du Vigean, and witnessing her entrance into a cloister, where she herself is destined at last to die. At the age of twenty-three years she marries M. de Longueville, who is forty-seven, and who, instead of making up for this disparity, by an assiduous tenderness, continues in the suite of the saddest coquette of the time, the famous Duchess de Montbazon. Outraged by this rival, unprotected by a husband, who is even incapable of jealousy, she yields little by little to the contagion which surrounds her; and returning to Paris, after passing some time amid the magnificent distractions of the embassy of Munster, she suffers herself to be captivated by the wit, grand air, and chivalrous appearance of Prince de Marcillac, afterwards Duke de La Rochefoucauld. This liaison shapes her life, and closes its first period in 1648.

The Fronde with its vicissitudes; love—such as it was understood at the hôtel de Rambouillet, the love of Corneille and Scudéry—with its enchantments and its griefs, mingled with dangers and glory, crossed by a thousand adventures, the vanquisher of the rudest obstacles, and yielding to its own infirmities—in fine, exhausting itself;—such is the second period, so short and so full, beginning in 1648, and closing in the midst of 1654.

From this time the whole life of Madame de Longueville is one long, austere penance, performed successively in Normandy, near her aged husband, among the Carmelites, at Port Royal, and finally concluded in 1679.

Thus at first a spotless reputation, then faults, then expiation divide the career of Madame de Longueville.

It is in this order that we have collected, and that we shall present all that patient research has enabled us to gather concerning Madame de Longueville. We shall give political and religious writings, and especially confidential letters, thrown off from her pen during every important moment of her life, and which exhibit it in a manner equally faithful and agreeable.

But if the writings and letters which we are about to publish, elucidate the character of Madame de Longueville, it is quite as true that the character, well comprehended, explains them and places them in their true light. To introduce and give interest to a work, it is usual to begin with some details respecting its author; and as in this case the author is a woman, it is necessary to become acquainted with her person, as well as with her mind and her heart.

I.

Anne Geneviève de Bourbon was the daughter, as we have said, of that Charlotte Marguerite de Montmorency, Princess de Condé, who had turned the head of Henry IV., and whom, it is said, he wished to snatch from the hands of her jealous husband, at the risk of setting all Europe in commotion. The daughter was at least as beautiful as the mother, and this was a principal advantage of Madame de Longueville, which, we confess, possesses for us no ordinary attractions.

Beauty extends its prestige to posterity itself, and attaches a charm, for centuries, to the name alone of the privileged creatures upon whom it has pleased God to bestow it. But I speak of true beauty. This is not less rare than genius and virtue. Beauty has also its epochs. It does not belong to all men and to all ages to taste it in its exquisite truth. As there are fashions which spoil it, there are periods which affect its sentiment. For example, it became the eighteenth century to invent pretty women—those charming dolls, perfumed and powdered, affecting the attractions which they do not possess under their vast hoops and great furbelows. It was quite sufficient to prattle in a *salon*, to write *Lettres peruviennes*, to serve as models for the heroines of the younger Crébillon, and to turn the heads of the heroes of Rosbach. Those of Rocroy and of Lens, the contemporaries of Richelieu, of Descartes, and of Corneille, the energetic and somewhat rude men who preceded Louis XIV., and who delighted in a life of agitation, but to end it like Pascal and Rancé, would not have been tempted to bend the knee before such frail idols. Let us dare to say that the foundation of true beauty, as of true virtue, as of true genius, is force. Shed over this force a ray of heaven, elegance, grace, delicacy, and you have beauty. Its perfect type is the Venus of Milo;[1] or again, that pure and mysterious apparition, goddess or mortal, which is called the Psyche, or the Venus of Naples.[2] Beauty is certainly to be seen in the Venus de Medicis, but in this we feel that it is declining, or about to decline. Look at, not the women of Titian, but the virgins of Raphael and of Leonardi: the face is of infinite delicacy, but the body evinces strength; they will disgust you forever with the shadows and

---

[1] Quatremère de Quincy: *Dissertation upon the Antique Statue of Venus, discovered in the Island of Milo*, in 4°; and *Collection of Archeological Dissertations*, 1836, in 8°, p. 143.

[2] Millengen: *Ancient Unedited Monuments*, in fol.: London, 1826, p. 15, plate viii.

monkeys *à la Pompadour*. Adore grace, but do not in every thing separate it too much from force, for without force grace soon shares the fate of the flower that is separated from the stem which animates and sustains it.

It was Florence, it was its artists and its princes, that carried into France the sentiment of true beauty. Here it was rapidly developed, and, for various reasons which I cannot now even point out, it reigned among us until near the close of the XVIIth century.

What a train of accomplished women this century presents to us! women who were loaded with admiration, drawing after them all hearts, and spreading from rank to rank that worship of beauty which throughout all Europe received the name of French gallantry! They accompany this great century in its too rapid course; they mark its principal epochs, beginning with Charlotte de Montmorency, and finishing with Madame de Montespan. Between these place the lady of the High Constable of Luynes, afterwards Duchess de Chevreuse, Madame de Hautefort, Madame de Montbazon, Madame de Guéménée, Madame de Châtillon, Marie de Gonzague, afterwards Queen of Poland, her sister the Palatine, and so many others, among whom, to my extreme regret, I dare not mention Mademoiselle de

La Vallière, and yet am compelled to place Madame de Maintenon.

Madame de Longueville has her place in this dazzling gallery. She had all the characteristics of true beauty, joining to it a peculiar charm.

She was of good stature and of an admirable form. Embonpoint with all its advantages were not wanting to her. She possessed, as I cannot doubt in examining the authentic portraits before me, that kind of attraction so much prized during the XVIIth century, and which, with beautiful hands, had made the reputation of Anne of Austria. Her eyes were of the most tender blue. Her fine light hair, descending in large ringlets, displayed the graceful contour of her face, and overspread her admirable shoulders, much exposed, according to the fashion of the times. Behold the foundation of true beauty. Add to it a complexion whose whiteness, delicacy, and tempered lustre have given it the name of pearly. This charming complexion displayed every shade of sentiment that crossed her soul. In speech she was most gentle. Her gestures, with the expression of her countenance, and the sound of her voice, produced the completest music; such is the language of a disinterested contemporary, a Jansenist, Nicole, perhaps, who describes her as "the most perfect actress in the world." But her peculiar charm consisted in a graceful ease, a languor, as all her contemporaries expressed it, which would change to the highest degree of animation when passion seized her, but which usually gave her an air of indolence and aristocratic carelessness, mistaken sometimes for *ennuie*, sometimes for disdain. I have observed this air in but one person in all France, and this person has left a memory so pure, I may say so holy, that I dare not name her in this connection, even to compare her with Madame de Longueville.

Believe me, I am not drawing upon my fancy for a portrait. I confine myself strictly to the best authorities. I will cite them, if necessary, to prove my perfect exactness.

Let us begin with him who knew her best, and who certainly has not flattered her. "This princess," says La Rochefoucauld in his *Mémoires*,[1] "had all the advantages of mind and beauty in such perfection, that it seemed as if nature had in her taken peculiar pleasure in forming a masterpiece."

Listen also to Cardinal de Retz, a very good judge in such matters, and who would have gladly taken the place of La Rochefoucauld. "In regard to Madame de Longueville, the small-pox had marred

---

[1] The only two good and complete editions are those of Renouard, 1804 and 1817, and that of the collection of Petitot. See this last vol. 51, p. 455.

her original beauty,[1] but it had left her nearly all its brilliancy, and this brilliancy, joined to her quality, her wit, and her languor, which in her possessed a peculiar charm, rendered her one of the most amiable persons in France."[2] And elsewhere: "She had a languor in her manner more touching than the animation of those who were more beautiful."

After consulting her male contemporaries, let us examine the opinions of those of her own sex. We may, it would seem, believe them when they eulogize the beauty of another. Observe what Madame de Motteville says in several places concerning that of Madame de Longueville: "Mademoiselle de Bourbon was beginning to display the first charms of that angelic face which has since become so celebrated."[3] "If Madame de Longueville[4] exerted great influence in this way (by her mind and fortune), the influence of her beauty was not less powerful; for although the small-pox had, since the regency, somewhat injured the perfection of her complexion, the brilliancy of her charms attracted those who saw her; and she possessed in the highest degree what the Spanish

---

[1] This disease attacked her during the year of her marriage. Scarcely any trace of it remained.

[2] Retz, Amsterdam, 1731, vol. i., p. 185. Ibid., vol. iv., p. 219.

[3] *Memoirs*, Amsterdam, 1750, vol. i., p. 44.

[4] Vol. ii., p. 16-17.

language expresses by those words—*donayre*, *brio*, *y byzarria* (gallant air). She had an admirable form, and her personal appearance had a charm whose power extended even over our own sex. It was impossible to see her without loving her, and without desiring to please her. Her beauty, however, consisted more in the coloring of her face than in the perfection of her features. Her eyes were not large, but beautiful, soft, and brilliant, and their blue was admirable; it was similar to that of the turquoise. Poets could compare the white and incarnation of her face to lilies and roses only; and the light shining hair which accompanied so many other wonderful things, made her resemble an angel, such as our feeble nature can conceive one, rather than a woman:

> 'Poca grana y mucha nieve
> Van competiendo en su cara,
> Y entre lirios y iasmines
> Assomanse algunas rosas.' "

To these different passages from Madame de Motteville, we would add a single line from the great Mademoiselle, who was not troubled with extreme benevolence: "Madame de Longueville was old; Mademoiselle de Bourbon was young and beautiful as an angel."[1]

---

[1] *Memoirs*, Amsterdam, 1735, vol. i., p. 45.

And the angelic air as well as the pearly complexion must have belonged to Madame de Longueville in a peculiar manner, since we again find these expressions in an unpublished letter[1] of another female of the same period, Mademoiselle de Vaudy, who writes to Madame de Longueville in 1655: "Though your Highness had not the tint of the pearl, the mind and the sweetness of an angel. . . . ." Does not this unintentional agreement of different persons prove the general effect produced by Madame de Longueville, and the justness of the comparisons naturally suggested by her beauty?

This fortuitous and striking harmony authorizes and fully justifies the language, which might otherwise be suspected, of Scudéry, in the dedication of *Artamène ou le Grand Cyrus:* "The beauty which you possess in the highest degree . . . . is not the most remarkable of your gifts, although an object of wonder to all the world. Doubtless we realize in your Highness the most perfect idea, whether it be of form, of which yours is so beautiful and so noble, or of majestic bearing, or of beautiful hair, or of bril-

[1] Library of the Arsenal, Manuscripts of Conrart, in fol., vol. viii., p. 145. On Mademoiselle de Vaudy, the relative and friend of Madame the Countess de Maure, see Mademoiselle, vol. iii., p. 58, and vol. v., p. 25, as well as her portrait among the portraits of Mademoiselle. See also Tallemant, vol. ii., p. 334.

liancy, as well in the eyes, in the clearness and vivacity of complexion, in the just proportion of all the features, and in that modest and gallant air, which is the soul of beauty."[1]

Not content with this description, Scudéry has taken it up again, and, as we would now-a-days say, illustrated it with a portrait of Madame de Longueville, just as Chapelain, in dedicating *La Pucelle* to her husband, placed the portrait of that prince at the beginning of his work. This leads us to say a few words in regard to the different portraits which we have seen of Madame de Longueville; they pre-

[1] In an obscure work, entitled, *The Life of Pierre Dubosc, Minister of the Holy Gospel, enriched with Letters, Harangues*, etc., Rotterdam, 1698, in-8o, I find a speech made to Madame de Longueville, at Caen, in June, 1648, in which the good Protestant minister speaks of her very much like Scudéry, p. 328: "The portrait, Madame, which fame has made of you, is known throughout the world; and it is so full of marvels that every one supposes the original to be flattered until he has the happiness of seeing you. Then all admit that what the public voice says of your Highness is but a pencil-sketch of what you are. . . . It is impossible to paint too well that agreeable mixture of sweetness and majesty which tempers your countenance, and which at once gives boldness and fear to those who have the honor to approach your person. It is impossible to express that inimitable address which appears in all your actions, that brilliant vivacity so admired in your words, that graceful and grand air which causes your silence to be respected. And what pencil can represent that mind, formed by the hand of the Graces and cultivated by that of the Muses, which produces nothing in you but that is judicious, delicate, brilliant, which gains for you the admiration of the age, the rapture of the court, the applause of the provinces, which has even merited the homage of enemies at Munster, bringing them to your feet, while they refused peace to all Europe."

sent her to us in the gracefulness of youth, in the full splendor of all her charms, in her maturity.

King Louis-Philippe conceived the happy idea of assembling at Versailles, in the galleries of the second floor, all the portraits which he could collect of the celebrated personages of France. Among them we find[1] a portrait of Madame de Longueville in youth, by the side of her father, Henri de Bourbon, and of her mother, Charlotte de Montmorency. It is unfortunately a copy. A note placed behind the frame says that this copy was made from an original painting of Ducayer executed in 1634. Mademoiselle de Bourbon, born in 1619, was then but fifteen years old. It is impossible to see or to imagine a more charming creature. All the signs of her future great beauty are already visible; certain attractions are still wanting, but the strength which promises and assures them is stamped upon every part.

We again behold her, after her marriage, and during the embassy of Munster, in 1646 and 1647. She is now twenty-seven or twenty-eight years of age. Anselm Van Hull is the author of this portrait. It is a bust, with a highly ornamented frame. The young woman has well preserved all that the young girl promised. The forms of beauty are developed.

---

[1] Attique du Nord, No. 2178.

Her tresses are magnificent. She has the collar of pearls, which seldom quits her. This portrait is engraved in the collection of the negotiators of Munster.[1]

That which is prefixed to the first volume of the *Grand Cyrus* represents Madame de Longueville in 1649.[2] Her age at this period is thirty years. This engraving is by Regnesson, brother-in-law of Nanteuil, after Chauveau. There are also two other engravings, slightly differing from each other, one by Moncornet, the other by Frosne. Among the enamel pictures of Petitot, in the museum of the Louvre, is one, in our opinion, ordinary enough, marked No. 50, which is referred to Madame de Longueville. All these portraits are of nearly the same period, and give her the same character of beauty, strength, and ampleness of form, face more full than in Van Hull, and a more marked embonpoint. To the honor of Scudéry, it must be said that the passages from the dedication of the *Grand Cyrus*, which we have quoted, may serve as a faithful text to the engraving

---

[1] *Pacificatores orbis Christiani, sive icones principum, ducum et legatorum qui Monasterii atque Osnabrugæ pacem Europæ reconciliarunt, quosque singulos ad nativam imaginem expressit Van Hull, celissimi principis Auriaci dum viveret pictor*, in folio, Rotterodami, 1697. This portrait has been often reproduced, among others, in the *Europe illustre* and the Collection of Odieuvre.

[2] This is, in fact, the date of the first edition of the first part, as given in the patent, printed January 7, 1649.

which accompanies them. Here are those light tresses, those eyes so soft, that complexion of dazzling brightness, and I may add that graceful and noble dress so becoming to beauty, even as the female dress of the eighteenth century seems to have been invented for ugliness itself.

Finally, the museum of Versailles[1] contains another portrait of Madame de Longueville, attributed to Mignard. It is easy to recognize in it the noble lady, whose image is prefixed to the *Grand Cyrus.* It is truly Madame de Longueville, with that grand air and amiable languor, which every one attributes to her. She is sitting, dressed in a rich court costume, and holding a bouquet of flowers in her hand.

Let us not forget to mention a beautiful silver medallion,[2] without date, and without engraver's name, which represents her at nearly the same age as the portrait of Versailles, in her beautiful maturity, and in the opulence of her charms.[3]

---

[1] Gallery of the first floor, No. 2195.

[2] Cabinet of Medallions, with this inscription: An. Gen. Borbonia, D. Long, S. P. Novi Castri. On the other side of the medal is the portrait of her husband.

[3] There should be at the Chateau d'Eu a portrait of Madame de Longueville, 22 inches by 18, which comes from the old collection of the Duchess de Montpensier. See vol. ii., p. 124, the work of M. Vatout, entitled, *Historical and Descriptive Catalogue of the Pictures belonging to his Royal Highness the Duke of Orleans.* 4 vols., in-8°, 1823. It is so long since we have seen this portrait, that we cannot say at what period it represents Madame de Longueville, wherein it differs from or resem-

Even after her conversion, and when she had entirely renounced the world, she preserved a portion of her beauty; and a gentleman who saw her at this time at the house of her brother, the Prince de Condé, declared[1] that the progress of age was scarcely visible upon her; that her piety became her; that her candor, her modesty, and her sweetness, ennobled by her air of dignity, rendered her at this period as capable of pleasing as ever.

II.

In describing the person of Madame de Longueville, we find ourselves tracing the character of her mind and of her soul.

Her mind has received the homage of the most delicate connoisseurs. We have seen that La Rochefoucauld, Retz, and Madame de Motteville praise it as much as they do her beauty. Retz urges particularly that this mind owed every thing to nature, and almost nothing to study, its indolence removing it from every effort in ordinary things. "Madame de

---

bles other portraits of her, or by what hand it was produced. It is perhaps the portrait which is at Versailles. Father Lelong mentions the following portraits of Madame de Longueville: 1, Van Hull; 2, Poilly, in fol. (We have not found this portrait in the work of Poilly in the Stamp-Office. See note, p. 363.) 3, Frosne; 4, Moncornet; 5, the collection of Odieuvre.

[1] Villefore, 2d part, p. 170.

Longueville," says he, "has naturally a great fund of wit, but she has still more finesse and tact. Her capacity, which has not been aided by her indolence, is not exercised upon business matters,[1] etc." And speaking of the languor of her manners: "She had even a languor of the mind, which was charming, because it had, if we may so speak, luminous and startling awakenings." Madame de Motteville coincides with the Cardinal de Retz: "This princess . . . was very indolent."[2] The occupation furnished by the applause of the great world, which ordinarily regards with too much admiration the fine qualities of persons of rank, had deprived Madame de Longueville of opportunities for reading and for storing her mind sufficiently to be called learned.[3] She was indeed far enough from this, and did not pique herself at all upon her acquirements. While her two brothers, the Prince de Condé and the Prince de Conti, had studied assiduously with the Jesuits of Bourges and of Paris, Mademoiselle de Bourbon had received, under the direction of her mother, nothing more than the simple instructions given in those times to women. A happy disposition and social intercourse with the choice spirits around her supplied every thing. Even at an early age she

[1] Retz, vol. i., p. 219.

[2] Ibid., vol. iii., p. 59.

[3] Retz, vol. ii., p. 18.

acquired a great reputation, and I find that while yet a child she was loaded with praises and even with dedications. I have now before me a *pastoral tragic comedy*, entitled *Uranie*,[1] which a certain Bridard dedicated to her in 1631, that is, when she was twelve years old. This Bridard says to her: "The most perfect courtiers know that you have a mind far before your years. I can myself testify to this, having heard you recite verses with so much grace, that one might suppose that an angel, borrowing your beauty, had descended upon the earth to discourse upon the wonders of heaven." I quote this passage from that book forgotten, and justly forgotten, because it forestalls all those of Madame de Motteville, of Mademoiselle de Montpensier, and of Mademoiselle de Vaudy. At twelve years we find her an *angel*, and so called ever afterwards. From early youth she had, with her brother, the Duke d'Enghien, frequented the hôtel de Rambouillet; and the *salons* of the Rue Saint Thomas du Louvre were not the most proper school for a mind characterized by grandeur and finesse, but a grandeur tending to the romantic, and a finesse often degenerating into subtility—a mind, too, like that of Corneille, the perfect representative of its epoch. It

---

[1] In-12. We possess the copy of the dedication which belonged to Mademoiselle de Bourbon, and which bears her arms.

seems, however, that the hôtel de Rambouillet did not fasten upon her its likes and dislikes, for one day, while listening to the reading of *La Pucelle* of Chapelain, so praised in this quarter, and hearing the remarks upon its pretended beauties—"Yes," said she,[1] "it is very beautiful, but it is very tiresome!" Somewhat in the same manner her brother, the great Condé, defended Corneille against the rules, exclaiming that he could not pardon rules which forced the Abbé d'Aubignac to write such bad tragedies. She was everywhere proclaimed the sovereign judge of all writings, the queen of wit, the arbiter of taste and of elegance, as Horace says. In 1649, in the quarrel concerning the two sonnets of Benserade and of Voiture, the whole court took the part of Benserade; but Madame de Longueville having declared herself in favor of Voiture, every one went over to her side. And at this period of her life she must have yielded to the prevailing taste, and must have been somewhat of a *précieuse*, for Madame de Motteville, in speaking of the principal beauty of her mind, which lay in delicacy of thought, accuses her of affectation, adding immediately, as if to excuse herself for finding any blemish in so accomplished a person: "All men partake of that clay

---

[1] Villefore, p. 75.

from which they originate, and God alone is perfect."[1]

All agree in saying that she conversed divinely, and with an exquisite mixture of vivacity and sweetness. The charm of her conversation must have been very extraordinary to have survived her youth and her worldly life, and still subsist in devotion and penitence. The Jansenist writer who left us a portrait, or, as it was then called, a *character* of Madame de Longueville,[2] does not hesitate to compare, and almost prefer her, to one of the most intellectual men, and most celebrated cenversationists, of the XVIIth century, M. de Tréville.[3] "The manner in which Madame de Longueville conversed is something to be studied. . . . Every thing that she said was so well said, that it would have been difficult, even with much study, to say it better. There were more lively and rare things in what M. de Tréville uttered, but there was more delicacy, and more spirit and good sense in Madame de Longueville's manner of expression."

---

[1] Vol. ii., p. 19. [2] Ibid., p. 7.

[3] Boileau, in his letter to Perrault, places the Count de Tréville among the nicest judges of wit. Saint-Simon undertakes to paint him, vol. iv., p. 184, and thus finishes his portrait, vol. vi., p. 372: He had belonged "to the great world, at one time a courtier, then a devotee and recluse, again, by degrees, an active member of the best society, always gallant, full of wit, and of the most refined taste." He had loved Madame, the amiable Henriette, and the beautiful de Ludre. See the

But to speak and to write are two very different things, each demanding a particular cultivation; and that Madame de Longueville did not study, is evident as soon as she takes up the pen. Her great natural qualities showed themselves with difficulty through the faults of every kind which resulted from her inexperience. It is in fact no small affair to express one's sentiments and ideas in a natural order, with their true shades, and in terms neither too nice nor too vulgar, terms which neither exaggerate nor enfeeble them. It is not unusual to find men full of wit, enthusiasm, and grace when they speak, and who, when they take up the pen, become contemptible. It is because writing is an art, a very difficult art, and which must have been learned. Madame de Longueville was entirely ignorant of it, and so were the most eminent women of her time. I have elsewhere[1] spoken of Madame Angelique Arnaud and of Jacqueline Pascal, who, though highly gifted, have left but very imperfect works. All are unanimous in representing the Princess Palatine as a per-

---

Memoirs of Lafare and Madame de Sévigné, letter of the 18th March, 1671. It is said that the observation, *he talks like a book*, was first made concerning him. He is the *Arsène* of the *charactères* of La Bruyère. I have seen some of his unpublished letters; the language is the best, but for any thing else they are not remarkable.

[1] IVth Series of our works, LITTÉRATURE, vol. ii., *Jacqueline Pascal*, p. 20.

son of great mind, who treated the greatest men as their equal. Retz[1] and Bossuet[2] affirm this, and I believe them, for in this matter they were better judges than I. Read, however, some of the manuscript letters of the Palatine. They are not, certainly, deficient in respect to solidity, finesse, and ingenuity; but I am forced to admit that they are often full of inaccuracies, that their construction is very awkward, and that the most common rules of orthography are sometimes outrageously violated. I do not conclude from this that the Palatine had not a mind of the first order, but simply that she had not been taught the art of writing properly her sentiments and thoughts. In this Madame de Longueville was no better skilled. Thus, all that we shall publish from her pen exhibits at once the beauty of her genius and the defects of her education.

With these women who write so well and so badly, we may contrast Madame de Sévigné and Madame de La Fayette, who always write well. To be just, however, it seems to me that we should take into consideration two very important things.

In the first place, these two ladies had received an

---

[1] *Memoirs*, vol. i., p. 221: "I do not believe that Queen Elizabeth of England had more capacity for State affairs."

[2] *Oraison funèbre de la Princesse Palatine.*

education altogether different from that given to Madame de Longueville; they had been under the tuition of skilful masters of language and of literature, among whom was one of the most learned men of the seventeenth century, who at the same time made the greatest pretensions to wit, gentility, and gallantry. Ménage had, during their youth and even after their marriage, taught Mademoiselle de Rabutin, and afterwards Madame de Lavergne, not only the French language as it was spoken and written by the Academy, but the language of the wits of the time, the Italian, and even somewhat of the Latin; he excused them from the Greek alone. He exercised them in writing, pointing out their errors, cultivating their happy instincts, polishing and regulating their mind and style. He retained them for a considerable time under this discipline, which was indeed highly agreeable to himself. Their professor was also their Platonic admirer, more Platonic than he perhaps desired. He addressed to them stanzas, sonnets, idyls, madrigals, and all sorts of verses in French, in Italian, and in Latin. He celebrated by turns the *formosissima Laverna* and the *bellissima Marchesa di Sevigni.*[1] He certainly would not have

---

[1] Ægidii Menagii Pœmata, since the first edition, which is of 1652, in-4°, Ægidii Menagii Miscellanea, until the Elzeverian edition, more complete, of 1663. In this there are more than twenty French, Latin,

taken the trouble to compose, in honor of their wit and charms, Latin and Italian verses which they might have been unable to comprehend. On the contrary, both of them wrote very well in Italian.[1] In a manuscript correspondence of Madame de La Fayette, lately in my possession, I have found more than one allusion to the time when, thus to speak, she pursued her studies under Ménage.[2] Nature had

---

and Italian pieces to Madame de La Fayette before and after her marriage. Madame de Sévigné does not appear so often; but, as an offset, she is seen in the edition of 1652, both under her own name and under that of Uranie. The study of the different editions of the poems of Ménage would not be useless in a history of Madame de Sévigné and of Madame de La Fayette.

[1] See the Italian Sonnet of Madame de Sévigné, published by M. de Montmerqué.

[2] This correspondence was sold at Sens, in 1849, at the sale of M. Tarbé. I examined it for several hours. It is composed of about seventy-six letters, all unpublished, and runs over almost all the life of Madame de La Fayette. We here find that Ménage felt a passion for his beautiful pupils. Repulsed and discouraged rather quickly by Marie de Chantil, he turned to her relative, Mademoiselle de Lavergne, with no better fortune, but without experiencing so much neglect. The intercourse of Ménage with Mademoiselle de Lavergne continued even after her marriage to the Count de La Fayette, became more intimate during her widowhood, and continued even until her death. Madame de La Fayette coquetted evidently with her Latin and Italian master, and for some time their relations were intimate but not tender. Finally, they became good and perfect friends. Several letters show with what care Madame de La Fayette had studied under Ménage the poets and good writers, both ancient and modern. She consults him, and refers to their disputes in regard to the use of such and such an expression. She speaks continually of their common friend, Huet, who wrote for *Zaïde* a dissertation on the origin of the romance. There are a few lines about Segrais. I do not remember seeing the name of La Rochefou-

done every thing for Madame de Sévigné: it had given her perfect exactness and solidity, with inexhaustible playfulness and sparkling vivacity. Art and genius united, made of her the incomparable letter-writer who left Balzac and Voiture a thousand leagues behind, and whom Voltaire himself has not surpassed. Like a mad and ignorant person, she appears to defy every thing; but in her boldest strokes she never miscalculates, which is an infallible sign of a finished art. Observe again, that if Madame de Sévigné wrote well, it was because she knew that her letters would be shown; but of this she does not betray the least suspicion: it is true that she wrote nothing but letters; I even doubt whether she could have written a book, and I could not imagine her engaged upon a romance, or upon any work whatever, except, perhaps, memoirs and satires, like those of her Cousin Bussy or Saint-Simon, or perhaps upon theological treatises like those of her daughter,

---

cauld once mentioned. This was perhaps a delicate subject, upon which the beautiful lady did not consult her learned friends. What existed between the duke and the countess did not concern the Abbé Huet and the Abbé Ménage. It was only to the Marchioness de Sévigné, or to the Marchioness de Sablé, that she would speak on such a matter. Besides, in this collection, we have only the letters or rather notes of Madame de La Fayette; not one of Ménage. Most of them are autographs, some dictated and signed, all perfectly authentic. M. Tarbé made a copy of this correspondence, which was sold with the autographs. It belongs now to M. Feuillet.

Madame de Grignan.[1] This was not the case with Madame de La Fayette. She was not only a person of great wit and information, but she was also an author. It is not surprising that she knew how to write, since she made a profession of it. An exquisite polish is her prominent characteristic, and it may be in part referred to the literary discipline which she preserved much longer than her friend; it may also be accounted for by the fact that she never wrote a word without submitting it to that same Ménage, to Sagrais, who resided with her, and who, if he did not lend her his pen, aided her with his counsels and his name, to Huet, or to La Rochefoucauld. Madame de La Fayette is certainly far superior to Madame de La Suze, to Madame de Brégy, to Madame Deshoulières, to Mademoiselle de Scudéry, to Madame d'Aulnoy, to Madame Lambert, but she belongs to their family. Although she passed her life with Madame de Sévigné, she differs from her essentially, and she belongs, too, to a very different world from that of Madame de Longueville.

But it is important to remember that Madame de Longueville preceded, by several years, the two il-

[1] See the dissertation of Madame de Grignan on the *Pure Love* of Fénelon, in vol. x. of the works of Madame de Sévigné, p. 518, edition Montmerqué.

lustrious friends, and that, early separated from the world, and buried in retirement during the last twenty-five years of her life, she was unable to profit by the then rapid progress of language and taste. There are in fact two very different parties in the literature of the seventeenth century: that of Louis XIII. and of the Regency, represented by Corneille and Pascal; and that which is particularly the work of Louis XIV., of which Racine and Fénelon are the most accomplished expression. In one we find a grandeur somewhat uncouth; in the other a charming art, sometimes felt too sensibly. In the style as well as in the conversation of the women of the seventeenth century, we observe prolixity, carelessness, and even incorrectness, for the language which they write or speak is not settled. They are neither able to choose between their thoughts, nor to give them that happy turn, that precision and elegance which, thanks to the superabundance of genius, became so common at the close of the century. But their attainment to all great things, political and religious, worldly ambition and holy penitence, gave their minds a much harder tempering than that possessed by the women who came after the Fronde, and who, with all France, were stamped with the taste of Louis XIV. Madame de Sévigné, born and formed in the first epoch, became fully developed in the second. Her heart is with the first, her genius springs from it; the second gave her its polish without depriving her of its vigor and its original fervor.[1] Madame de Longueville was in full splendor under the Fronde; afterwards she lived among the Carmelites and at Port-Royal; the cultivation of her taste ceased about the year 1650. Let us not then demand in her qualities which she cannot possess. Let us recognize in her a mind of the first rank, but still the mind of a woman—of a great lady, of a very indolent princess, who has not made the least improvement of her talents, and who shows equally her merits and defects, which are also the merits and defects of the times in which she lived, namely, an uncultivated grandeur, a refined delicacy, with a perpetual negligence.

---

[1] We shall often return in this work, for example, 1st Part, chap. ii., to this difference between the literature of Louis XIII. and that of Louis XIV. We have elsewhere said, Fourth Series, vol. ii., of the illustrious women of the seventeenth century, p. 18: "Let us go on and examine the age of Louis XIV. An end has come to the manly vigor of the times of Richelieu; the freedom of the Fronde has ceased; Louis XIV. has made politeness and dignity, tempered by good taste, the order of the day. Fortunate are the minds which have been formed in the strength and liberty of the preceding age, which receive the polish of the new epoch! This was the privilege of Madame de Sévigné, as well as of Molière and of Bossuet."

III.

If the mind of Madame de Longueville displays the woman, her soul especially is in the highest degree feminine, and, far from accusing, I desire to praise her for it. Yes, Madame de Longueville belongs to her own sex; she possesses its adorable qualities and its well-known imperfections. In a world in which gallantry was the order of the day, this young and ravishing creature, married to a man already old and even otherwise connected, followed the universal example. Naturally tender, the senses, according to her own most humble confession, had no part in the affairs of her heart; but, overwhelmed with homage, she yielded to it. Amiable, she made her happiness in being loved. The sister of the great Condé, she was not insensible to the idea of playing a conspicuous part; but far from pretending to rule, she was so much the woman, that she permitted herself to be governed and guided by him whom she loved. While around her, interest and ambition so often took the colors of love, she listened to her heart alone, and devoted herself to the ambition and interest of another. All authors are unanimous in this particular. Her enemies reproach her with severity for not having a proper aim, and for having despised her own interests. They do not suspect that in the expectation of overwhelming her, they elevate her; and even they themselves take care to conceal her conduct and her faults, which, after all, may be reduced to a single one.

She could even be touched by the devotion of Coligny, who shed his blood to avenge her of the outrage of Madame de Montbazon;[1] for a moment she listened[2] heedlessly to the gallantries of the brave and intellectual Moissons, afterwards Marshal d'Albret; still later she compromised herself somewhat with the Duke de Nemours; but the only person that she loved truly was La Rochefoucauld. She devoted herself to him entirely; she sacrificed every thing to him; her duty, her interests, her repose, her reputation. For him she staked her fortune and her life. She exhibited the most equivocal and the most contrary conduct. It was La Rochefoucauld, who caused her to take part in the Fronde, who, according to his liking, made her advance or recede, who united her to, or separated her from, her family, who governed her absolutely. In a word, she consented to be in his hand a mere heroic instrument. Pride and passion had doubtless something to do with this life of adventure and this contempt of peril. But of what stamp must have been the soul that could find consola-

[1] Part i., chap. iii. [2] Ibid., chap. iv.

tion in this! And, as often happens, the man to whom she devoted herself was not wholly worthy of her. He had infinite spirit; but he was profoundly selfish, meanly ambitious; he measured others by himself; he was as subtile in evil as she was in good; he was full of refinement in his self-love, and in the pursuit of his own interest; in reality, the least chivalrous of men, although he affected all the appearance of the highest chivalry. So, as soon as he believes that Madame de Longueville has left him for a moment, and listened too long to the Duke de Nemours, he returns against her, and pursues her with the most pitiful resentment. He blackens her character in the eyes of her brother; he reveals the weaknesses of which he himself has taken advantage; and when she is devoted to the task of repairing the errors of her life, when she is expiating them by the severest penitence, he seeks, by publications in a foreign land, which he dares not own,[1] to blast her name, just as at a later period he will cause Madame de Sablé to print to his glory newspaper articles, which his own hand will correct, and carefully relieve of the little criticisms, inserted for the purpose of adding weight

[1] No one has been duped by the disavowal which he made, for political purposes, of the passages of these memoirs which concern Condé and his sister; for they are the very ones which most betray his hand. They shocked the public conscience, whose interpreter is Madame de Motteville, vol. v., pp. 114, 115, and 182.

to the praise;[1] so that the poor woman on returning from the Carmelites or from Port-Royal was forced to encounter in the few *salons* which she still entered, the history of her amours and the narrative of her errors penned by the hand of him who should have died in her defence, even, if necessary, against the truth. On the breaking up of the Fronde, La Rochefoucauld managed his affairs so well as to retain a good position with the court; he entered the carriage of Mazarin, uttering those famous words: "Every thing happens in France;" he solicited and obtained great favors for his son; he sought for himself the situation of governor of the Dauphin, which was given to Montausier; he knew how to surround himself with amiable women, who bestowed upon him their admiration and their little cares, and one of whom, Madame de La Fayette, consecrated to him her life, and took the place of Madame de Longueville. How different the conduct of Anne de Bourbon! Love had drawn her into the Fronde, love had there retained her; when love no longer exists, she knows not where she is. The proud heroine, who, to war upon Mazarin, had sold her jewels, pledged her fortune, risked her life in a frail bark upon the sea, aroused the South, and held in check the royal power, as soon as she finds that her exertions must avail

[1] See Part iii.

herself alone, withdraws into obscurity, and, at the age of thirty-five years, in all her beauty, plunges into solitude to grieve, like Mademoiselle de La Vallière, over the errors of her past life. Ah! doubtless it would have been better to struggle against the heart, and by force of courage and vigilance to fly all weakness. We bow the knee before those who have never transgressed; but when, with Mademoiselle de La Vallière, or with Madame de Longueville, one would compare Madame de Maintenon, with the endless calculations of her worldly prudence, and the tardy scruples of her piety, which ever come to the aid of her fortune, we protest with all our soul. We speak boldly in behalf of the sister Louise de la Miséricorde, and for the penitent of M. Singlin and of M. Marcel. We prefer a thousand times the opprobrium with which they sought in vain to cover themselves, to the vain consideration which, in a degenerate court, surrounded Madame Scarron, who became privately the wife of Louis XIV. Two things only move us—virtue and true passion: the one is above all things else, and can be recompensed worthily by God alone; the other should not be too much celebrated; but it has its excuse in the grandeur of its disinterested transports, in its sacrifices, in its sufferings, and, above all, in its expiations.

Let us endeavor to comprehend Madame de

Longueville. She was not a politician like the Palatine; she had no true business tact. It is folly to accuse her of not having consistency and personal character. Her true character and the unity of her life should be sought where they are—in her devotion to him whom she loved. It is there wholly and always the same, at once consistent and absurd, and touching even in her follies.

I attribute all her disorderly movements to the uneasy and fickle spirit of La Rochefoucauld. He it is who is ambitious; he it is who is full of intrigues; he it is who wanders at random here and there, according to circumstances, solely occupied with his own interests, and without any other great merit than a mind fertile in expedients of every kind, and a dashing courage, without military talents. And I attribute to Madame de Longueville—to the blood of the Condés, to that great heart which she ever exhibited—I attribute to her boldness in danger, a certain secret contentment in the excess of misfortune, and after reverses a pride before the victors which yields not to that of the Cardinal de Retz. Madame de Longueville, therefore, did not cast down her eyes; she lifted them to a more worthy object. Stripped of what was her all, she bid adieu to the world, and, making no apology to the court, went to ask pardon of God alone.

This considered, all the criticisms which have been lavished upon Madame de Longueville, result in her favor.

La Rochefoucauld, after having eulogized Madame de Longueville in the words which we have quoted, adds: "But these fine qualities were rendered less brilliant by a stain which was never seen upon a princess of such merit, which found no imitations on those who entertained for her a particular adoration; a stain which so transformed her in their sentiments that she did not recognize her own. At this time the Prince de Marcillac shared her mind, and as he joined his ambition to his love, he inspired her with a desire for business to which she had a natural aversion." This stain, with which La Rochefoucauld here reproaches her, is precisely her glory—the affection of a loving and devoted woman.

The future author of the *Maximes* has no difficulty in confessing that he was attached to her as much from interest as from affection. After such a delaration, we cannot admit the chivalrous exclamation:

> That I might win her heart, be pleasant in her eyes,
> War I've waged with kings, I would have storm'd the skies.

No, it was not to please her that you entered the Fronde; it was a passion for movement and intrigue that prompted you to take part in it. You know that she had a natural aversion to business, and that contrary to her taste and her manifest interests, she entered into it for your sake alone.

La Rochefoucauld relates, in the new part of his *Memoires*, how and with what intentions he became connected with Madame de Longueville. He was striving to revenge himself of the queen and of Mazarin; to accomplish this he had need of the Prince de Condé, and he sought to secure the brother by means of the sister. But let us permit him to speak for himself: "So much unprofitable labor and so much weariness, finally gave me other thoughts, and made me attempt dangerous ways in order to show my resentment to the queen and the Cardinal Mazarin. The beauty of Madame de Longueville, her wit and the charms of her person attached to her all who could hope for her favor. Many men and women of quality sought to please her; and in addition to the charms of this court, Madame de Longueville was upon such good terms with all her house, and so tenderly beloved by the Duke d'Enghien, her brother, that the esteem and friendship of this prince could be safely counted upon by any one fortunate enough to secure the approval of his sister. Many people uselessly attempted this game, mingling other sentiments with those of ambition. Miossens, who afterwards became marshal of France, persisted longest, and with similar success. I was one of his particular friends, and he informed me of his designs. They were soon destroyed of themselves. He knew it, and told me several times that he had resolved to renounce them; but vanity, which was the strongest of his passions, prevented him often from telling me the truth, and he dissembled hopes which he had not, and which I knew he ought not to have entertained. Some time passed in this way, and finally I had reason to believe that I could make a more considerable use than Miossens of the friendship and confidence of Madame de Longueville. I convinced him of this. He knew my position at court. I told him my views, stating that consideration for him would always restrain me, and that I should not seek to form a connection with Madame de Longueville without his permission. I confess that to obtain this, I purposely excited him against her; not, however, by uttering any thing untrue. His full consent was finally obtained; but he repented of having given it to me when he saw the result of this connection."

The declared enemy of Madame de Longueville was her daughter-in-law, Madame de Nemours, whose character was entirely the opposite of her own. She was judicious but severe. She was quite naturally on the side of M. de Longueville, her father, whom she endeavored to withdraw from the influence of his wife. In her *Memoires* she recognizes the perfect disinterestedness of Madame de Longueville, her sincere attachment to her brother, and her want of taste for politics: "It is certainly astonishing[1] that Madame de Longueville should have been one of the first (to take part in the Fronde), she who had nothing to hope from this party, and who had no reason to complain of the court. . . . The prince entertained an extreme tenderness for his sister. She, on her side, managed him less from interest than for the particular esteem and tender friendship which she felt for him. . . . Madame de Longueville knew very little about politics." At the same time she accuses her of being fond of show, of having no weighty motive for her conduct, of having sacrificed fortune and repose to a false glory, and all under the influence of La Rochefoucauld. "It was," said she, "M. de La Rochefoucauld who inspired this princess with so many foolish and false sentiments. As he had a very great power over her, and as, besides, he thought only of himself, he engaged her in all the intrigues with which she was connected, only to promote his own selfish designs. . . Marcillac, who ruled her absolutely, and who wished that others should have no credit with her, or even to appear to have any, alienated her from the deputy, who would

---

1 *Mémoires*, edit. of Amsterdam, 1783, p. 12.

not have been sorry to rule her also. . . Marcillac, to promote his own interest, showed Madame de Longueville. . . As soon as Marcillac, who urged on Madame de Longueville only to procure sooner what had been promised to him by the court, had obtained what he desired, he thought no more of the interests of others; he found in his own all that he sought. He even persuaded Madame de Longueville that she herself was little thought of."

Retz confirms the insinuations of Madame de Nemours concerning himself, and takes good care to explain her pretensions, and even her expectations. He thus concludes the portrait which he has traced of Madame de Longueville: "She would have had few defects had it not been for gallantry. As her passion compelled her to make politics a secondary matter, instead of the heroine of a great party, she became its adventurer."

To justify the sentiments of Madame de Longueville, we might have limited ourselves to quoting two decisive passages from the most impartial witness of the things and persons of this period, Madame de Motteville:[1] "In attaching himself politically to the prince, Marcillac devoted himself to Madame de Longueville in a manner somewhat more tender, uni-

[1] *Mémoires*, vol. ii., p. 15.

ting the sentiments of the heart to the consideration of grandeur and fortune. It was quite apparent to the whole court that this princess treated him with great attention. In all that she afterwards did, it was clearly seen that her mind was not solely occupied with ambition, but that the interests of the Prince de Marcillac filled a prominent place therein. For him she became ambitious; for him she ceased to love repose, and, in order to be sensible to this affection, she became too insensible to her own glory. . . . The wishes of the Prince de Marcillac, as I have said, were not displeasing to her; and this nobleman, who was perhaps more selfish than tender, anxious to benefit himself through her, thought it his duty to inspire her with the desire of ruling the princes her brothers."

Let us crown all these quotations with one from Guy-Joly: "The Prince de Marcillac managed her with care, judging that she would have particular consideration in the party, by reason of the ascendency which she had over the Princes de Condé and de Longueville, and that, being in her good graces, it would be easy for him to obtain great advantage whenever it might be necessary for him to treat with the court."[1]

---

[1] *Mémoires de Guy-Joly*, collection Michaud, 3d Series, vol. ii., p. 15.

Thus, by the admission of every one, La Rochefoucauld pursued in the Fronde his own interest alone, and Madame de Longueville pursued only the interest of La Rochefoucauld.

But we must not stop here; we must establish, by undoubted facts, and present clearly the point of view which we have just indicated. La Rochefoucauld himself, closely interrogated, testifies that, far from having been drawn into the Fronde by Madame de Longueville, as some have been pleased to represent, it was he himself who drew her in, and he himself who directed all her movements.

It is he himself who informs us of the motive which prompted him to the connection which he formed with Madame de Longueville at the close of 1647, or at the beginning of 1648. He continued wonderfully faithful to the plan which he had proposed to himself.

1st. At the close of 1647, La Rochefoucauld was irritated because he could not obtain from the cardinal either the place of Governor of Havre or that of a colonel of cavalry. He succeeded in turning Madame de Longueville against Mazarin, by making her believe that Condé had not received all that was due to him. "Madame de Longueville, whose entire confidence I possessed, felt as keenly as I could desire the conduct of the cardinal towards the Duke d'Enghien."[1] In 1648, before embracing the party of the Fronde, La Rochefoucauld tried for the last time to gain Mazarin, and demanded "for his house the same advantages which had been accorded to those of Rohan, of La Trémouille, and some others." "I found myself," said he,[2] "so removed from favor that I stopped here. I spoke of it to the cardinal in leaving him. He promised positively to grant my request in a short time. On my return I should have received the title of duke in order that my wife might have the privilege of sitting in the presence of the king. I went to Poitou with this expectation, and there I quelled the disorders (the first movements of the Fronde); but I saw that the cardinal, far from keeping his promise, had granted dukes' patents to six persons of quality, without remembering me." And then he engaged in the sedition. Madame de Longueville, following the instructions which he had given to her, had commenced laying snares for the deputy and the parliament, had overcome Conti, gained her husband, and circumvented Condé; but she held so loosely the reins of this intrigue, that she wrote to La Rochefoucauld, submitting to him her own proceedings, and begging him to come and decide what should be done. The pas-

---

[1] Petitot, vol. li., p. 396. [2] Ibid., p. 398, 399.

sage from La Rochefoucauld on this subject is very curious, and deserves to be quoted.[1] "I was in the first transports which a treatment so extraordinary might be expected to produce, when I learned from Madame de Longueville that the whole plan of the civil war had been resolved upon at Noisy between the Prince de Conti, the Duke de Longueville, the Deputy of Paris, and the most prominent members of the parliament. She informed me that there was hope of gaining the Prince de Condé; that she did not know precisely what to do at this juncture, being ignorant of my sentiments, and she besought me to come by diligence to Paris, that we might decide together whether she ought to push or delay this project. This news consoled me in my chagrin, and I felt myself able to convince the queen and the cardinal that it would have been well for them to humor me. I asked leave of absence; I had difficulty in obtaining it; and it was granted only on condition that I would not complain of the treatment which I had received, and that I would not insist upon my pretensions. It was easy to promise all this, and I arrived in Paris full of the resentment which I had a right to feel. I there found things precisely in the condition described by Madame de Longueville; but

---

[1] Petitot, vol. li., pp. 398, 399.

I found less excitement, either because the first steps had been taken, or because the diversity of interests and grandeur of the design had diminished the ardor of those who had undertaken it. Madame de Longueville herself had purposely raised difficulties, in order that I might have time to make my appearance, and to render myself competent to decide. I did not hesitate to do it, and I felt great pleasure in knowing that, to whatever extremity the severity of the queen and the hatred of the cardinal might reduce me, I had still the means to be revenged."

2. Thus engaged in the Fronde, Madame de Longueville appeared to become entirely reckless. She delivered the Prince de Conti into the hands of La Rochefoucauld; she conspired to lead away M. de Longueville; she deceived her mother by refusing to accompany her to court, under pretence of sickness; she went so far as to commit herself, notwithstanding her approaching confinement, to the hands of the people at the Hôtel de Ville. She did more: for the sake of La Rochefoucauld, she became embroiled with her brother Condé, for whom she entertained the greatest affection; she strove to draw him into the Fronde; he became angry with her; hence that rupture so astonishing after such tender friendship, and those outbursts of wrath now so easily accounted for. "The Prince de Conti . . . was

weak and fickle; he depended entirely upon Madame de Longueville, and she left to me the care of guiding him.[1] The Duke de Longueville possessed mind and experience; he entered easily into the parties opposed to the court, and left them still more easily. . . . He was continually raising obstacles, and repenting of his engagements in it. I was afraid that he might do more, and discover to the prince what he knew of the enterprise. With this apprehension, I sent Gourville to Paris to notify Madame de Longueville and the deputy of the suspicion which there was reason for entertaining of the Duke de Longueville. . . . The Marquis de Noirmontiers and myself were constrained to tell him that we were going to carry away the Prince de Conti, and that we would declare to the world that he alone had shown a want of fidelity to his friends, after engaging them in an undertaking which he abandoned. He could not bear these reproaches, and suffered himself to be led as we desired. . . . The king, followed by the queen, the Duke d'Orleans, and the prince, set out secretly from Paris at midnight, near the close of the year 1649, and went to Saint-Germain. All the court followed in great disorder. The princess wished to carry along Madame

---

[1] Petitot, vol. li., p. 399, etc.

de Longueville, who was on the point of being confined; but she feigned illness, and remained at Paris. . . . The Prince de Conti and Madame de Longueville, in order to give more confidence, lodged in the Hôtel de Ville, and committed themselves entirely into the hands of the people." . . . In another place he says:[1] "Madame de Longueville was again obliged to reside at the Hôtel de Ville as a pledge of the fidelity of her brother and husband to the people, who are naturally suspicious of the great, because they are ordinarily the victims of their evil doings. . . . The Prince de Condé[2] . . . had taken measures with the court. The connection which I had with the Prince de Conti and Madame de Longueville was not agreeable to him. . . . The cardinal was preparing to quit the kingdom; but the prince soon reassured him; and the bitterness which he exhibited towards the Prince de Conti, towards Madame de Longueville and myself, was so great, that the cardinal could not doubt that it was genuine."

3. At the end of this first Parisian war, in 1649, the Prince de Condé became reconciled with his family, and even with La Rochefoucauld. The latter was included in the treaty which was consummated; he obtained for his house "the same advantages of

---

[1] Petitot, vol. li., p. 462. [2] Ibid., p. 401.

rank that had been accorded to those of Rohan, of Foix, and of Luxembourg." Such is the declaration of La Rochefoucauld;[1] but the truth is, that it was Madame de Longueville who claimed for him these advantages, and who labored energetically in his interests. So Madame de Mottville asserts: "Madame de Longueville[2] omitted nothing in her efforts to secure the favor of the court for the Prince de Marcillac. . . . To satisfy[3] her fully it was necessary to promote the Prince de Marcillac, and in this conjuncture she procured for his wife the right of sitting in the royal presence, and of entering the Louvre in her carriage. These advantages placed him above dukes, and upon an equality with princes, though he was neither the one nor the other: he was not a member of the royal family." Madame de Nemours goes still farther:[4] "Madame de Longueville interfered in this settlement, and it is even pretended that M. de Marcillac received some money." What a part in all this affair was that of La Rochefoucauld! Madame de Longueville is at least disinterested. She at the same time suffers herself to be eclipsed and to be compromised, anxious only to serve and to please.

4. In 1650, Mazarin thinking that he ought to re-

---

[1] Petitot, vol. lii., p. 9. [2] Vol. iii., p. 295. [3] Ibid., p. 398.
[4] *Mémoires*, p. 47.

voke the favors which Madame de Longueville had obtained for La Rochefoucauld, all minds became exasperated: troubles recommenced; the princes were put in prison; the arrest of Madame de Longueville was contemplated, and an order was issued directing her to appear before the Queen at the Palais-Royal. "Instead[1] of obeying, she resolved, by the advice of the Prince de Marcillac, to set out at once, with all speed, for Normandy, for the purpose of engaging that province, and the parliament of Rouen, on the side of the princes, and of securing in her friendship the fortresses of the Duke de Longueville and of Havre-de-Grace. . . . The Prince de Marcillac accompanied her in this journey." I ask, which of the two drew the other into this second war, much more serious than the first? But I hasten to say that on this occasion both conducted themselves equally well. While Madame de Longueville was pledging her jewels in Holland for her defence at Sténay, La Rochefoucauld was also exposing his fortunes in Guyenne. It was the saddest and the most touching moment in the history of their loves and their adventures. They were separated from one another, but still they loved; they served with ardor the same cause; they struggled and they suffered together.

[1] Mémoires de La Rochefoucauld, Petitot, vol. lii., p. 24.

5. In 1651, after the deliverance of the princes, La Rochefoucauld grew weary of war, into which he seems to have engaged only to please Madame de Longueville. "The Duke de La Rochefoucauld[1] could not testify so openly his repugnance to this war; he was obliged to consult the feelings of Madame de Longueville, and all that he could then do was to try to make her desire peace." What then were the feelings of Madame de Longueville? Did she wish to continue the war for the sake of playing a conspicuous part, and with a view to gratify that ambition of glory with which she has been so often reproached? By no means. Her thoughts were much more humble. Still attached to La Rochefoucauld, she contemplated with pain a peace which threatened to separate them. Madame de Longueville[2] knew that the deputy had embroiled her irrevocably with her husband, and that after the impressions made upon him as to her conduct, she could not return to him in Normandy without at least hazarding her liberty. The Duke de Longueville, however, wished to keep her near him, and she had no pretext for avoiding this dangerous journey, except the desire of instigating her brother to carry on a civil war. "At the same time La Rochefoucauld

[1] Mémoires de La Rochefouc., Petitot, vol. lii., p. 72. [2] Ibid., p. 71.

informs us that he persuaded her to avoid such a responsibility, to retire to Montrond with the Princess de Condé, and to allow matters to unravel themselves. He[1] showed Madame de Longueville that her removal from Paris alone could satisfy her husband, and prevent him from making the journey which she dreaded; that the prince might easily grow weary of the protection which he had until then afforded her, having a pretext so specious as that of reconciling a woman with her husband, and especially if he thought that he might thereby attach to himself the Duke de Longueville; besides, that she alone would be accused of fomenting disorder; that she would be, in various ways, held responsible both to her brother and to the world, for kindling in the kingdom a war whose results might be grievous to her house and to the State .... In fine, to avoid so many difficulties, he advised her to ask the prince to permit the princess, the Duke d'Enghien, and herself to retire to Montrond, in order that he might not be embarrassed in a precipitate march if he found himself obliged to depart, and in order that he might have no scruple in deciding either to fire the kingdom by a civil war, or to risk his life, his liberty, and his fortune, upon the doubtful faith of Cardinal Maz-

[1] Mémoires de La Rochefoucauld, Petitot, vol. lii., pp. 79, 80.

arin. This advice met the approbation of Madame de Longueville, and the prince soon after consented to have it followed.

Madame de Longueville, in this instance, as in all the others, did not then lead away La Rochefoucauld; she permitted herself to be guided by him; she obeyed his counsels, which to her were laws.

Here again is the true and perfect unity of her conduct: Madame de Longueville pursues the course marked out for her by another, with an indefatigable constancy, amid all intrigues and dangers, and, as it were, with her eyes shut to the motives which actu ate La Rochefoucauld.

Her blindness is for a long time complete; but, as she united great shrewdness to great passion, after they had been long separated, and when she was no longer under the charm or under the yoke of his presence, her eyes became partly opened; and in the voyage from Guyenne, having encountered the Duke de Nemours, who showed every appearance of perfect chivalry, and who was then said to be very attentive to Madame de Châtillon, absence, the void already in her heart, the innate love of pleasing, the desire of showing the power of her charms, and of troubling somewhat a rival who wished at the same time to retain both Nemours and Condé, in short, the feeling of liberty inspired by a voyage rendered her more open than she should have been to the addresses of the young and handsome cavalier. There is no proof that she was beyond temptation.[1] Scarcely had he returned to Paris when M. de Nemours forgot her, submitted to the chains of Madame de Châtillon, who triumphed, with her accustomed perfidy, over the sacrifice which had been made to her. Justly wounded, La Rochefoucauld falls out with her forever. It is said[2] that he seized with joy this occasion for separating himself from her, as he had long desired it. Let this be so; he might have stopped there; it was unnecessary to calumniate her in the mind of Condé, to impute to her the base design of having wished to ruin the party and betray her brother in order to serve the interests of the Duke de Nemours,[3] an absurd accusation, and one which her whole conduct falsifies, and to paint her as a vulgar creature, capable of going to the same extremities for another, if that other so desired; it was unneces-

---

[1] See Part ii.

[2] *Mémoires de Madame de Nemours*, p. 150.

[3] La Rochefoucauld, p. 198 of the edition of 1664: "The Prince de Condé was warned of the design which she had to ruin his party, by very extraordinary means, for the interest of Nemours, and feared, that similarly prejudiced in behalf of another, she might go to the same extremities if this one should so desire it." *Was warned*, and by whom, if not by La Rochefoucauld, who then enjoyed the entire confidence of Condé? La Rochefoucauld perceived so plainly the odiousness of this passage, that he afterwards modified and softened it, as may be seen in the editions of Renouard and Petitot.

sary, as Madame de Motteville so well says,[1] "from a lover to become an enemy, from an enemy an ingrate," and to suffer himself through revenge to commit offences which went, as Madame de Motteville again says, "beyond what a Christian owes to God, and a man of honor to a lady."

Is it possible, in fact, that resentment, of which wounded self-love was the occasion (for then La Rochefoucauld loved Madame de Longueville very feebly, if ever he loved[2] her truly), could have degraded a man of honor like him so far as to make him engage in the shameful plots of Madame de Châtillon? Madame de Motteville exhibits, as if with regret, the conduct of La Rochefoucauld in this affair:[3] "Madame de Châtillon made use of the Duke de La Rochefoucauld and of his passions. . . . M. de La Rochefoucauld told me that jealousy and revenge made him act carefully, and that he did all that she desired." Now, what Madame de Châtillon desired,

---

[1] Vol. v., pp. 114, 115.

[2] Madame de Sévigné doubts it very much. Letter of October 7, 1676: "I do not believe that he was ever in love." He says himself in making his own portrait: "I who know whatever is delicate and strong in the sentiments of love, if ever I happen to love, it will certainly be in this manner. But in one of my make, I do not believe that this knowledge which I possess ever passes from the mind to the heart." Segrais, (Mémoires, Anecdotes, edit. d'Amsterdam, 1723, p. 113): "M. de la Rochefoucauld said that he had never found love except in romances; as for him, he had never felt it."

[3] Vol. v., p. 132.

was to humiliate Madame de Longueville, to keep Nemours for her pleasures, and Condé for her fortune. La Rochefoucauld has in so small a degree the sentiment of the good and the bad, of the honest and the dishonest, that he relates what he has done with a sort of satisfaction; he appears to triumph in an intrigue so skilfully planned. "Madame de Châtillon[1] brought about a desire for peace by very agreeable means. She believed that so great a good ought to be the work of her beauty, and mingling ambition with the design of making a new conquest, she wished at the same time to triumph over the heart of the prince, and to draw from the court all the advantages of the negotiation. These were not her only reasons for entertaining such thoughts: a desire to gratify vanity and revenge actuated her as much as any thing else. The emulation which beauty and gallantry often produce among ladies, had caused an extreme bitterness between Madame de Longueville and Madame de Châtillon; they had long concealed their feelings, but they finally made a full exhibition of them; and Madame de Châtillon did not content herself with compelling M. de Nemours to break off all commerce with Madame de Longueville; she wished, besides, to obtain the sole

---

[1] Edit. of 1664, pp. 229–232; Petitot, pp. 156–158.

disposal of the conduct and interests of the prince. The Duke de Nemours, who had a perfect understanding with her, approved this design; he thought that, being able to regulate the conduct of Madame de Châtillon towards the prince, she would inspire him with such sentiments as he could wish to give him, and that thus he would be able to dispose of the prince by the power which he possessed over Madame de Châtillon. The Duke de la Rochefoucauld was much deeper than any one in the confidence of the prince, and was, at the same time, very closely connected with the Duke de Nemours and Madame de Châtillon. . . . He induced the prince to engage with her and to give her, in her own right, the lands of Merlou; he disposed her also to humor the prince and M. de Nemours, so that she might preserve them both, and made M. de Nemours approve this connection, and even appear not to suspect it, since he was to make his account in it and make use of it for obtaining the principal part in affairs. This machine being conducted and regulated by the Duke de La Rochefoucauld, gave him almost the entire disposition of all that composed it, and thus these four persons therein equally finding their advantage, it would have doubtless had the success which they contemplated, had not fortune opposed it." Let us finish this picture by a stroke which La

Rochefoucauld has forgotten, and which Mademoiselle furnishes: "Madame de Châtillon,[1] MM. de Nemours and de La Rochefoucauld, who expected great advantages by a treaty, the first a hundred thousand crowns, the other a government, and the last a similar sum, thought only of making peace for the prince."

Thus, in the end as well as in the midst and at the beginning of his connection with Madame de Longueville, the only motives of La Rochefoucauld were interest and self-love. One day in his *Maximes* he will thereunto reduce all human nature, inclosing it within the precincts of his own person, and giving as limits to the moral world those of his very small experience as a frondeur and a courtier.[2]

Truly we may smile to hear the author of the *Mémoires* and the *Maximes* say in the portrait which he has left us of himself: "Ambition does not move me . . . I have virtuous sentiments . . . I can keep a secret, and I have less difficulty than others in keeping to myself what has been told me in confidence. . . . I love my friends, and my love is of such a nature that I would not hesitate to sacrifice my

---

[1] *Mémoires*, vol. ii., p. 129.

[2] Some time ago I expressed the same opinion in regard to La Rochefoucauld, and, as may be seen, I still hold it. See 1st series of my works, vol. iv., p. 200; 4th series, vol. i., p. 51, and vol. ii., p. 8.

interests to theirs." Segrais was hard to suit with eulogy, or he had not read the above passages, when he said that La Rochefoucauld never praised himself.[1] Madame de Longueville would have recognized La Rochefoucauld by the following traits: "I am not incapable of avenging myself if I have been offended, and when it concerns my honor to resent an injury committed against me; on the contrary, I should be sure that duty would perform so well in me the office of hatred, that I would pursue my revenge with greater vigor than another." The true portrait of La Rochefoucauld is that which has been drawn by Retz.[2] "There has always been something indescribable in M. de La Rochefoucauld: he took pleasure in intrigues at an early age, and at a time when he did not trouble himself with little things, never a weakness with him, and at a time, too, when he was unacquainted with great ones, which were not his forte; he never had much capacity for business . . . his views were not sufficiently extended . . . he always had an habitual irresolution . . . he was never a warrior, though a very good soldier; he was never of himself a good courtier, although he had the best intention to be one; he was never a good party man, though all his life a partisan. . . . All

---

[1] Mémoires, Anecdotes, p. 81.

[2] Vol. i., p. 217.

these things, together with his *Maximes*, which do not exhibit much faith in virtue, and his policy which has always been to withdraw from business with as much impatience as he engaged in it, makes me conclude that he would have done much better to have known himself, and to have passed, as he might have done, for the most polished courtier, and for the most civil man in common life which his century produced."

As to Madame de Longueville, she is certainly far from being perfect, and perhaps she would have been less loved had she been so; but amid the follies into which passion plunged her, we feel at least that interest is nothing to her. The defect of which she continually accuses herself, is the desire of pleasing and of appearing. The only injury which she committed against La Rochefoucauld was that momentary display of giddiness and coquetry during the journey from Guyenne. This was her real stain. All the rest of her conduct in the Fronde is explained and easily defended when viewed as we have indicated.

Besides, no one's conduct in the Fronde should be regarded in too serious a light, for the Fronde was not a serious affair;[1] it was a series of intrigues, in

[1] On the Fronde and its general causes, see Part i., chap. 4.

which no one had any other object than interest, vanity, love of importance, with gallantry, and pleasure. Princes thought only of themselves, of increasing their authority and their fortune; and to this end, they went by turns from one party to another according to events and to the daily changes around them. Condé, the prominent person in the drama, and the only one who with his rival Mazarin merits a place in history, despised at bottom all parties; but in the end he fixed his mind upon a place incompatible with royal grandeur. His natural inclination was to the side of the Court: the Fronde, properly speaking, and the parliament were odious to him, and he never served them except with great disrelish. His chief spring of action was war, for which he had a genius; and this it was which, after much deliberation and hesitation, finally carried him away. The parliament, forgetting its part and its duties, was agitated by young lords—burlesque tribunes. The people of Paris were set in commotion: they were excited against the Court; but as soon as serious reforms and a convocation of the States-General were talked of, the parliament took alarm, and receded as well as the opposing party.[1] The only use of the Fronde,

[1] See thereon a curious passage of Madame de Motteville, vol. iv., p. 359, etc.

in the admirable economy of our history, has been to strengthen the royal power, to make every one sensible of its absolute necessity, and to promote, perhaps to excess, the work of Louis XI., of Henri IV., and of Richelieu. Under the League, two great opinions, two great causes, were in hostility. The League also produced minds, stamped characters, was a school of politics and of war, and formed the strong men of the first half of the seventeenth century. The Fronde is in our annals an episode without grandeur; it formed no one, either a warrior or a statesman; the nation took very little part in it, because it felt that in it no great interest was at stake; it was a pastime for gentlemen, for wits, and belles. To the ladies especially the Fronde belonged: they were at once its motive power and its instruments, its most interested actors; and among them Madame de Longueville played the most conspicuous part.

IV.

We should be tempted to be more severe towards the faults of more than one kind into which she was drawn by her sad connection with La Rochefoucauld if she herself had felt less remorse, if her repentance had not been so long and so severe. Her errors began at the close of 1647, or during the first months of 1648—they did not extend beyond 1652; her remorse ceased only with her life in 1679. Madame de Longueville was roused to reflection in 1653: she became converted in the middle of the year 1654. At this period she was thirty-five years of age, and in all the splendor of her beauty. For a long time yet she might have enjoyed the pleasures of life and of the world. She renounced them to devote herself unreservedly and forever to God. During twenty-five years, in Normandy, among the Carmelites, and at Port-Royal, she lived only for duty and repentance, seeking to become dead to every thing that had formerly occupied her life—the cares of her beauty, the tendernesses of the heart, the graceful employments of the mind. But in the dress of haircloth as well as in fashionable attire, among the Carmelites and at Port-Royal as well as at the hôtel de Rambouillet and in the Fronde, she preserved what she could never lose—an angelic face, a mind charming in the most extreme negligence, with a certain loftiness of soul and character. This third and last epoch of the life of Madame de Longueville, will here be presented as fully as the subject demands: therein we shall see, in all its truth, a devotion continually increasing, and more and more scrupulous, sometimes reducing her to the most pitiful condition, sometimes elevating her to an admirable grandeur; as, for example, in her struggles, after the death of her husband, with her brother Condé, in regard to her two sons, and in the defence which she undertook of persecuted Port-Royal.

We do not think that we debase Mademoiselle de Lavallière by comparing with her Madame de Longueville. It is true that the loves of Mademoiselle de Lavallière move us in a very different manner from those which we shall have to relate. In setting aside the circumstance of royalty, which in this case forms the disagreeable side, and which is always somewhat injurious to true and disinterested love, Louis XIV. was much better calculated to please than La Rochefoucauld; he was much younger and much more handsome; he was, or appeared to be, a great man and a hero. He adored Mademoiselle de Lavallière at once with an impetuous ardor and with the most delicate tenderness, and his passion continued for a long time. Mademoiselle de Lavallière loved the king as she would have loved a simple gentleman. It is this which gives her a separate place among the favorites of Louis XIV., and places her far above Madame de Montespan, and especially above Madame de Maintenon. It cannot be denied that Madame de Longueville loved with the same disinterestedness and the same abandonment; but her affection was ill bestowed, but she mingled with it wit and vanity, but she became giddy and coquettish. Thus far the comparison is entirely against her. But, besides, she was far superior to Mademoiselle de Lavallière. She was incomparably more beautiful and more intellectual. Her soul was also more proud. At the least suspicion of change in the affection of Louis XIV., she would have fled from the court; while Mademoiselle de Lavallière remained in it some time, in the presence of her proud, triumphing rival, thinking that by force of humility, of patience, and of devotion, she would reconquer the heart that she had lost. And then, what better could she do than to enter a cloister? Would she not have rendered herself contemptible by remaining in the world, by giving to society the spectacle of a favorite of the king consoling herself, like Madame de Soubise, for the inconstancy of her royal lover, in the enjoyment of a fortune sadly acquired and shamefully preserved! In entering the convent of the Carmelites, Mademoiselle de Lavallière did no more than she was compelled to do. There is in the conversion and retirement of Madame de Longueville something more free and more unusual, and to glorify her penitence, nothing is wanting but the voice of Bossuet. If the incomparable orator who had consecrated to God Louise de La Miséricorde, and who, at a later period, had made his words equal in greatness to the actions of Condé, if his voice had been heard at the celebration of the obsequies of

Anne de Bourbon, Christian letters would have counted another masterpiece, of which the funeral oration of the Princess Palatine may give us some idea, and the name of Madame de Longueville would be surrounded with an immortal halo.

THE YOUTH OF MADAME DE LONGUEVILLE.

CHAPTER I.

1619 to 1635.

Mademoiselle de Bourbon in her family—Her mother, Charlotte de Montmorency—Her father, M. the Prince—Her brother, the Duke d'Enghien—Her religious education—The convent of the Carmelites of the Rue Saint-Jacques—The four great prioresses—Mademoiselle d'Epernon—Mademoiselle de Bourbon at the ball of the Louvre, February 18, 1635—Her portrait at the age of fifteen years.

I SHALL some day attempt to make known in Madame de Longueville the heroine, or, if you prefer, the adventuress of the Fronde, casting herself amid dangers and intrigues of every kind in order to serve the interests and the passions of another. I shall afterwards show her overcome, disabused, her soul at once wounded and bereaved, turning its regards towards the only side that cannot deceive her, towards duty and God. At present, I would recount her life before the Fronde, and even before the unequal marriage imposed upon her by her family, the source, indeed, of her errors and her misfortunes. I would paint the youth of Madame de Longueville, show Mademoiselle de Bourbon in her days of innocent splendor, yet bearing in herself all the seeds of a stormy future; born in a prison, and leaving it to mount almost upon the steps of a throne; surrounded early by the most gloomy spectacles, with all the felicities of life, beautiful and intellectual; proud and tender, ardent and melancholy, wishing to bury herself at fifteen in a cloister, and, once thrown, in spite of herself, into the world, allowing herself there to be intoxicated with her own success; becoming the ornament of the court of Louis XIII. and of the hôtel de Rambouillet, eclipsing the most accomplished beauties by a peculiar sweetness and a ravishing languor; giving ear to two proposals, but still pure and free; and advancing, apparently, towards the most beautiful destiny, under the wing of a mother like Charlotte de Montmorency, by the side of a brother like the Duke d'Enghien.

I agree that this picture of a brilliant but fortunate youth, without adventures and without blemishes, may seem somewhat tame to readers accustomed to the great bustle and the sudden turns of fortune in fashionable romances. In order to indemnify them, I shall place with this picture another more highly colored. After the young girl growing up innocently between religion and the muses, as heretofore described, I shall exhibit the young woman, rushing, in her turn, into the arena of gallantry, scattering around her conquests and quarrels, and becoming the subject of the most famous of the great duels which, during so many years, reddened the Place-Royal, and were not arrested even before the implacable axe of Richelieu. These will be scenes sufficiently animated; but, while waiting for the tragi-comedy, endure, a little while, the pastoral. It was then a necessary interlude, and I beg you to assume for a moment with me the taste and the manners of the seventeenth century.

Anne Geneviève de Bourbon was born August 28, 1619, in the tower of Vincennes, where her father and mother had been prisoners for three years.

Her mother was Charlotte Marguerite de Montmorency, granddaughter of the high constable, and, according to unanimous testimonies, the most beautiful person of her times. Dazzling in her early youth, she preserved even in advanced age a remarkable beauty. In addition to her portraits, we have two faithful descriptions, one by Cardinal Bentivoglio, who knew her and loved her, it is said, at Brussels, where he was apostolic nuncio in 1609, when she was nearly sixteen years of age; the other, by the hand of Madame de Motteville, who has portrayed her as she saw her later at the court of Queen Anne. "She had a complexion," says Bentivoglio,[1] "of extraordinary whiteness, eyes and features full of charm; she was graceful in gestures and manner of speaking; and all her different qualities heightened each other, because she added to them none of the affectations of which women are accustomed to avail themselves." Madame de Motteville thus expresses herself:[2] "Among the princesses, she who was first had also the most beauty; and, though not young, she still caused admiration in those who saw her. . . I wish to testify that her beauty was still great, when, in my infancy, I was at court, and that it endured to the end of her life. We praised her during the regency of the queen, at fifty years of age, and we praised her without flattery. Her complexion was fair; she had blue and perfectly beautiful eyes. Her mien was lofty and full of majesty, and her whole person, which was in every way agreeable, always pleased, except when she proudly and sharply opposed those who dared to displease her." When, at fifteen years of age, she appeared at the court of Henry IV., she turned the head of the old

---

[1] We borrow the translation that Villefore has given of this part of the Italian narrative of the cardinal, Part 1st, p. 22.

[2] Part 1st, p. 44.

king. He married her to his nephew, the Prince de Condé, in the hope of finding him a convenient husband; but he, proud and amorous, was clearly of the opinion that he had married the beautiful Charlotte for himself; and, seeing the king more and more inflamed, he found no other means of extricating himself from his difficult position, than by taking his wife and flying with her to Brussels. We know all the follies that Henry IV. then committed, and to what extremities he was about to go when he was assassinated, in 1610.[1]

Henri de Bourbon, Prince de Condé, was no ordinary man. He owed much to Henry IV., and he expected much from him; but he had not the courage to peril the fortune of his house by voluntarily exiling himself; and later he compromised himself anew by his resistance to the tyrannical conduct of Marshal d'Ancre, under the regency of Marie de Médicis. Arrested in 1616, he did not leave his prison until the end of 1619, and from that time he no longer thought of any thing but his fortune. Born Protestant, he had embraced Catholicism

[1] See, in the Library of the Arsenal, Manuscripts of Conrart, in-4o, vol. xvi., p. 642, an unpublished letter of Henri de Bourbon to his mother, upon the assassination of Henri IV., which proves how absurd it is to accuse him of having been concerned in that assassination. The same volume contains different writings of the same prince against Marshal d'Ancre.

through policy, after the example of Henry IV. His wife had brought to him a great part of the immense riches of the Montmorencys. He submitted himself to Luynes, and served Richelieu. He forced his son, the Duke d'Enghien, to espouse a niece of the all-powerful cardinal, who had just decapitated his brother-in-law. As avaricious as ambitious, he amassed property and heaped up honors. At the death of Richelieu, he became the chief of the council, and displayed in that difficult conjuncture a fortunate mixture of prudence and firmness. He sustained the regency of Anne of Austria, and saved France from the first perils of the long minority of Louis XIV. He merits a place in the gratitude of his country, for having given to it twice, as it were, the great Condé, by imposing upon that nature of fire—a nature wholly made for war, the severest military education that ever prince received, and by preparing him to take, at twenty-one years of age, the command in chief of the army, on which rested, in 1643, the destinies of France.

When Henri de Bourbon, who was called M. the Prince, was arrested, he preferred but one petition, and that was dictated by jealousy and love; he demanded that his wife might be allowed to share his prison. Charlotte de Montmorency was scarcely twenty-one years of age; she did not love her husband,

and they did not live agreeably together; but, without hesitation, she besought the king in person to permit her to imprison herself with her husband, accepting the condition of remaining a prisoner as long as he should be the same. This captivity, at first very hard at the Bastile, then a little less rigorous at Vincennes, continued three years. The young princess was often ill; she was several times unfortunately the mother of untimely children.[1] Finally, August 28, 1619, between mid-

---

[1] We find in regard to all this, new and curious details in a *Journal historique et anecdote de la cour et de Paris*, t. xi., in-4°, manuscripts of Conrart. This unpublished journal commences January 1, 1614, and goes to January 1, 1620.

M. the Prince was arrested September 1, 1616, by order of Marshal d'Ancre, favorite of the queen regent, Marie de Médicis.

"September 11. Madame the young Princess arrives very much afflicted. It is said that M. de Montmorency was not pleased that the queen was unwilling to permit her to see M. le Prince.

"May 19, 1617. M. le Prince petitions the king to do a charitable deed by delivering to him his wife, that she might remain a prisoner with him.

"May 26, 1617. Madame the Princess de Condé goes to salute the king and supplicate him to let her enter as a prisoner in the Bastile with M. the Prince. The king grants it to her, and permits her to take with her only one damsel. Upon which her *petit nain*, having supplicated the king to be pleased that he should not abandon his mistress, his majesty also permitted him. The same day, after dinner, Madame the Princess entered the Bastile, where she was received by M. the Prince with all the testimonies of friendship that can be imagined; and he gave her no repose until she had said to him that she pardoned him." In this same journal, there has often been a question of the bad conduct of the prince towards his wife, in regard to which there is not one word of blame.

night and one o'clock, she gave to the world Anne Geneviève. It seems as if the birth of this child brought good fortune to her parents; for two months

---

"August 31, 1617. The undertaking to save the prince from the Bastile discovered.

"September 15, 1617. M. the Prince taken from the Bastile to the wood of Vincennes. . . . A long time before he had asked that he might be placed there in order to have better air. M. de Modène said to him that, mindful of that, he had pressed the king so much upon the subject, that at last he had obtained it. M. the Prince responded that in the mean time he had become accustomed to the air of the Bastile; and thereupon resisted all that he could, until it was necessary to go. Madame the Princess also went with him in a coach, having been unwilling to enter a litter. It is said that in the beginning M. the Prince only thought it was desired to deprive him of his wife. M. de Vitry, M. de Persan, M. de Modène, were with him in the coach. After his arrival at the wood of Vincennes, it was permitted him, about the beginning of October, to walk upon the top of a thick wall, which is in the form of a gallery. M. de Persan dwelt in the tower of the wood of Vincennes, in order to guard the prince with the greatest part of the soldiers that he had with him in the Bastile, and M. de Cadenet (afterwards Duke and Marshal de Chaulnes, brother of Constable de Luynes), with a dozen companies of the regiment of Normandy, kept guard in the court of the château, which the soldiers are not permitted to leave.

"About December 20, 1617. Madame the Princess very sick. She is put to bed in the wood of Vincennes, at seven months, of a still-born child, and was more than forty-eight hours without motion or feeling. Never was a person in greater extremity without dying. Among other physicians, M. Duret and M. Pietre assisted her with extreme care. When M. the Prince desired that there should be obsequies for this little infant, M. the Bishop of Paris assembled some theologians, who judged that, since, not having received baptism, it had not entered into the Church, no ceremonies ought to be used on the subject of its death.

"September 5, 1618. Madame the Princess is put to bed of two dead boys. The king shows great displeasure thereupon. Several persons had permission to go to see her.

"March 21, 1619. M. the Prince falls sick. Tuesday, April 2. MM.

had not passed away, when the Prince de Condé left prison with his wife and daughter, and resumed his rank and all his honors.

Hatin, Duret, and Seguin came to the Louvre to represent the state of the malady. The cause was attributed to profound melancholy. For several days he was regarded as hopeless. Madame his mother, Madame the Countess, Madame de Ventadour, Madame the Countess d'Auvergne, Madame de la Trémoille, Madame de Fontaines, Madame la Grande, etc., were allowed to go and visit him. Monday, April 8, the king sent to him his sword by M. de Cadenet, and wrote to him: 'My cousin, I am very much grieved at your illness. I pray you to be comforted. As soon as I shall have set in order my affairs, I will give you your liberty. Be rejoiced then, and have the assurance of my friendship. I am, etc.'

"August 28, 1619. Between midnight and one o'clock, Madame the Princess was put to bed of a daughter, in the wood of Vincennes.

"October 17, 1619. Council held, in which is taken the final resolution of releasing M. the Prince.

"October 18. The king goes to Chantilly, to await there M. the Prince.

"19th. M. de Luynes goes to find M. the Prince at the wood of Vincennes.

"20th. M. de Luynes goes early in the morning to the wood of Vincennes, and gets into a carriage with M. the Prince and Madame the Princess, in which were also MM. de Cadenet and de Modène. He goes to Chantilly to find the king, and sees him in a cabinet, where, it is said, he falls upon his knees, and makes extreme protestations of fidelity, and feeling of obligation, which he had for him.

"22d. The king returns to Compiègne, accompanied by M. the Prince. Madame the Princess arrived there and saw the queen the same day."

In the xvi. vol. of the same manuscript, p. 933, a French diplomatic agent transmits the reports spread abroad in the Low Countries, on the subject of the Prince and Princess de Condé, prisoners at the Bastile or in Vincennes: "The Princess de Condé, the younger, has written from there to her own *femme de chambre* married in that city, that M. the Prince de Condé was under the impression that he had been poisoned by his head-cook, named Baucheron, who had practiced and received money for that purpose, and had escaped; and because he might take refuge in that country, she charges her to inform the Prince and Princess of Orange, in order to arrest him if possible. The people of the so-

Anne Geneviève passed very soon from the tower of Vincennes to the hôtel de Condé. There, two years afterwards, September 2, 1621, was born the brother, who was destined to give such lustre to the name of Condé, Louis, Duke d'Enghien; and later, in 1629, another brother still, Armand, Prince de Conti. This last was not wanting in spirit; but he was feeble in body, and even considerably deformed. He was destined for the Church. He pursued his studies at the college of Clermont, with the Jesuits, in company with Molière, and studied theology at Bourges, under Father Deschamps. He made his appearance in the world in the early part of 1647, a little previous to the Fronde. The Duke d'Enghien, charged with sustaining the greatness of his house, was brought up by his father with the masculine tenderness already spoken of, the fruits of which have been too great to allow us to show them in a single moment.

M. the Prince gave no governor to his son; he chose to direct his education himself, calling to his aid two gentlemen, one for exercises of the body, the other for those of the mind. The young duke pur-

---

called Prince of Orange also say, that M. the Prince de Condé has thought of escaping, and has been betrayed and discovered by one of his domestics, but that he has still other means for regaining his liberty."

sued his studies, under the Jesuits of Bourges, with the greatest success. He maintained there, with a certain *éclat*, philosophical theses. He learned the principles of law under the celebrated Doctor Edmond Mérille. He studied history and mathematics, without neglecting the Italian, dancing, boxing, horsemanship, and the chase. On his return to Paris, he saw again his sister, and was charmed with her grace and spirit: he bound himself to her in a most tender friendship, which suffered some changes, but resisted all trials, and, after the passionate age, became as firm as at first it had been ardent. At the hôtel de Condé, the Duke d'Enghien learned, in the company of his sister and his mother, politeness, elegant manners, and gallantry. His father placed him at the academy, under a renowned master, to whom he gave absolute authority over him. Louis de Bourbon was there treated as severely as a simple gentleman. He had at the academy the same success as at college, which he left, the most capable of all those that were there with him. Let us listen to the words of Lenet,[1] the reliable witness of all that he recounts:

"No one had yet seen a prince of the blood brought up and instructed in that common manner;

---

[1] *Mémoires de Lenet*, collection of Michaud, 3d series, v. ii., p. 448.

nor had any one seen a prince who, in so short a time, and in such extreme youth, exhibited so much knowledge, so much experience, and so much address in every thing. The prince, his father, skilful and enlightened in all matters, believed that in the açademy he would be less diverted from that occupation, so necessary to a young man of birth, than in the hôtel. He also thought that those lords and gentlemen who were there, and who had entered it in order to have the honor of his company, would be servants and friends, who would attach themselves to his person and his fortune. During all those days devoted to work, nothing could divert his mind. The whole court admired his air and his grace in skilfully managing a horse, in running at the ring, in dancing and fencing. The king himself compelled him, from time to time, to give an account of his conduct, and often praised the profound judgment of the prince his father in every thing, and particularly in the education of the duke his son, saying to everybody that in this he wished to imitate him, and to have Monsieur the Dauphin instructed and brought up in the same manner." . . . .

. . . . "After the young duke had remained at this excellent school the time necessary to perfect himself, as he did, he left it; and after having been some months at court and among the ladies, where, in the beginning, he exhibited that noble and gallant air so universally admired, the prince his father persuaded the king and Cardinal Richelieu—that powerful, skilled, and authoritative minister—to send him into his own government of Burgundy, with letters-patent, to command there in his absence." . . .

. . . "The troops often traversed Burgundy, and frequently made it their winter-quarters. There the young prince began to learn the manner of properly establishing and governing them, that is, of giving subsistence to the troops without ruining the places where they sojourned. He learned how to mark out lines of march and places of bivouac, and to make soldiers live with order and discipline. He received the complaints of all, and caused justice to be done them. He found a manner of satisfying the soldiers and the people. He often received orders from the king, and letters from the ministers; he was punctual in replying to them; and the court, like the province, saw with astonishment his application to business. He entered the parliament when important subjects rendered his presence necessary, or when the discussion of some interesting question excited his curiosity. The intendant of justice completed nothing without rendering an account of it to him. He began from that moment, whatever might be his confidence in his secretaries, to sign no order, no letters, which he had not previously commanded, which he had not read from end to end. . . . These great and serious occupations did not interfere with his amusements, and his pleasures were no obstacle to his studies. He found days and hours for all things. He went to the chase, and was among the best at shooting on the wing; he gave balls to the ladies; he looked after the management of his servants; he danced; he continued to learn languages and read history; he applied himself to mathematics, and especially to geometry and fortifications; he planned and raised a fort of four bastions, a league from Dijon, in the plain of Bloye; and such was his eagerness to see it completed and in readiness for attack and defence—as was the case several times with the young lords and gentlemen who rendered themselves assiduous about him—that he had his table removed thither, and took there most of his meals."

Thus prepared, the Duke d'Enghien went, during the summer of 1640, to serve, in the capacity of volunteer, in the army of Marshal de La Meilleraye. The marshal wished to take his orders, and to have the appearance at least of depending on him. The young duke firmly refused, saying that he had come to learn his trade, and wished to fulfil all the functions of a volunteer, without regard to his rank. In one of the first engagements, La Ferté-Senneterre was wounded, and had his horse killed by a cannon-shot. The Duke d'Enghien was so near him, that the blood of the horse covered his face. At the siege of Arras, he was everywhere seen at the head of the volunteers. He was found at all the sallies made by the besieged. He rarely left the trench; often slept there, and had his food brought there. Three engagements took place during this siege. The young duke distinguished himself in all. "The great heart which he showed upon these occasions," says Lenet;[1] "the obliging manner with which he treated every one; the liberality with which he assisted friends who were in need, wounded officers and soldiers; the secrecy which he observed in rendering them assistance, made the clear-sighted predict that he would some day be one of the greatest captains of the world."

It was in the winter of 1641, that he was compelled to espouse Mademoiselle de Brézé, niece of Richelieu. The Duke d'Enghien did every thing in his power to shun an alliance which was repugnant to his heart as well as to his ambition. He had cast his eyes upon Mademoiselle, then the only daughter of the Duke of Orleans, beautiful, young, rich, and intellectual. He had already allowed his soul to be penetrated

---

[1] *Mémoires de Lenet*, Michaud, 3d series, vol. ii., p. 458.

with a particular sentiment for another person, whom he at length adored. He yielded only after a long resistance, protesting officially and before a notary, that he gave way to force and to the deference that he owed to the will of his father. He fell sick, and was even in danger, when, suddenly, the report was spread abroad that the campaign was about to be opened, and that the army of Marshal de La Meilleraye was marching into Flanders, to attack the stronghold of Aire. This news reached him when still so feeble that he could scarcely quit his bed. "He sets out immediately," says Lenet.[1] "The prayers of his family, the tears of his mistress, the command of the king himself are not able to arrest him. He learns on his march, being at Abbeville, that the cardinal was approaching from the besieged place in order to attack the lines. He quits his coach, mounts a horse at the same hour with the Duke de Nemours, his intimate friend, a handsome prince, full of spirit and courage, whom death took from him soon after.[2] He passes in the night by Hesdin, so near the enemy that one might almost say that he passed through

[1] *Mémoires de Lenet*, Michaud, 3d series, vol. ii., p. 455.

[2] His eldest brother, who, having taken his title after his death, was also distinguished for his beauty, his bravery, his gallantry, played an important part in the life of Madame de Longueville, and perished in a senseless duel with the Duke de Beaufort, his brother-in-law.

their army, and arrives fortunately in the camp, where he is received with testimonies of joy that it would be difficult to express. This fatigue, which might have been expected to cause a relapse in a feeble and reduced convalescent, gives to him new strength, and from that moment he is seen exposing himself to all the perils of war. He often sleeps in the trench; he eats there; and there is no work, however advanced, where he is not seen taking part like a simple soldier. . . . At the siege of Bapaume, the duke wished to end the campaign as he had commenced it; that is, by going everywhere, and incurring all the hazards and all the perils of the trench and ádvance works. It was not possible for him to leave the army as long as he thought there was any thing of importance to undertake."

Some time after, he followed the Cardinal de Richelieu and the king to the siege of Perpignan. He was there wounded, and there covered with glory; so that no one was astonished when, in 1643, after the death of Richelieu, Louis XIII., also near his death, at the same time that he established the Prince de Condé chief of council, named the Duke d'Enghien Generalissimo of the principal army of France, destined to defend the frontier of Flanders, menaced by a powerful Spanish army. The Duke d'Enghien was not twenty-two years of age. A month afterwards he gained the battle of Rocroy, soon to be followed by those of Friburgh, Nortlingen, and Lens.

Such was the brother. The sister had not disregarded the examples of her house, but on the contrary had rapidly attained, by her wit and her beauty, a renown sufficiently great.

From her infancy, great lessons had never been wanting to her.

She was eight years of age in 1627, when one of the near relatives of her mother, Montmorency-Boutteville, was beheaded in the Place de Grève, for having fought a duel in spite of the edict of the king, leaving, under the protection of Madame the Princess, his widow and three young children,—Marie-Louise, afterwards Marchioness de Valençay; Isabelle-Angélique, afterwards Duchess de Châtillon; and Fançois-Henri de Montmorency, born after the death of his father, who became the Duke Marshal de Luxembourg, one of the most faithful friends and best lieutenants of Condé.

She was thirteen in 1632, when the own brother of her mother, the Duke de Montmorency, ascended the scaffold at Toulouse for having revolted against the king, or rather against Richelieu, upon the uncertain faith of Gaston, Duke of Orleans. This terrible catastrophe, which resounded from one end of France to the other, filled the hôtel de Condé with mourning, and made a profound impression upon the delicate and proud soul of Mademoiselle de Bourbon. She was so troubled by it, that her grief, adding new ardor to the piety in which she had been nourished, caused her to think seriously of quitting the world and becoming a Carmelite in the great convent of the Rue Saint-Jacques.

What religious education had Mademoiselle de Bourbon received, then, that such a thought should come to her at thirteen or fourteen years of age? How did she know the convent of the Carmelites—what ties had she already formed there, which attracted her so powerfully?

It was the time when the religious spirit, after having gone astray in the civil wars, and produced the great crimes and the great virtues of the League, refined, but not enfeebled, by the Edict of Nantes and the policy of Henry IV., found in peace new strength, and covered France, no longer with inimical parties armed against each other, but with pious institutions, in which weary souls were eager to seek an asylum. Everywhere the ancient orders were reformed, and new orders were founded. Richelieu courageously undertook the reformation of the clergy, created seminaries, and above these, as their model and tribunal, raised the Sorbonne. Bérulle instituted the *Oratoire*, Çesar de Bus the *Doctrine chrétrienne*. The Jesuits, who sprang up in the middle of the sixteenth century, and who spread themselves so rapidly over France, at first decried and even banished for their participation in culpable excesses, little by little regained favor under the protection of the immense services which their heroic skill daily rendered, beyond the ocean, to Christianity and civilization. The order of Saint Benedict engaged in a salutary reform, and the Benedictines of Saint-Maur gave the prelude to their gigantic works. But who can enumerate the fine institutions, designed for women, that were founded on every hand by Christianity, during the first half of the seventeenth century? The two most illustrious, after reformed Port-Royal, are the Sisters of Charity about 1640, and the Carmelites in 1602.

The first convent of the Carmelites was established at Paris, in the Faubourg Saint-Jacques, under the auspices and by the munificence of that house of Longueville, into which Mademoiselle de Bourbon was destined to enter. Her mother, Madame the Princess, was one of the benefactresses of the rising institution. There she had an apartment, where she often retreated for a long time. At an early period, she thither led her daughter, and there filled her soul with the principles and the devotional habits of the times. Mademoiselle de Bourbon grew up in the shade of the holy monastery. There she beheld the reign of virtue, goodness, concord, peace, silence: there she was loved, and there she was called. It is, then, natural that at the first sight of the tempests which menaced all the great things of the earth, and struck the most illustrious members of her own family, she should think of forestalling her destiny, and seek a shelter under the humble roof of the Carmelites. She had there sweet and noble friendships, which she never abandoned. We possess a multitude of letters, addressed by her to the Carmelites of the convent of the Rue Saint-Jacques, at all the epochs of her life, before, during, and after the Fronde. We feel that they were written to persons who had her entire confidence and whole soul. But what were those persons? She calls them sometimes the Mother Prioress, sometimes the Mother Sub-prioress, Sister Marthe, Sister Anne-Marie, Mother Marie-Madeleine, Mother Agnes, etc. One could wish to pierce the veil that covers the family names of all these nuns. We doubt much whether the friends of Mademoiselle de Bourbon and Madame de Longueville could have been common creatures; and as we know that many women of the first quality and of noblest heart found a refuge among the Carmelites, as the name of Sister Louise de La Miséricorde has become the popular symbol of disinterested and unfortunate love, a curiosity, somewhat profane but very natural, leads us to inquire what these nuns, so dear to the sister of the great Condé, were in the world.

Hitherto we have been reduced to conjectures, suggested to us by bringing together different passages from Madame de Sévigné, Madame de Motteville, and Mademoiselle. The French Carmelites have no history. Faithful to their vow of obscurity, these worthy daughters of Saint Theresa have passed away without leaving any traces of themselves behind. As during their life, an impenetrable cloister shut them out from all eyes, and buried them in advance, so the genius of their order seems to have taken care to annihilate them in the memory of men. At long intervals have appeared a few memoirs of the Carmelites, consecrated to edification, filled with holy maxims, void of human facts, and almost with out dates. At the beginning of this century, a priest, M. Boucher, in a new *Life of the blessed Sister Marie, of the Incarnation, Madame Acarie, Foundress of the reformed Carmelites of France*,[1] has, for the first time, thrown a little light upon the origin of that holy house, presenting, or rather withholding, in the notes of his work, a few short biographies of the principal nuns. The national library, so rich in manuscripts of every kind, possesses

[1] Paris, 1800, in-8°.

none that comes from the Carmelites of the Faubourg Saint-Jacques, or that relates to them. The general Archives have inherited all their principal titles. We have studied them sufficiently to give the assurance that a record[1] of the greatest interest might be formed of them. Among other precious pieces, we may designate an inventory of paintings, by different celebrated masters,[2] statues,[3] and objects of art which the liberal and generous piety of the faithful of every rank had, during two centuries, accumulated for the Carmelites, and which were again noticed in 1790. But there were other treasures which we had wished to discover—we desired an exact list of all the nuns of that convent during the seventeenth century, with their religious and their

[1] There is a constant demand for a collection of the cartularies of the old abbeys. Why will not some friend of religion and letters occupy himself with filling up the lacunes, so much to be regretted, of the *Gallia christiana*, by bringing together, under the name of the Cartulary of the convent of the Carmelites of the Faubourg Saint-Jacques, a multitude of pieces which we have held in our hands, which would establish, upon authentic monuments, the history of that interesting congregation, from the first years of the seventeenth century to the French Revolution? All the notes, extracts, and copies, that we have amassed, belong to him who will undertake to enrich with a new volume of this kind the *Collection des documents inédits relatifs à l'histoire de France.*

[2] For example, Guido, Champagne, and Lebrun.

[3] Among others, a statue, in white marble, representing the Cardinal de Bérulle on his knees. This beautiful work is by Jacques Sarrazin, and is still to be seen in the chapel of the Carmelites.

family names, the date of their profession and that of their death. We placed a particular value upon knowing the succession of prioresses who had, by turns, governed the convent, spoken or written in its name. It was conceived, in fact, that without these two documents, the friendships of Mademoiselle de Bourbon and Madame de Longueville would remain, for us, almost impenetrable.

Light has come to us from a quarter where we had not, at first, sought for it.

In the ruins of the convent of the Faubourg Saint-Jacques, spared by the revolutionary tempest, yet barely standing, some poor nuns, having escaped a stupid persecution, have been trying, for fifty years past, to collect the traditions of the Carmelites, and they continue it in obscurity, prayer, and toil:

> Præcipites atra sue tempestate columbæ,
> Condensæ et divûm amplexæ simulacra sedebant.

Weary of uselessly searching archives and libraries, I addressed myself to these good nuns, and they responded to me with the most graceful kindness. The two documents that I needed were sent to me, with manuscript annals, and a collection of biographies ample and full of details. Thanks to these precious communications, it is easy to make out the history of the Carmelites of the Faubourg Saint-Jacques. Under the pious designations and mystic symbols of Carmel, we recognize more than one person who has already been met in the memoirs of the times. Instead of beings in some sort abstract and anonymous, we have before us animated and living creatures, whose regards were doubtless finally directed towards heaven, not to be turned thence, who, nevertheless, for a longer or shorter period, inhabited the earth, knew our sentiments, felt our weaknesses, and, always remaining pure, sometimes felt sorely tempted, and shared our humanity. Some day we shall deliver to the public the key that has been lent us, which will give the secret of many mysterious things in the intimate history of the manners of the seventeenth century. Here we shall allow ourselves only a few rapid sketches that can throw light upon the obscure part of the youth and of the whole life of Madame de Longueville.

Saint Theresa, who died in 1582, had refounded in Spain the ancient and degenerate order of Carmel. The saintly renown of the new Carmelites of Spain spread itself rapidly in Italy and France. An admirable woman, Madame Acarie, afterwards Sister Mary of the Incarnation, conceived the idea of sending to Spain for some disciples of Saint Theresa, and of establishing them at Paris in the Faubourg Saint-Jacques. Such was the origin of the first convent of French Carmelites.

There are two Princesses de Longueville who obtained from Henri IV., in 1602,[1] the necessary letters-patent, Catherine and Marguerite d'Orleans, daughters of Henri, Duke de Longueville, who died unmarried,—Marguerite in 1615, Catherine in 1638, both buried in the convent whose second founders they were called, the title of first founder having been reserved for Marie de Médicis. And when, in 1617, the young institution was already strong enough to need another house at Paris, it was again a Princess de Longueville who defrayed the expense of the new establishment, in the Rue Chapon,[2] to wit, the sister-in-law of Marguerite and of Catherine,[3]

---

[1] General Archives, demesnial section, 1st file, letter C: "Letters-patent of King Henry IV. for the establishment of the order of the nuns of Notre-Dame of Mount Carmel, verified in parliament October 1, 1602, at the very humble petition of our dear well-beloved cousin, Demoiselle de Longueville." And in other pieces it is also said: "The said lord (King Henry), favorably disposed to the petition of Catherine d'Orleans, daughter of the late Henri d'Orleans, Duke de Longueville and de Touteville. . . ."

[2] Since that time the convent of the Rue Saint-Jacques has been called the Great Convent, to distinguish it from the house in the Rue Chapon.

[3] The act of donation which is in the General Archives, was made in the name of the duchess dowager de Longueville, as well as in the name of her son, the future husband of Anne de Bourbon. "Madame Catherine de Gonzagues and de Clèves, Duchess de Longueville and de Touteville, widow of the late very powerful prince Henri d'Orleans, during his life, Duke de Longueville and de Touteville, sovereign Count of Neufchâtel and Valengin, in Switzerland, also Count of Dunois and Tancarville, etc., dwelling at Paris, in his hôtel de Longueville, Rue des Poulies, parish of Saint-Germain de l'Auxerrois, as well in his own

the widow of their brother, Henri d'Orleans, first of the name, and the mother of Henri II., who espoused Mademoiselle de Bourbon. Madame the Princess de Condé was not backward in bestowing her benefits on the convent of the Rue Saint-Jacques, and she became especially attached to it. So it may be said that Mademoiselle de Bourbon was, in advance, consecrated in every way to the Carmelites.

Let us endeavor to represent what was, in the seventeenth century, the convent of the Carmelites, where Mademoiselle de Bourbon wished to conceal her life, where Madame de Longueville returned to die. It was situated in the street of the Faubourg Saint-Jacques, directly opposite to Val-de-Grâce. It ex-

---

name as in that of Monseigneur Henri d'Orleans, his son, also Duke de Longueville and de Touteville." . . . Catherine de Gonzagues and Clèves was sister of Charles de Gonzagues, Duke de Nevers, the father of Marie and Anne de Gonzagues, the Queen of Poland and the Palatine. Her son, Henry II., exercised himself much in playing at tennis, and one of his shoulders became larger and more elevated than the other. All the skill of the physicians was powerless. The desolate mother addressed herself to Madame Acarie, then sister Marie de l'Incarnation. She engaged in prayer previous to the holy sacrament, and the next day the form of the youth was very much improved. Through gratitude, the mother and son founded the house of the Rue Chapon, endowed it with ten thousand crowns in silver, and two thousand livres a year. The Duke de Longueville testified to this fact before the Apostolic Commissioners, charged with the beatification of Madame Acarie. Catherine de Gonzagues died in 1629. We find in the Archives different acts which prove that the niece of Richelieu, Madame the Duchess d'Aiguillon, was also one of the benefactresses of both convents. "Marie Vignerot, Duchess d'Esguillon, dwelling in her hotel, situated in Saint-Germain-des-Prés, parish of Saint-Sulpice." . . .

tended from the Rue Saint-Jacques to the Rue d'Enfer, and finally embraced, with all its dependencies, the vast space which, from the garden and inclosure of the Oratorian seminary of Saint-Magloire, at present the Sourds-Muets, ascends to the buildings now occupied in the Rue Saint-Jacques and in the Rue d'Enfer, by the establishment called the brew-house of Luxembourg. There were two entrances, one from the Rue Saint-Jacques, the other from the Rue d'Enfer. The entrance from the Rue d'Enfer still exists, at No. 67, and is now what it was two centuries ago. It led into the existing court, which served as a public passage to the Rue Saint-Jacques. Almost opposite, a little to the right, was the church; a little farther to the right, on the grounds where the wholly new street of Val-de-Grâce has been opened, were vast gardens, with numerous chapels, the monastery itself, and, entirely upon the Rue d'Enfer, the infirmary and the apartments reserved for particular persons. On the other side, to the left, towards Saint-Magloire, were the different main-houses of the monastery and their dependents.[1]

But the monastery had thus increased only with time.

The first seat of the community had been the an-

---

[1] See Gomboust's plan of Paris, in 1652, and the plan called Turgot's, of Paris, in 1740.

cient priory of Notre-Dame-des-Champs, whose church was of the time of Hugh Capet, and, according to ancient tradition, was established upon the ruins of a temple of Ceres, where Saint Denis had already taken refuge when he preached the gospel at Paris. At least, excavations made in 1630, have brought to light some remains of pagan antiquity. There was, therefore, already some mystery about the new establishment at the beginning of the seventeenth century.[1]

---

[1] See Malingre, *Antiquités de la Ville de Paris*, in-fol., Paris, 1640, pp. 152 and 153, also pp. 501 and 503, *Nouveaux Mémoires concernant la maison des Carmélites*; a few lines in the *Histoire de la Ville de Paris* of Felibien and of Lobineau, vol. ii., pp. 1268-1271, and some records in vol. iii. of the *Preuves et Pièces justificatives*, p. 144. Sauval contains but a page on the Carmelites, vol. i., p. 450. The best thing in regard to this convent is found in the *Curiosités de Paris*, 1771, vol. i., pp. 459-463. We take from it the following description of the church: "Although the main body of this church is very ancient, it is one of the best decorated in Paris. The great altar is formed of four marble columns, and is reached by twelve steps, very ingeniously placed, with a balustrade of marble. All the ornaments of this altar are of bronze gilded; the tabernacle, which represents the ark of the covenant, is all of silver; the bas-relief in front is highly wrought, and represents the Annunciation. Nothing is more sumptuous than this altar on feast-days. You then see a sun, bright with stones of great value, accompanied by candlesticks, vases, and other pieces of goldsmith's ware, whose quantity equals its magnificence. The picture is by Guido, and represents the Annunciation.

"The choir is separated from the nave by four beautiful columns of sea-green marble, surmounted by flames of gilded bronze of wonderful beauty and size. The crucifix of bronze, which you see on the door, is one of the best and highly esteemed of the works of Sarrazin.

"The vault of the church, upon which numerous stories from the Holy Scriptures are represented, was painted by Champagne, through the liberality of Marie de Médicis. Observe in it an excellent piece of per-

If it was the Spanish Carmelites who founded the convent of the Rue Saint-Jacques, and established there the spirit and rule of Saint Theresa, it must be

---

spective, designed by Des Argues: it is a crucifix, with the Holy Virgin and St. John, so artistically painted by the same Champagne, that, on entering the church, they appear upon a perpendicular plane, although horizontal, which produces an agreeable and singular effect.

"Above the door of this church there is a beautiful gallery, containing statues of Saint Peter, of Saint Paul, and of Saint Michael overcoming the devil.

"All the chapels are magnificent: the most beautiful pictures and gildings adorn all parts of it; neatness and good taste reign throughout.

"The twelve pictures ornamented with gilded frames, which are placed under the windows, represent subjects drawn from the New Testament, and were painted by very skilful masters. The first, at the right on entering, represents the *Resurrection of Lazarus;* the second, *The Circumcision of our Lord;* the third, *The Adoration of the Magi;* the fourth, *The Assumption of the Holy Virgin;* the fifth, *The Descent of the Holy Ghost upon the Apostles;* the sixth, *The Birth of our Lord.* These six pictures were also painted by the celebrated Champagne, and are very highly esteemed. On the other side, the first represents the *Miracle of the Five Loaves*, by Stella; the second, *The Madeline at the feet of our Lord, at the house of Simon the Pharisee*—it is one of the finest works of the famous Le Brun; the third, *The Entry of Jesus Christ into Jerusalem*, by La Hire; the fourth, *Christ at the side of Jacob's well, talking with the Samaritan woman*, by Stella; the fifth, *Christ served in the Desert by Angels*—this is also by Le Brun; the sixth, *The Appearance of our Lord to the three Marys*, by La Hire.

"Opposite to the choir of the nuns, observe the great picture representing *the Annunciation;* it is an excellent work by Guido, who painted it for Queen Marie de Médicis.

"Look afterwards at the chapel of Sainte-Marie-Madeleine; it is one of the most ornamented. You will there see the statue of Cardinal de Berulle, made in marble by Sarrazin, in 1657; it is raised upon a marble pedestal, upon which are excellent bas-reliefs, by Lestocart, a famous sculptor. These bas-reliefs represent the Holy Sacrifice of the Mass, and that also performed by Noah, when he left the ark. You will also see in this chapel, all covered with pictures, one of the most perfect

remembered that, those nuns having left France in 1618, to return to Spain, or to end their days in Belgium in the monasteries of their order, it was the French genius which early took possession of the convent of the Rue Saint-Jacques, and made it what it became.

In the number of the prioresses who governed it, may be distinguished four, who aided the rising congregation to advance rapidly towards the perfection which it attained at the close of the seventeenth century. These were Mademoiselle de Fontaines, the Mother Madeleine de Saint-Joseph; the Marchioness de Bréauté, Marie de Jésus; Mademoiselle Lancri de Bains, Marie-Madeleine; and Mademoiselle Bellefonds, the Mother Agnès de Jésus-Maria. Mademoiselle de Bourbon knew them all, and some of them were her friends.

Mademoiselle de Fontaines was the first French head-prioress. She was of an excellent family of Touraine. Her father had been ambassador to Flanders, and her mother was sister to the wife of Sillery the chancellor. It was the Cardinal de Bérulle who, meeting her at

---

paintings ever produced by the famous Le Brun; it represents the *Penitent Madeleine.* Grief and repentance are so vividly expressed in this, and the skill of the excellent master so well proved by all the accompaniments, that you can find nothing more finished and more perfect. The life of this saint is represented in the wainscot of this beautiful chapel."

Tours, and seeing her there young and already filled with holy thoughts, pointed out to her the Carmelites of the Rue Saint-Jacques as the way to the perfection after which she aspired. She did not walk thither, but ran, as Madame Acarie says of her. And yet she loved her family so tenderly that she felf a poignant grief in leaving it, and, as she herself said at a subsequent period, the coach that took her to the Carmelites seemed to her like a car that carries criminals to punishment. Touched by her example, two of her sisters followed her to the Carmelites.[1] She joined them at twenty-six years of age. For some time she had before her the Spanish mothers, and from them caught that holy ardor which excites and vivifies, and can alone surmount the difficult commencements of every great establishment. She was constantly faithful to the device of Saint Theresa: Endure or die. She is the Saint Theresa of France. The nun who succeeded her has thus painted the effects of the government of Mother Madeleine de Saint-Joseph: "When she was prioress, I can truly say the monastery resembled a paradise, so much fervor and desire for perfection of heart was seen. The question was who should be the most humble, the most penitent, the most subdued, the most collected,

---

[1] *Histoire manuscrite*, t. ii.

the most meditative, the most solitary, the most charitable; in brief, who should be most conformed to our Lord Jesus Christ; and all this, too, with a peace, an innocence, a beatitude, and an elevation to God that surpass the power of expression. This servant of God was among us like a torch that gave us light, like a fire that warmed us, a living rule by whose example we could learn how to become saints." Some admirable words of hers have been preserved. We will cite but a single sentence: "Yes," said she to her daughters, who for the most part were of high rank, "yes, we are of a very good house; we are daughters of a king, sisters of a king, spouses of a king; for we are the daughters of the Father Eternal, the sisters of Christ, and the spouses of the Holy Spirit." She had one of those great hearts that make heroes of every kind, and which are the primary source of miracles. She therefore performed miracles like Saint Theresa: like her she had ecstasies and visions. It was the heart in her that warmed the imagination, and, in fact, the heart is the sacred source of all great things. What[1] philosophy would interpose here its

[1] We have elsewhere established that of the three sources of human knowledge, intuition, induction, and deduction, the first is much the most fertile and the most elevated. It is intuition, which, by its own spontaneous power, discovers directly and without the aid of reflection, all essential truths; it is the source of light to the human race; the voice that speaks to prophets and poets; the principle of all inspira-

miserable objections! Be on your guard; those objections would turn against Socrates and his demon, as well as against the good angel of Mother Madeleine de Saint-Joseph. That good angel was at least the inner vision, the secret and truly marvellous voice of a great soul.

Mother Madeleine de Saint-Joseph was born in 1578, entered the convent in 1604, pronounced her vows in 1605, and died in 1637.[1]

Marie de Jésus is a nun of a wholly different character.

Charlotte de Sancy was daughter of Nicolas de Harlay, Lord de Sancy, who was under Henri IV. ambassador, superintendent of the finances, and colonel of the Swiss. The two sons of Harlay de Sancy, after having occupied important positions, retired to the Oratoire. His first daughter was married to M. d'Alincourt, grandfather of Duke de Villeroy; the second, Charlotte, was married to the Mar-

---

tion of enthusiasm, and of that unalterable and sure faith, that astonishes reasoning which is compelled to treat it as a folly, because it cannot account for it by its ordinary processes. See the *Cours de Philosophie*, particularly, First Series, vol. v., p. 301; and Second Series, vol. i., Lecture vi., pp. 131-141, etc.

[1] *See the Vie de la Mère Madeleine de Saint-Joseph, religieuse Carmélite déchaussée*, by a priest of the Oratoire (Father Senault): Paris, 1655, in-4°. There is a second edition, of 1670, augmented. The Carmelites still have the head of their venerable mother. It is powerful and large. A portrait of her, preserved by the convent, exhibits in her face great strength of character. It has been many times engraved.

quis de Bréauté. Having remained a widow twenty-one years—beautiful,[1] spirituelle, of a charming temper, she was the delight of her family, and one of the ornaments of the court of Henri IV. Two circumstances conspired to snatch her from the pleasures that surrounded her. One day, at Spa, while dancing at a ball during a storm, she heard a clap of thunder, and wished to retire. The gentleman who was her partner laughed at her fright, and retained her. At the same instant the thunder again sounded, and the man by her side was struck dead. Some time afterwards she met with the writings of Saint Theresa, read them, and was so touched by them, that, young as she was, she resolved at once to quit the world. She entered among the Carmelites, and took the veil, under the name of Marie de Jésus, the same year with Mademoiselle de Fontaines. She preserved in the cloister that winning gentleness which, in the world, added to the effect of her beauty, and subjected to her all hearts. She was adored by her new companions, as she had been at the court. Her particular gift was, with sweetness and humility, a boundless charity, which was especially exercised in the salvation of souls. She excelled

[1] The Carmelites have a small portrait, painted on wood, of Mother Marie de Jésus, somewhat advanced in life, but of a noble and sweet visage. It has been engraved by Regnesson.

in the art of bringing sinners to God. These were her miracles. Here is one of them that the tradition of the Carmelites has preserved for us :[1]

A man of merit, who possessed goods and important occupations, formed a culpable connection. His mother was in distress about it, and often went to pour her grief into the bosom of her daughter, a nun at the convent of the Rue Saint-Jacques. One day when she was in the parlor, Marie de Jésus was inspired to go to her and console her. She gave her Saint Augustine's *Confessions* and Saint Theresa's *Way to Perfection*, asking her to make her son promise to read them for a quarter of a hour only every morning. He made the promise, but did not keep it for eight days. One night, feeling urged to keep his word, he arose and read some pages of these books. As he continued reading, God enlightened him, and so touched him, that he shed tears for several hours, troubled and agitated lest he should lose the Holy Spirit. Finally he became calm, and, during several nights, was penetrated, and, as it were, inundated with light in regard to the perfection of God. One morning, at the break of day, he drove to the Place de Grenelle with the person who held him captive. There he announced to her that he

---

[1] *Histoire manuscrite*, vol. ii.

should never see her again. He left her his carriage to drive where she wished. Returning home on foot, he went to the Carmelites to visit his sister, whom he had not seen for many years. She called Marie de Jésus, and said to her brother: Behold your benefactress! Marie de Jésus had not ceased to pray for him. She lavished upon him the most affectionate counsels, which she renewed regularly once a week for several years. He followed them with great docility, and made such progress in virtue, that, giving up his charge, and renouncing all the pleasures of life, he retired into a country-place, lived there in penitence, and died in the love of God.

Marie de Jésus was loved much by Anne of Austria, who often went to see her, accompanied by Louis XIV. and his brother the Duke d'Anjou. She contributed largely to the aggrandizement and embellishment of the monastery, which lost her in 1652.

In the year 1620, the Carmelites acquired a worthy sister in one of the maids of honor of Queen Marie de Médicis, Mademoiselle Marie Lancri de Bains. In order to show what Mademoiselle de Bains was, we shall avail ourselves of a manuscript life, composed by a Carmelite who knew her perfectly well.[1]

---

[1] *Histoire manuscrite*, vol. ii.

"Madame de Bains had her daughter brought up among the Ursulines: she removed her from their charge at the age of twelve years, to place her at court, hoping that her beauty and acquirements might procure for her an establishment, little reflecting upon the perils to which she exposed her by leaving her to herself in a place so full of dangers. But God, who had already appropriated this soul, kept watch over her, and preserved her, without a stain, in the midst of that court. Her virtue was there admired as much as her perfect beauty; her portrait passed even into foreign lands, where the most famous painters emulously drew it, in order to exhibit the skill of their pencil. She afterwards declared that until the age of fifteen years, she never reflected upon this advantage, but that she then saw herself with the same eyes as the public. The attractions of her person, and still more her sweetness and modesty, won the esteem and affection of the queen. Mademoiselle de Bains never gloried in any thing but in doing good to the unfortunate. This generosity had its source in a noble, tender, constant heart, united with a mind solid, judicious, capable of great things; and it seemed as if the Creator had been pleased to prepare in this masterpiece of nature the triumph of grace. So many amiable qualities attracted the attention of the whole court. A number of lords, as the Duke de Bellegarde, the Marshal de Saint-Luc, etc., sued for an alliance so desirable. But He who had elected her from all eternity for his bride, did not allow that heart, worthy of himself alone, to be shared by any creature. Divine Providence continued to bring upon her at the same time some mortification (we are ignorant of its nature), which began to open her eyes, and to give her some slight idea of a calling for the religious life."

Mademoiselle de Bains never accompanied the Queen Marie de Médicis to the Carmelites, without wishing to remain there. A sickness which she had at eighteen years of age, redoubled her fervor, but she was opposed by the efforts of the whole court to retain her, especially by the entreaties and tears of her mother. When Mademoiselle de Bains threw herself among the Carmelites, at scarcely twenty years of age, her mother followed her thither. "She conducted her daughter to the bottom of the garden, and there, during three whole hours, employed all the persuasives that tenderest love could suggest. After having exhausted endearments, and tried to move her conscience by telling her that it was her duty to help her widowed mother in her old age, finally, getting beside herself, she fell at the feet of her daughter, drowned in tears. What a trial for Mademoiselle de Bains, who loved that tender mother as much as she was loved by her! Her recourse to God enabled her to come out victorious from that first contest, which was not the last, for, during the entire period of her novitiate, Madame her mother often returned to the charge."

For some time the convent of the Rue Saint-Jacques was besieged by noblemen of the first rank, who went to offer their alliance to the beautiful novice. Her constancy was not in the least shaken, and she would have refused all these visits if the mother prioress had not, in order to prove her, constrained her to receive them. She pronounced her vows in 1620, under the name of Marie-Madeleine de Jésus.

Her beauty must have had something very extraordinary in it, to judge by the following anecdote, related by the pious author of whom we avail ourselves: "Humility being the foundation of every spiritual edifice, Sister Marie-Madeleine de Jésus seized with avidity every means of destroying, in her own eyes and in the eyes of others, the gifts of nature and of grace with which God had favored her. She was not contented with refusing the visits of the great, as well as of all her friends, but desirous of being forgotten, and of removing from their sight every thing that might remind them of her, she endeavored, under different pretexts, to recall her portraits from their hands, in order to burn them. One of these portraits having been sent to Mother Madeleine Saint-Joseph, she amused herself by showing it to the assembled community. At the sight of it all the nuns, not recognizing it at first, were touched, and besought God not to leave in the world that masterpiece of nature, worthy of himself alone, but to bestow her upon Carmel. One of them, Marie de Saint-Theresa, daughter of Madame Acarie, offered herself to God, to suffer every thing that it might please him to inflict in return for such a grace. Then Mother Madeleine de Saint-Joseph, smiling and touching her on the shoulder, told her that the goodness of God had anticipated her desires, that the person for whom she trembled was already in the order, and that it was only necessary to ask for her perseverance."[1]

Sister Marie-Madeleine passed rapidly through all the grades of the order. Elected prioress in 1635, and often re-elected, she witnessed, in 1637, the death of the venerable Mother Madeleine de Saint-Joseph, in 1652 the death of Mother Marie de Jésus, and suc-

---

[1] The Carmelites were very willing to let me see the portrait, painted upon canvas, of Mother Marie-Madeleine, which does not belie her reputation for beauty. The face is of the most perfect oval; the eyes are of the finest and deepest blue; the forehead is noble; the general aspect is full of grandeur and grace. It would be difficult to find any thing more beautiful.

cessively the death of the head visitors of the order and of the instructors of the holy monastery.[1] The wars of the Fronde were to her a perilous trial, wherein she often found herself sharing danger with Queen Anne and the Princess de Condé, the two protectresses of the convent. She was obliged to quit for some time the house in the Rue Saint-Jacques, which was too much exposed to the soldiery, to send a part of the community to Pontoise, and to take the rest to the Rue Chapon. It required great firmness to maintain religious discipline in the midst of such trouble. Through fear of the least abatement, she continually applied herself to renew the fervor of the primitive spirit in the souls committed to her charge. It is said that she then spoke to her daughters with words of fire, which filled them with a holy emulation. She displayed usually a sweet and majestic cheerfulness, a charming affability, with an intrepidity that was proof against every trial when the question was con-

---

[1] We will mention the best known of the general visitors of the order: in 1614, the Cardinal de Bérulle; in 1619, Father de Condren, the second general of the Oratoire; in 1627, the Abbé de Bérulle, nephew of the cardinal, etc. Among the superiors of the monastery, we find, in the earlier period, Father Gibieuf, a learned oratorien, one of the correspondents of Descartes; later, in 1662, M. Ferret, doctor in theology, and curate of Saint-Nicholas-du-Chardonnet; in 1678, M. Pirot, a doctor of the Sorbonne; in 1715, M. Vivant, grand vicar of Cardinal de Noailles; in 1747, the Bishop of Bethlehem, celebrated for having extirpated Jansenism, which had been introduced among the Carmelites at the close of the preceding century.

cerning the interests of God, of those of the order, or of the salvation of souls. On such occasions, says our manuscript, without being surprised or arrested, she would have overcome a world of opposition, and sacrificed her own life. So much virtue united with so much sensibility, had acquired for her such an ascendancy over the hearts and minds of her daughters, that one of them wrote that if she had undertaken to persuade them that white was black and day night, they would have believed her, so thoroughly were they convinced that she could not be deceived. In fine, she possessed in the highest degree the gift of governing. It was to her that so many persons of highest birth, wounded or repentant hearts, intrusted themselves, seeking refuge among the Carmelites.

Marie-Madeleine, born in 1598, lived a long time, and died in 1679, the same year with Madame de Longueville. She had found an admirable assistant in Mademoiselle de Bellefonds.

Judith de Bellefonds was born in 1611. Her father, governor of Caen, was the grandfather of the marshal of that name. Her mother was the sister of the wife of Marshal de Saint-Géran, and she herself was sister to the Marchioness de Villars, mother of the vanquisher of Denain, celebrated for graces of mind.[1]

---

[1] Her letters from Spain to Madame de Coulanges, are, for attractiveness of style, much superior to those of Madame des Ursins. Letters

She was as handsome[1] as her mother, as spirituelle as her sister, and she possessed all the requisites for pleasing. She had the greatest success at the court of Queen Marie de Médicis. Going with her to the Carmelites, she met Madame de Bréauté, Marie de Jésus, who, like her, had known all the attractions of the world, and by her entreaties and her example persuaded her to renounce it, and to give herself to God alone. Mademoiselle de Bellefonds joined the Carmelites in 1629, at seventeen years of age, choosing Saint Agnès as her patron saint, from whom she took the name of Agnès de Jésus-Maria. Her first years at the convent being spent with Mother Madeleine de Saint-Joseph, who had become very infirm, she was penetrated with the spirit of that great servant of God, and promptly showed all the qualities requisite for a great prioress. She was elected sub-prioress at thirty years of age, prioress three years afterwards, and she discharged the duties of one or the other of these offices for thirty-two years, her life being prolonged until near the close of the century. She found the French Car-

---

de Madame de Villars, etc., Paris, 1806 and 1823, and what Madame de Sévigné says of her, letters of October 8, 1679, and February 28, 1680.

[1] The painted portrait that has been shown me, represents her in fact as having the most happy face, with charming blue eyes and beautiful forehead, and a look at once lively and agreeable.

mel established by the eminent virtues of those who had preceded her—she had simply to sustain it. Her dominant qualities were firmness and moderation. With equal facility she dealt with great and small things; always mistress of herself, even-tempered, sensible, and enlightened, speaking of every thing with justice and simplicity, and removing difficulties with an astonishing precision. She who, by the elevation and charms of her mind, seemed born only for the people of the world and important things, was still more admirable with the simple and the poor. She used their ills, to which she was sensible, to elevate them to God, yet ceased not in her endeavors to console them. The happy also found near her protection against the dangers of fortune. The Queen of England, in the midst of her terrible trials, often went to the Carmelites to find consolation with Mother Agnès. The chancellor, Le Tellier, often consulted her. Courted on all sides for the charm of her conversation, she sought solitude, and endeavored to make it loved by her companions. Mademoiselle de Guise having offered 100,000 livres to obtain the privilege of often entering the convent, Mother Agnès refused that sum, saying that 100,000 livres could not repair the injury thereby certain to be done to the spirit of the institution, which can be preserved only by seclusion and separation from the world. Her charity was such that after her death the mother who succeeded her, being blamed for bestowing alms a little too freely, replied: "You are very fortunate that Mother Agnès is no more; she would have left on this occasion neither communion-cup nor vessel of silver in our church." It must be perceived in Madame de Sévigné, how much she made of Mother Agnès: "I was ravished," wrote she to her daughter,[1] "with the spirit of Mother Agnès." Elsewhere she speaks of the vivacity and the charm of her speech.[2] But all eulogies pale before that touching letter of Bossuet, written to the prioress who succeeded her:[3] "We shall then see her no more, that dear mother; we shall no longer hear from her mouth those words that charity, that gentleness, that faith, that prudence dictated and rendered worthy of being listened to.[4] This was the sensible person who believed in the law of God, and faithfully kept it. Prudence was her companion, Wisdom her sister. The joy of the Holy Spirit did not leave her. Her balance was always just; her judgments were always right. Her counsels never led astray; they were preceded by her

---

[1] Letter of January 5, 1680.
[2] Letter of November 22, 1688.
[3] Edition of Lebel, vol. xxxix., p. 690.
[4] Varying from our manuscripts: *weighed.*

example. Her death was tranquil as her life, and she rejoiced in the last day. I thank you for remembering me upon this sad occasion. My spirit unites with yours in the prayers and sacrifices that are offered for that soul blessed of God and men. I join you in the pious tears that you shed upon her tomb, and take part in the consolations with which faith inspires you."

Such was the convent where Mademoiselle de Bourbon received those impressions that decided her whole life; such were the women whom she saw and heard, when she accompanied the princess her mother to the sacred house. She perceived, moreover, the venerable looks, the already transfigured face of Mother Madeleine de Saint-Joseph, and listened to her powerful speech, for Mother de Saint-Joseph was the friend and counsellor of Madame the Princess. She felt, too, the penetrating sweetness of the conversation of Marie de Jésus. She knew that Marie-Madeleine, who was so dangerous in the world by her beauty, so edifying and powerful in the cloister. With her she formed a connection which ceased only with life. But it was, above all, Mademoiselle de Bellefonds, the Mother Agnès, who attracted and charmed her. They were almost of the same age, and the free and joyous temper of the young and spiritual nun established between them, at an early period, an intimacy whose traces are found even in the letters subsequently addressed by the unfortunate and repentant princess to the great prioress, wholly occupied with her difficult duties. The following note,[1] written during their youth, will give an idea of the intimacy of their relation, and show the natural graces of Mademoiselle de Bourbon's mind. It bears the date of 1637. She was then seventeen years of age. These are the earliest lines of hers that we have been able to find. Did Marie de Rabutin write in a more amiable manner at the same age?

"To my Sister Agnès de Jésus-Maria.

"My very dear Sister:

"I write this to you to give you a severe reprimand. I think you will be much astonished at it; but it seems to me that I am not wrong. I must tell you, in order not to leave you any longer in suspense, that, since the death[2] of our blessed mother (Madeleine de Saint-Joseph), our mother (Marie-Madeleine) has promised me her picture. It is three or four days since I reminded her of this promise, and she has sent me word that it was not her fault, but that

---

[1] An autograph billet, for which we are indebted to the Carmelite ladies.

[2] This fixes the date of the note: it is therefore a little while after the death of Mother Madeleine de Saint-Joseph; that is, in 1637.

you had prevented her from giving me what she had promised, and that I must tease you for it. I am therefore resolved to give you no peace until you put me in possession of the portrait. If you wish, I will allow you to have it copied, but if you are not quick about it, you will see that we shall be on bad terms. You know that it would not take much to embroil us, since we are very much inclined to hate each other. It seems to me that I have gone bravely through my reprimand, and that it is very severe. I think it will put you in great alarm, and you will consequently be in much fear of losing my good graces.[1] . . . When the picture is finished, send to me for whatever it costs. (Take care), if you please, to have it made very near the size of that of my Sister Catherine[2] de Jesus, or a little larger.

"Your very affectionate sister and servant,

"Anne de Bourbon."

And observe that I have here spoken only of the most em■ent prioresses, without saying a word of so many other nuns of the highest rank and the most

---

[1] Several lines effaced and wholly illegible, and half of a page cut.

[2] Mademoiselle Nicolas, born at Bordeaux, agreeable in person and mind, say our manuscripts, and pleasing to everybody. Having read, when quite a child, the Life of Catherine de Sienne, she devoted herself to imitating her, and joined the Carmelites at nineteen, and died at thirty-three. There is a small portrait of her, very well made, representing her in ecstasy.

amiable character, who were in the convent of the Rue Saint-Jacques during the youth of Madame de Longueville: Madame Séguier d'Autry, mother of Chancellor Séguier, the Mother Marie de Jésus-Christ; Madame La Rochefoucauld de Chandenier, Sister Marie de Saint-Joseph; Mademoiselle Le Bouthillier, Sister Philippe de Saint-Paul; Mademoiselle d'Anglure de Bourlemont, niece of Pope Urban VIII., Sister Geneviève des Anges; Madame de Brienne, the Mother Anne de Saint-Joseph; the Countess de Bury, left a widow at nineteen years of age, Sister Madeleine de Jésus; Mademoiselle de Lenoncourt, the Mother Charlotte de Jésus; Mademoiselle de Fieubet, Mesdemoiselles de Marillac, and somewhat later, names still more illustrious, hearts still nearer that of Mademoiselle de Bourbon, who, at the first impressions of passion or unhappiness, sought an asylum in the holy solitude.

Among those noble penitents, we must distinguish a particular friend of Madame de Longueville, whose rank was nearly equal to her own, who was, like her, sensitive and proud, who, wounded early in her affections, retired from the world before her, and heard the noise of the Fronde only through the walls of the convent of the Rue Saint-Jacques, where, several years before, she had fled the threat of a throne and the perils of her own heart. That friend to whom

Madame de Longueville wrote more than one letter, was Sister Anne-Marie de Jésus, that is, Anne Louise-Christine de Foix de La Valette d'Epernon, sister of the Duke de Candale, daughter of Bernard, Duke de La Valette d'Epernon, and of Gabrielle de Bourbon, legitimate daughter of the Duchess de Verneuil and Henri IV.

We have a sufficiently full life of Mademoiselle d'Epernon, from the hand of the Abbé de Montis.[1] But edifying lives must be distrusted almost as much as the histories of Tallemant des Réaux. This person looks for scandal only, and nowhere sees any thing but the evil. The pious panegyrists are quite as credulous in regard to the good. Evidently the Abbé de Montis did not know every thing, or was unwilling to tell every thing. He seems to have read neither the Memoirs of Mademoiselle nor those of Madame de Motteville. He paints with truth the person and the character of Mademoiselle d'Epernon. He is deceived when he imagines that the instinct of Christian perfection alone led her to the Carmelites. This instinct was nourished and supported by the experience of the vanity of human affections; it shone forth, and suddenly threw Mademoiselle d'Epernon among the Carmelites, in conse-

[1] Paris, 1774, in-12.

quence of a cruel loss, the death of a person to whom she had given her heart. This death, with the great error that preceded it, induced her to quit the world; and neither the long resistance of her family, nor even the hope of a crown could change her resolution.

For the sake of brevity, we shall confine ourselves to the collection of a limited amount of testimony. That of the veracious Madame de Motteville is decisive: "The Chevalier de Fiesque, who was killed at the siege of Mardyck, in 1646, had, according to the opinion of his friends, great spirit and valor. He was regretted by a young lady of high birth, who honored him with a tender and virtuous friendship. I know nothing of it in particular; but, according to the general opinion, it was founded upon piety and virtue, and consequently somewhat unusual. This virtuous lady began, soon after the death of De Fiesque, to despise the pleasures of the world, and finally forsook them all, as unworthy to occupy a place in her soul; she gave herself to God, entering the great convent of the Carmelites, where her pious life is an example to all."[1]

Mademoiselle,[2] who knew Mademoiselle d'Epernon well, and loved her tenderly, takes up matters farther

---

[1] Vol. 1st, p. 369. [2] Ibid., p. 74.

back: "It was principally at these balls (during the winter of 1644), that the Chevalier de Guise (afterwards the Duke de Joyeuse) testified, without any reserve, his passion for Mademoiselle d'Epernon. . . . The malady[1] of Mademoiselle d'Epernon gave me much pain. The Chevalier de Guise took every care of her imaginable. The danger to be apprehended in approaching those who have the small-pox, did not hinder him from visiting her every day. He manifested for her an incredible passion, which lasted during the whole of the following winter." The marriage failed; not at all, as the Abbé Montis says, through the refusal or the indecision of Mademoiselle d'Epernon, but through the intrigues of Mademoiselle de Guise, who tried to marry her brother to Mademoiselle d'Angoulême.

After the death of Chevalier de Fiesque, killed at the siege of Mardyck, Mademoiselle d'Epernon appeared wholly changed. She, so recently given up to display, so carried away with pleasures, no longer thought of any thing but her own salvation, "which displeased and surprised me," says Mademoiselle.[2] "I had seen her very far from the austerity which she was continually preaching; she no longer spoke of any thing but death, contempt for the world, and

[1] Vol. 1st, p. 79.

[2] Ibid., p. 124.

the happiness of the religious life. . . . The morning of her departure for Bordeaux (whither she was called by her father, Governor of Guyenne), which was the day of Saint Theresa, she came to bid me adieu. She found me in bed; fell upon her knees by my side, and told me that the goodness which I had always shown towards her, and the reciprocal confidence which had existed between us, obliged her to reveal to me the resolution which she had taken of joining the Carmelites, and the hope she entertained of carrying this resolution into execution. Such was my tenderness for her, that I could not help being moved. Touched by her design, I could not speak of it without weeping. I used every reason that I could to dissuade her from it. . . . She had already taken her resolution too firmly to listen to any thing that might change it. . . . The cardinal had been consulted[1] concerning the marriage of Prince Casimir, brother of the King of Poland,[2] and now himself king, with Mademoiselle d'Epernon. . . . I confess, that when I heard this news, I had the greatest joy. Although the emperor was married, he had a son, who was King of Hungary, of an age proportionate to mine,

---

[1] Vol. 1st, p. 146.

[2] The King of Poland, Wladislas, had just espoused Marie de Gonzague, daughter of the Duke de Nevers, sister of the Palatine. After the death of this first husband, she passed with the crown to his brother Casimir, whom Mademoiselle d'Epernon had refused.

and a prince of good promise. Thus the proximity of Germany and Poland made me believe that my good friend and myself might pass our days together. She would be amply avenged of Mademoiselle de Guise and M. de Joyeuse. In this affair there was nothing to displease me; and it may be seen from the manner in which I wrote to her concerning it, that I strove to hinder her from becoming a Carmelite. The conjuncture was most favorable. . . . The devotion of Mademoiselle d'Epernon defeated this design, and she preferred the crown of thorns to that of Poland. Although she seemed to receive this proposition as a high honor, she feigned sickness, and caused the waters of Bourbon to be prescribed for her, in order to enter the first convent of the Carmelites that she should find on the way. . . . Madame d'Epernon[1] took her on this journey in utter ignorance of her design. They proceeded to Bourges, where the next day she joined the Carmelites. Here she took the habit with one of the domestics of Madame d'Epernon. . . . She wrote me from Bourges,

[1] Her mother-in-law, Marie de Cambout, niece of Richelieu, whom the cardinal had married to the Duke d'Epernon, as he had married another of his nieces, Mademoiselle de Brézé, to the Duke d'Enghien. Madame d'Epernon was ill-treated by her husband, and died in retreat, in 1691. She was sister of the Abbé du Cambout de Pontchâteau, a celebrated Jansenist. See two portraits of her among the portraits of Mademoiselle.

informing me that she was coming to the great convent at Paris. . . . Mademoiselle d'Epernon could not be better situated. It is a great house, well located, and filled with young ladies of quality and spirit, who have left the world which they knew and despised. Now, it is this that makes great nuns. . . . When she had arrived, she requested me to pay her a visit. I went angry enough, grieved indeed to the very heart. When, however, I saw her, I was touched with the utmost tenderness, and all other feelings yielded so thoroughly thereto, that it was impossible for me to conceal it from her, my tears and my extreme grief not even leaving me power to speak; these tears did not cease during the two hours that I was with her, though I was unable to say a single word. . . . Time has taught me in turn the happiness which she enjoyed."

Mademoiselle d'Epernon, born in 1624, entered among the Carmelites at twenty-four years of age, in 1648; took the veil in 1649; spent many years in penitence and religious training, and died in 1701, at the age of seventy-seven years, having passed fifty-three in the monastery of the Rue Saint-Jacques. She desired to live the most obscure life, and was not even sub-prioress.[1]

---

[1] It is worth while to see, in the Abbé Montis, the great resistance

Like Mademoiselle d'Epernon, Mademoiselle de Bourbon thought of laying the storms that awaited her, in the peaceful retreat where she had so many

---

which Mademoiselle d'Epernon had to overcome from her brother, the Duke de Candale, and especially from her father, who appealed to the parliament and to the pope; the death of the Duke de Candale, his remains carried to the Carmelites; the conversion of the duke through the instrumentality of his daughter, the finest portions of her life and her pious death. She was one of the benefactresses. *Histoire manuscrite*, vol. 1st, p. 558. "The gifts bestowed by Anne-Marie de Jésus amounted to more than a hundred and fifty thousand livres. Besides this immense sum, the Duke d'Epernon, her father, dying in 1661, without heirs, bequeathed to it a hundred thousand livres over and above the sixteen thousand which he left as a pious legacy. This lord had already assigned to the house, during the life of our very honored Sister Anne-Marie, three thousand livres pension, finding that the sixteen thousand livres, which were regarded as her dowry, was too slender a sum, and sufficient only to endow a lady who had followed her." The lady here alluded to, and of whom Mademoiselle also speaks, was named Bouchereau. "Being," says the Abbé Montis (p. 84), "of an agreeable form, she occupied herself with things quite as fragile; but she finally turned her attention to religion, and, desiring to become a nun, and guessing the views of Mademoiselle d'Epernon, she opened her heart to her, and begged to be allowed to follow her, which was readily granted." Mademoiselle Bouchereau died during her novitiate, before making a profession.

It is through error that, on the faith of the Abbé Montis, in the abridged Life of the Mother, joined to that of Mademoiselle d'Epernon, p. 291, the learned editor of the works of Bossuet supposes, vol. xxxiv., p. 690, the beautiful letter on the Mother Agnes is addressed to Madame d'Epernon, prioress of the Carmelites of the Faubourg Saint-Jacques," for Mademoiselle d'Epernon—it was thus that she was called—and not Madame d'Epernon, was never prioress. Bossuet wrote to the prioress who succeeded the Mother Agnes, either the Mother Claire du Saint-Sacrement, who died as he entered upon his office; or rather to the one who almost immediately took her place, that is, the Mother Marie du Saint-Sacrement; in the world, Madame de La Thuillerie, who took her vows in 1654, was prioress from 1691 to 1700, and died in 1705. Our manuscripts contain several ancient copies of the letter of Bossuet, all bearing the inscription: *To the Mother of the Saint-Sacrement.*

friends. There she enjoyed herself, and passed the greater part of her life; for her mother, the Princess de Condé, always made her a companion in her frequent visits to this convent. This princess, as was not rare in those times, possessed at once great ambition, with a piety that bordered upon superstition. Contrasts abounded in her character. She never loved her husband very much, and at twenty-one years of age had imprisoned herself with him at the Bastile and Vincennes, for three long years. She was vain enough of her great beauty, taking great pleasure in making conquests; that of Henry IV. had

---

In 1680, Madame de Sévigné, accompanying Mademoiselle to the Carmelites, there saw Mademoiselle d'Epernon, and found her very much altered. Letter of the 5th of January, 1680: "I was yesterday at the convent of the Carmelites with Mademoiselle, who was good enough to ask Madame Lesdiguières to take me there. We entered this holy place. I was delighted with Mother Agnes. She spoke to me of you, whom she seemed to know through her sister (Madame the Marchioness de Villars). I saw Madame de Stuart, beautiful and contented (she made a profession this very year, say our manuscripts, under the name of Sister Marguerite de Saint-Augustin, and died in 1722). I saw Madame d'Epernon. . . More than thirty years had elapsed since we had seen one another: she seemed to be horribly changed."

And nevertheless, without being a great beauty, she was the worthy sister of the beautiful Candale. The convent of the Carmelites possesses several pictures of her. One is quite large, representing her between forty and fifty, pale and sick, but still agreeable. The best and most perfectly preserved, represents her young and charming. Her figure is delicate and graceful, but of that fragile grace which years do not respect. She is painted with a smile upon her lips, and such as she was in the world. It is probably the portrait of Beaubrun, engraved by Edelinck.

at least flattered her; she had been very much sought after, much praised, and her life had always been free from scandal. She had a pride that passed all bounds when any want of proper respect was shown towards her; but when this pride was undisturbed, she was amiable and at ease. She was not destitute of greatness of soul or spirit. She destined her daughter for the highest position; but, observing her great beauty, and knowing, by her own experience, the perils thereof, she took care to arm her against them, by planting in her heart a serious piety, and by surrounding her with the most edifying examples. Not content with going often to the convent of the Carmelites, she wished to be able to go there at any hour; to remain there—she and her daughter—as long as she liked; to have an apartment there like the queen herself; and, to that end, she took upon her burdens onerous enough, as appears from an authentic act, passed November 18, 1637, in her own name, and in the name of Mademoiselle de Bourbon, from which we give the following extract:

"We, present in person, the reverend Mothers Marie-Madeleine de Jésus (Mademoiselle de Bains), humble prioress; Sister Marie de la Passion (Mademoiselle de Machault), sub-prioress; Sister Philippe de Saint-Paul (Mademoiselle de Bouthillier), and Sister Marie de Saint-Barthélemy (Mademoiselle Guichard), depositaries, representing the community, . . who, advertised of the great desire that the high and powerful princess, Dame Charlotte-Marguerite de Montmorency, spouse of the high and powerful Prince Henri de Bourbon, first prince of the blood, and Demoiselle Anne de Bourbon, their daughter, have shown to be received as founders of the new house which the said reverends are at present constructing, and which they expect to join to their ancient cloister; after having proposed the business in full chapter, and with the permission of their superiors, . . . in consideration of the great piety professed by the said dame princesses, . . . and of the very charitable affection which they have always borne towards the order of the Carmelites, and particularly towards this monastery, have voluntarily admitted the said princesses as founders, granting them the enjoyment of all the privileges accorded to founders, . . . to wit, freely to enter the monastery whenever they wish; to drink, to eat, to sleep there; to be present at divine service and other spiritual exercises; to take part in all the prayers, vigils, and other pious works that are performed daily; we have moreover consented that the same dame princess may enjoy the privilege, which she has obtained from the Holy Father, of bringing two persons with her three times a month, as she has done thus far, . . . always on the condition that the said two persons shall not remain in the monastery after six o'clock in the evening during the winter, and after seven o'clock during the summer. . . . This being accepted, . . . the said dames are obligated to continue the honor of their benevolence to the reverends, and also to defray the costs and expenses of the building."

In consequence of this act, Madame the Princess gave more than 120,000 livres at different times, a quantity of precious stones, ornaments for the church, relics which she caused to be set with a magnificence corresponding with her piety and her position. At the same time, she was anxious to enjoy her rights, and, while awaiting the completion of the new building, she took an apartment at the convent, which she furnished somewhat like a Carmelite. Her bed and all her furniture were of brown serge. In this desert she sometimes spent a whole week or a fortnight; finding herself more happy, she said, than in the midst of the pleasures of the court. A simple nun could never have shown more respect for the regulations of the house. She subjected herself to long silence through fear of meddling with that which was prescribed. Sometimes finding herself alone in her chamber with the two nuns who kept her company, she declared that she was afraid, and that at evening she took them for phantoms, because they spoke to her only by signs, and for things absolutely necessary. Subsequently, she wished to have a cell in the dormitory, as simple as that of all the others. "She would," says the manuscript history[1] which has been confided to us, "have willingly employed all her goods for the use or the embellishment of the convent, if address had not been employed to conceal from her the knowledge of its most legitimate wants. Sometimes she complained with infinite grace: If your mothers were willing, I would do here a thousand things; but they cannot do this thing, they will not do that, and I can do nothing. This great princess, whom a natural pride sometimes rendered so formidable, here became the friend, the companion, the mother of whomsoever applied to her. Her power was never felt except through her benefits. The will of the mother prioress was her law: she called her our mother; rose up whenever she perceived her; submitted herself to her commands with a charming sweetness, and was seen in the choir, at morning prayers, at every service, in the refectory, practising ordinary mortifications, laying her natural greatness at the feet of the spouses of Jesus Christ, with a humility that rendered her to them still more noble."

Admitted with her mother into the interior of the monastery, Anne-Geneviève filled her soul with the

---

[1] Vol. 1st.

most edifying conversations, the gravest and most touching spectacles. Everywhere she met none but the living already dead and kneeling upon the grave. Here was the tomb of Michel de Marillac, keeper of the seals, who died in exile, at Châteaudun, in that same year, 1632, when Richelieu beheaded his brother, Marshal de Marillac, uncle of Mademoiselle de Bourbon, Duke de Montmorency; here were the funeral monuments of the two women of the house of Longueville, Marguerite and Catherine d'Orleans. She doubted not that she should one day see buried in this same place her brilliant friend, the famous Julie, Mademoiselle de Rambouillet, now Duchess de Montausier; that she should see carried to this place the heart of Turenne—that heart which, for a moment, she was destined to trouble and dispute with duty and the king; that here several of her own children should also have their tombs, and that here she herself should repose by the side of her mother, Madame the Princess, and of her sister-in-law, the sweet, pure, and graceful Anne-Marie Martinozzi, Princess de Conti.[1]

Mademoiselle de Bourbon wished, in her turn, to be one of the benefactresses of the Carmelites, and to

---

[1] L'Histoire manuscrite, vol. 1st, contains the epitaphs of Michel de Marillac, of Marguerite and Catherine d'Orleans, of Madame the Princess, of the Princess de Conti, etc. When the keeper of the seals, Marillac,

make such presents as would please them. She obtained from Pope Urban VII. the relics of seven martyr virgins, with a brief of the Holy Father attesting their authenticity, and that the names of each of these victims of faith had been found entire, or abbreviated on the stone that held their bodies inclosed in the catacombs. Let us transport ourselves to those times; let us place ourselves in a convent of the Carmelites, and we shall form some idea of the holy joy which filled the house on witnessing the arrival of this magnificent and august present. Queen Anne, touched with a pious emulation, placed with them some relics of Saint Paule, a Roman dame, and an illustrious friend of Saint Jerome. The body of Saint

---

was arrested, the Mother Madeleine de Saint-Joseph tried, in every way, to serve and console him in his misfortune. Regardless of the opinion of Richelieu, who was then more powerful than ever, and who was the protector of the order, she caused an exposition of the eucharist during sixty days and sixty nights; procured the offering of a large number of prayers; she wrote often to the pious exile; implored the cardinal to have him treated with less rigor; and after his death earnestly sought and obtained his body from Châteaudun; erected to him a tomb at the base of the sanctuary in the chaple of Saint Thérèse, and composed herself this epitaph: "Here lies Messire Michel de Marillac, keeper of the seals of France, who, having been raised to this and other dignities, has always preserved an esteem for true honors and eternal riches, doing many good works, loving justice, seeking the glory of God, sustaining his Church, succoring the oppressed, giving all that he had to the poor; and when he was, by Providence, deprived of all, he showed his great magnanimity and contempt of earthly things; living contentedly, and journeying on to a holy death, by which he passed from this world to another, in the year of grace 1632."

Rosalie, a grandchild of France, had just been found at Palermo. M. d'Alincourt obtained it, and sent it as an offering. Mademoiselle de Bourbon placed all these relics in a silver shrine, made in the form of a dome, surmounted by a lantern, and surrounded by four figures, representing the Evangelists.

The Duke d'Enghien seeing his sister, whom he adored, and whose spirit he knew, thus occupied with embellishing and enriching the convent of the Carmelites, where he was sometimes taken, felt his honor piqued, and wished to make his offering also. In order to divert him during his recovery from a severe illness, various curiosities of the day were brought and shown to him in his chamber, and among other things a reliquary, admirable for its design and richness. The Duke d'Enghien asked the purpose of this masterpiece. The goldsmith replied that it was for the Carmelites of the Rue Saint-Jacques, but that, not being in a condition to pay for such a piece of workmanship, they had left it on his hands. The young duke exclaimed that he wished the Carmelites could have this beautiful reliquary, and he found a very good way of realizing his wish. He took a purse in hand, and, extolling the curiosity, which he kept concealed, refused to show it to those who came to visit him, unless some pieces of gold or silver were put in his purse; and he succeeded in procuring the sum demanded, which was 2,000 louis.[1]

Thus passed the infancy and the youth of Mademoiselle de Bourbon, in the midst of the spectacles and practice of a true and profound piety. We must not be surprised, then, that this piety should at length induce her to renounce the world and become a Carmelite. She who was one day to be the ardent disciple and the intrepid protector of Port-Royal, was then in the hands of a Jesuit, Father Le Jeune. He encouraged her design; but in vain she addressed the most earnest supplications to her father, the Prince de Condé. Having other views in regard to his daughter, he complained to Madame the Princess; and in order to break the charm that attached Anne-Geneviève to the Carmelites, it was decided that she should be taken oftener into society. Mademoiselle de Bourbon obeyed; but, her mind being still filled with the images and the discourses of the Rue Saint-Jacques, she took no pleasure in these brilliant assemblages. When her mother found fault with her poor success, Mademoiselle de Bourbon is said to have replied to her:[2] "You have, madame, such touching graces, that, as I simply attend you, and appear after you, I am not noticed."

---

[1] *Histoire manuscrite*, vol. 1st, pp. 491, 492.

[2] Villefore, p. 18.

This manner of justifying herself appeased Madame the Princess, who, in spite of her devotion, willingly suffered herself to be reminded that she had been and was still very beautiful.

Mademoiselle de Bourbon, during several years, followed her inclination; and, in order to make her renounce it, it was necessary to do her a sort of violence. Thus far she had found means of escaping the ball. Madame the Princess was obliged to employ her authority to make her go; and three days before its occurrence, she was commanded to prepare herself for it.

"Her first movement," says Villefore,[1] "was to go and tell this news to her good friends the Carmelites, who were very much afflicted at it, and embarrassed in replying to her, for she asked their advice as to her conduct at so difficult a conjuncture. A council was held in due form, over which presided, in religious habit, two excellent virtues, Penitence and Prudence; and it was resolved that Mademoiselle de Bourbon, before going to the assault, should arm her self, under her clothing, with a small cuirass, vulgarly called a hair-cloth, and that she should then lend herself, in good faith, to all the finery that was designed for her. As soon as her consent was obtained,

---

[1] Villefore, p. 14.

every thing was resorted to that could most enliven her natural graces, and nothing was forgotten to ornament a beauty more brilliant by its own splendor than by all the jewels with which it was loaded. The Carmelites had strongly recommended her to be on her guard, but her self-confidence misled her. From the moment she entered the ball-room, and as long as she remained there, the eyes of the whole assembly were fixed upon her. Admirers flocked about her, lavishing those subtle praises that easily lay hold of a newly enkindled self-love, which is suspicious of nothing. . . . On retiring from the ball, she felt her heart agitated by new emotions: she was no longer the same person."

It would not be without interest to know something about that ball where Mademoiselle de Bourbon was carried away as a victim, where she appeared to conquer, and which she left intoxicated; but Villefore gives us no information respecting it. We are therefore reduced to conjecture. Here is one which we give for what it is worth. We read in the manuscript memoirs of André d'Ormesson, and in the *Gazette de France*, of Renaudot,[1] that, February 18,

---

[1] Manuscript of André d'Ormesson, fol. 332, verso.—It was on the occasion of the ballet of the 18th of February, 1635, that the *Gazette de France* cited, for the first time, the name of Mademoiselle de Bourbon. The extra of the 21st of February, gives a full account of the fête of the

1635, there was given at the Louvre, under King Louis XIII., a grand ball, in which figured all the beauties of the day, and among the rest Mademoiselle de Bourbon. Observe that it is the first court-ball in which the name of Mademoiselle de Bourbon is found, both in d'Ormesson and the *Gazette.* Again, that the great violence, an account of which has been preserved for us by Villefore, could have been shown to the princess only on an occasion that demanded the infliction, and for a royal ball. If this conjecture were admitted, we should have the precise date of the conversion of Mademoiselle de Bourbon to worldly life, as we have of the date of her conversion to the religious life, which is certainly August 2, 1654, when she was thirty-five years of age: the first would be February 18, 1635, when Mademoiselle de Bourbon was sixteen.

18th. It describes all the scenes of the ballet of the king, names all the great lords who danced in it, and concludes thus: "Such was the grand ballet of the queen, which so delighted all who were present that they were unable to decide which was most charming, the beauties who adorned, the gems with which they glittered, or the figures which represented those *sixteen* divinities of which it was composed: the queen, *Mademoiselle de Bourbon*, Mesdames de Longueville (the first wife of the Duke de Longueville), de Montbazon, de Chaulnes, de La Valette, de Retz, Mademoiselle de Rohan, Mesdames de Lyancourt and de Mortemart, Mesdemoiselles de Senecé, de Hautefort, d'Esche, de Vieux-Pont, de Saint-Georges and de La Fayette, who did not quit it until three o'clock in the morning. Every one left this place of marvels with the feelings of Jacob, who, having seen angels in the night, thought that he was standing upon the spot where heaven and earth united."

It is to very near this age of Madame de Longueville that these words of Madame de Motteville refer: "Mademoiselle de Bourbon began, although very young, to exhibit the first charms of that angelic face which has since had such renown." In order to judge how faithful this slight sketch is, one must go to Versailles and see a portrait, by an old and excellent master, named Ducayer, representing Mademoiselle de Bourbon, at the age of fifteen years, by the side of her father and her mother, in 1634. She is here seen in all the freshness of her virgin beauty, but in court attire, and as if going to that ball which she so much dreaded, and which changed her soul and her life.

Mademoiselle de Bourbon did not, however, forget her friends of the convent of the Carmelites, and continued to visit them. Thus far she had experienced but one sentiment; from that time she had two,—love of God and of the Carmelites, with a taste for worldly success. She preserved the same piety, but that piety was henceforth combated by the desire of pleasure, the need of loving and being loved, the wish for applause upon that stage where she witnessed the success of so many persons who had neither her mirth, nor her spirit, nor her face. This combat continued a long time. We have letters addressed by her to the Carmelites, and in a tone of the most lively piety, even when she was allowing herself to be most carried away by her passions. Accuse neither her sincerity, nor the inefficacy of the best principles. We are really sincere when we express sentiments that are really in the heart, although we may not have strength to follow them; and these noble sentiments have also the precious advantage of mingling with our faults a remnant of virtue that hinders us from sinking to the bottom of the abyss, of uniting therewith a beneficent remorse that sustains the moral life, and of almost always achieving a triumphant restoration to well-doing. Let them sleep for a season in the soul of Madame de Longueville. There they will never be extinguished. At some future day they will be awakened, and we shall return to the convent of the Carmelites, in the Rue Saint-Jacques. But it is necessary to quit it, in order to follow Mademoiselle de Bourbon to the court, to Chantilly, to Ruel, to Liancourt, among beautiful companions, amid agreeable promenades, taking part in gallant conversations. We shall follow her first to Rue Saint-Thomas-du-Louvre, to the hôtel de Rambouillet.

CHAPTER II.

1635 to 1642.

Mademoiselle de Bourbon at the hôtel de Rambouillet—The Genre Précieux—Madame de Sablé, type of the true précieuse—Corneille and Voiture—Mademoiselle de Bourbon at Chantilly—At Ruel—At Liancourt—Her young friends—Mademoiselle du Vigean and Condé—Marriage of Mademoiselle de Bourbon.

It is an error too general, and recently fortified by M. Rœderer in his ingenious and learned memoir on *Polite Society in France*,[1] that the hôtel de Rambouillet was the first, and for a long time the only *salon* in Paris where good company ever assembled. No: the Marchioness de Rambouillet did not create, she simply followed up the happy revolution which caused a taste for intellectual things, delicate pleasures, elegant occupations to succeed, in France, the barbarity of the civil wars, and the license of manners too much allowed by Henry IV. This taste is the distinctive characteristic of the seventeenth cen-

---

[1] *Mémoire pour servir à l'histoire de la Société polie en France;* Paris, in-8°, 1835. See also M. Walckenaër: *Mémoires touchant la Vie et les Ecrits de Madame de Sévigné*, vol. 1st, chap. iv. and v.

tury; it is the pure and noble source whence issued all the wonders of this great period. Louis XIV., in 1661, received it wholly formed, illustrious on all sides by reason of the most brilliant military and political success, rich in masterpieces of every kind, when already the finest geniuses had finished or commenced their career; when Malherbe and Balzac, the founders of the new prose and of the new poesy, when Descartes, the founder of the new philosophy, had long been buried; when Le Sueur and Sarrazin were dead; when Pascal and Poussin were about to close their eyes; when Corneille was no longer but a shadow of himself; when Madame de Sévigné, La Fontaine, and Molière, were forty, and Bossuet thirty-six years of age. All these great minds have, in their style as well as in their thought, something artless and masculine, which betrays another epoch; an art and a literature developed under other auspices. The seventeenth century does not commence with Louis XIV., who crowns it, but with Richelieu, who inspired it. No one felt better than Richelieu the growing taste for politeness and letters. The foundation of this great soul was ambition: his true genius was for politics; but, eager for every kind of glory, he desired also to be, or to appear, one of the first wits of his time, and even an accomplished cavalier. Like all great men from Cæsar to Napoleon, he was very amiable when he wished to be so. It pleased him for a while to affect to be a discontented man of ambition, who was abiding his time under the appearance of a man of the world, seeking and obtaining the most brilliant success in society. As soon as he acquired power, he gave vogue to his own tastes; and in 1630 there was in Paris more than one hotel where there were assembled, for agreeable pastime, people of wit, of lofty and of low descent, military personages, lawyers and theologians, with their amiable wives, who naturally gave the ton. The hôtel de Rambouillet was the most considerable of all the rendezvous of the new spirit, and it continued to be the most celebrated, by reason rather of the defects than of the good qualities there encountered.

In fact, what idea is presented to the mind as soon as we hear mentioned the hôtel de Rambouillet? That of a choice reunion where the most exquisite politeness is cultivated, but where, little by little, the *genre précieux* enters and acquires full control.

And what was this *genre précieux?*

It was at first simply what is now called the style *distingué*. Distinction was what was sought above all things at the hôtel de Rambouillet: whoever possessed it, or aspired to it, from princes and princesses of the blood to lettered persons of the most humble fortune, was well received, attracted to, retained in the amiable and illustrious company.

But what must we understand by distinction? It cannot be defined in an absolute manner. Each epoch makes an ideal of distinction for its own use. Two things, however, almost always enter it, two things in appearance contrary, and which are combined only in choice spirits happily cultivated: a certain elevation in ideas and sentiments, with an extreme simplicity in manners and language. I suppose that with Aspasia, at Athens, Pericles, Anaxagoras, and Phidias talked of art, of philosophy, of politics, with no more effort and declamation, than workmen and merchants would have used in conversing about their ordinary occupations. Socrates was an accomplished model in this style, and the *Banquet* of Plato, wherein, after supper, discourse is held upon the most elevated topics in the most charming and most natural manner, gives us a perfect idea of what was then the *ton* of that particular atticism at Athens, and which, even at Athens, was the mark of distinction. It was the same at Rome with the Scipios, where an amiable badinage was often mingled with the gravest matters, a little less, perhaps, at the suppers of Cicero, when Cæsar was not present, the master of the house not being a sufficiently great lord to be always perfectly simple, and the new man,

—I do not say the parvenu—especially the orator and the man of letters, being a little too perceptible, even when he strove most to imitate Plato. It was this Roman urbanity, the somewhat degenerated daughter of Athenian atticism, that the hôtel de Rambouillet aimed at and contributed to spread.[1]

Grandeur was in some sort in the air from the very commencement of the seventeenth century. The policy of the government was grand, and great men sprang up in crowds to carry it out in the councils and on the battle-field. A mighty spirit pervaded French society. Everywhere were great designs in the arts, in letters, in sciences, in philosophy. Descartes, Poussin, and Corneille were advancing towards their future glory, full of bold thoughts, under the eyes of Richelieu. Every thing was turned to grandeur. Every thing was rude, even somewhat gross, mind as well as heart. Force abounded; grace was absent. In this excessive vigor, good taste was unknown. Politeness was necessary to lead the century to perfection. Of this the hôtel de Rambouillet was particularly the school.

The days of its greatest lustre begin in 1630, and extend to 1648, when the idol of the house, Mademoiselle de Rambouillet, married in 1645 to M. de

[1] The very word *urbanity* is from Balzac, one of the first and most illustrious frequenters of the house.

Montausier, follows him into his government of Saintonge and of Angoumois, at the commencement of the Fronde. The palmy days of the illustrious hôtel were then under Richelieu, and during the first years of the regency. For a score of years it rendered incontestable services to the national taste; but the good which it was able to do, was achieved in 1648. Already its defects had begun to appear and to encroach upon its good qualities. The inferior circles which had been formed in Paris and in the provinces, at first useful because they promoted politeness, had terminated in being dangerous by degenerating loftiness of ideas and sentiments into a false grandeur, extravagant and affected, especially by carrying affectation into simplicity. It was then that the *genre précieux*, becoming corrupted, the great master in fact of nature and truth, declared against it that pitiless war, opened by his comedy of *Les Précieuses Ridicules*, printed in 1660, and closed by that of *Les Femmes Savantes*, printed in 1673. But let us return to 1630.

In 1630 there was much originality in France, but it was an originality which showed the necessity of foreign models. At a later period, Molière, La Fontaine, Boileau, and Racine, those geniuses so eminently French, proposed the study of models; they sought them in antiquity, which they imitated without ceasing to be original, giving the French character to every thing that they touched. Their predecessors had addressed themselves to Italy and to Spain, in their eyes the two nations most advanced. The Médicis had introduced among us a taste for Italian literature. Queen Anne brought, or rather strengthened, a taste for Spanish literature. The hôtel de Rambouillet endeavored to unite them.

The Spanish style was, at the beginning of the seventeenth century, made up of high gallantry, languishing and Platonic; of a heroism somewhat romantic; a knightly courage; a lively sentiment of the beauties of nature, which developed itself in eclogues and idyls, both prose and verse; a passion for music and serenades, as well as for carousals, elegant conversations, and magnificent diversions. The Italian style was precisely the contrary of Spanish grandeur, or, if you please, bombast, wit, carried to refinement, raillery and jesting, which threatened to abase every thing. From the mixture of these two styles sprang the alliance, ardently pursued, rarely accomplished in a perfect proportion, of the grand and the familiar, of the grave and the pleasant, of the sprightly and the sublime.

At the hôtel de Rambouillet, it was not sufficient to be a hero; it was also necessary to be a gallant man, an *honnête* man, as was the appellation in 1630, and as it continued to be during the seventeenth century; an *honnête* man, new and piquant expression, mysterious type which it is difficult to define, and whose sentiment spread with inconceivable rapidity. The *honnête* man had elevated sentiments: he was necessarily brave, gallant, liberal; he had wit and fine manners, but all this without the least appearance of pedantry, and with an easy and familiar air. Such was the ideal which the hôtel de Rambouillet proposed for public admiration, and for the imitation of people who prided themselves on being *comme il faut.*

The women were naturally called upon to play the principal rôle in an enterprise like this, and the Marchioness de Rambouillet seemed formed expressly to preside over it. She was almost Italian: her father was Vivonne Pisani, and her mother, Savelli. Her husband was a very high lord, and had been ambassador extraordinary to Spain. They had already withdrawn from business, with a considerable fortune, to a beautiful hôtel near Paris, a magnificent country residence:[1] they were there in the way of no one, and drew about them a large circle. To finish the portrait of an accomplished hostess, add that Madame de Rambouillet, though very beautiful, had never been engaged in any intrigue, and that she was passionately

[1] The Château de Rambouillet, above Versailles, ten leagues from Paris. Francis I. died here.

fond of people of wit, though without any pretension thereto herself: in fact, only a few letters and two stanzas are all that can be found from her pen.[1]

She was also an object of admiration to all those who knew her. Tallemant des Réaux himself passes upon her the highest eulogy. He says that she was beautiful, virtuous, and sensible. "She has,"[2] observes he, "always loved beautiful things; and for the sake of reading Virgil, she applied herself to the study of Latin, but was prevented from accomplishing her design by sickness: she contented herself afterwards with learning Spanish. . . . She was in every thing a very clever person. . . . No one in the world was less selfish; she went farther than those who say that giving is a pleasure worthy of a king, for she said that it was a pleasure worthy of God. . . . There never was a mind more upright. . . . Never was there a truer friend." Her only defect which M. Rœderer has intentionally suppressed, and which Tallemant does not fail to notice, was an excessive delicacy in language. There were words which frightened her, and which found no favor with her,[3] so that there was

[1] One to Madame the Duchess d'Aiguillon, relating to a certain water-course: Tallemant, vol. ii., p. 228. The other, her epitaph, preserved by Ménage in his *Observations on the Poetry of Malherbe.*

[2] Vol. ii., p. 233.

[3] I do not know where M. Rœderer got the idea that Madame de Rambouillet wrote so simply. Here is one of her billets, which could not

already in Arthénice (the *nom de precieuse* of Madame de Rambouillet) something of Philaminte. Segrais speaks of her in terms similar to those of Tallemant:[1] "Madame de Rambouillet was admirable; she was good, gentle, beneficent, and warm-hearted, and she possessed a correct mind. It was she who corrected the bad manners then prevalent. She had formed her mind by reading good Italian and Spanish books; and she taught politeness to all

---

have led the person to whom it is addressed to speak of *simplicity*, as M. Rœderer does of the letters of Madame de Rambouillet, and of her daughter to Voiture; we speak from conjecture, for these letters have not been seen by us. The one we give here was found among the manuscripts of Conrart, in the Library of the Arsenal, vol. xiv., in-4°, p. 53; it is addressed to Godeau, by turns Bishop of Grasse and of Vence:

"SIR:—If my carabineer-poet or poetic carabineer (Arnault, Colonel of Carabineers, a distinguished warrior, a man of great wit, but a satirist, and a person enough like Bussy) was in Paris, I would reply to you in verse, and not in prose; but for myself I have no familiarity with the muses. I return a million thanks for your kind wishes; and in recompense, I wish every moment that you were in a lodge, where I am sure you would sleep better than you do at Vence. It is supported by columns of transparent marble, and was built above the mid-region of the air by Queen Zirfée. The sky there is always serene; clouds darken neither the sight nor the understanding, and thence quite at my ease I have considered the downfall of the terrestrial Angel. It seems to me that on this occasion fortune has shown that it is a slander to say that she favors only the young. And because I am no more the subject of change than my lodge, you may rest assured that I shall continue so as long as I live.

"Sir,

"Your very humble servant,

June 26, 1642. OC (Catherine) DE VIVONNE."

[1] The works of Segrais, Amsterdam, 1723, vol. 1st. *Mémoires Anecdotes*, p. 29.

those who frequented her company. Princes visited her, though she was not a duchess. She was also an excellent friend, obliging to every one. The Cardinal Richelieu held her in the highest esteem. . . . Madame de La Fayette learned much from her." One of her daughters, the celebrated Julie, possessed a most remarkable mind, and, in default of great beauty, a very fine form and noble air. She understood how to make agreeable the house of her mother, and she was ably seconded by her brother, the Marquis de Pisani, as intellectual as he was brave; also by her numerous sisters, especially by her who was the first Madame de Grignan.[1]

We may find anywhere a description of the hôtel de Rambouillet, and of that famous blue chamber, which was in some sort the sanctuary of the temple of the goddess of Athens, to speak like Mademoiselle in *La Princesse de Paphlagonie*.[2] It was a large *salon*, the decorations of which were all of blue velvet, set off with gold and silver, and whose large windows, opening from the ceiling to the floor, admitted abundance of light and air, and gave the prospect of a very beautiful and well-cultivated garden, which extended as far as the eye could reach.

---

[1] On Mademoiselle de Rambouillet, Pisani, and his sisters, see Tallemant, vol. ii., pp. 207–262.

[2] Edition of 1659, pp. 118–121.

The hôtel had been built upon a new plan, designed by Madame de Rambouillet herself. It was not very vast, but of a beautiful appearance. It was the last hôtel but one of the Rue Saint-Thomas-du-Louvre, on the side of the Place du Palais Cardinal, between the Quinze-Vingts, which occupied the corner of the street, and the hôtel de Chevreuse, afterwards the hôtel d'Epernon, and a little later, towards 1663 or 1664, the hôtel de Longueville.[1]

M. Rœderer has left hardly any thing to be done in cataloguing the great lords and ladies who frequented the hôtel de Rambouillet during the last half of its long and brilliant existence. I will limit myself to selecting, from the group of amiable women ever found there, one whom M. Rœderer has too much neglected, and who is, in my eyes, the model of a true and perfect *précieuse*, Madeleine de Souvre, Marchioness de Sablé, whose life is connected with that of Madame de Longueville, and of whom Madame de Motteville has left us the following portrait:

[1] See Saural, *Antiquités de Paris*, vol. iii., p. 200, and the plan of Paris by Gomboust. These hotels, or rather their ruins, have just entirely disappeared, with the Rue Saint-Thomas-du-Louvre, to the advantage of the Place du Carrousel. May this admirable place preserve its grandeur, so dearly bought, and no transversal building spoil the beautiful harmony of the Louvre and the Tuileries! May also some competent and industrious man, devoted to the study of Paris and its monuments, resolve not to let the Rue Saint-Thomas-du-Louvre perish without giving its description and a history faithful to the epoch of its greatest glory.

"The Marchioness de Sablé[1] was one of those whose beauty was creating the most sensation when the queen (Queen Anne) arrived in France (in 1615); but if she was lovely, she was still more desirous of appearing so. The love which this lady had for herself rendered her a little too sensible to that testified to her by the other sex. There were in France some relics of the politeness that Catherine de Médicis had introduced from Italy; and so much delicacy was found in the new comedies and in all other works, both prose and verse, which came from Madrid, that she conceived a very high opinion of the gallantry which the Spaniards had caught from the Moors. She was persuaded that men might, without crime, entertain the most tender sentiments for females; that the desire of pleasing impelled them to the greatest and handsomest acts, gave them spirit and inspired them with liberality and every virtue; but that, on the other hand, women, who were the ornament of the world, and made to be served and adored, ought to tolerate their respect alone. This lady, supporting her sentiments with fine wit and great beauty, gave them much authority in her time; and the number and consideration of those who continued to see her, perpetuated in our time what the Spaniards call *fucezas*."[2]

---

[1] *Mémoires*, vol. 1st, p. 18.

[2] Ed. of Amsterdam. Petitot, vol. xxxvi. of the collection, p. 341,

Madame de Sablé had been passionately loved by the brave, handsome, and unfortunate Duke de Montmorency, uncle of Madame de Longueville, who was decapitated at Toulouse in 1632. She responded to his passion; but Montmorency having raised his eyes upon the queen, Madame de Sablé, like a true Spaniard, broke connection with him. "I heard her say," says Madame de Motteville again, "that her own pride was so great, that, on the first demonstration made by the Duke de Montmorency of his change of affection, she wished to see him no more, being unable to receive agreeably devotion which she was obliged to share even with the greatest princess in the world."

The Marchioness de Sablé continued faithful to the manners of her youth, and, when the hôtel de Rambouillet was almost closed, she maintained something akin to it in her hôtel of the Place-Royale, with her intellectual friend, the Countess de Maure, and even in her retreat of Port-Royal, at the Faubourg Saint-Jacques. She kept up for a long time a school of *bon ton*, of *morale*, and of refined literature, whence originated the *Maximes* of La Rochefoucauld.

Among the people of letters who came often to the hôtel de Rambouillet, the two most cele-

---

proposes to read *husesas*, from *huso*, spindle. The true reading seems *finezas*.

brated are without contradiction Corneille and Voiture.

Corneille, with Descartes, is the highest expression of the literature of the first half of the seventeenth century. His qualities, like his defects, were in the most perfect harmony with his times. Hence a success which no one has since equalled. Under Louis XIV., what piece of Racine produced the impression made by the *Cid*, in 1636? It is necessary to read the writers of the times in order to obtain an idea of the enthusiasm which seized Paris and all France. They were true transports:

> All Paris for Chimène hath the eyes of Rodrigue.

Nothing more true. Because at this time there was not a gentleman in Paris who did not pretend to be a Rodrigue; not a woman of *bon ton* who had not at heart, or who did not affect the sentiments of Chimène. The more we study this admirable piece, which *Polyeucte* alone surpassed a few years after, the more we discover in it the traits of that great epoch forever gone, heroism and great gallantry; that point of honor which doubtless shed much blood, but promoted the warlike spirit; in ripe men and in chieftains, serious interests and energetic passions clashing with each other; in youth, the generous struggle of love and duty, which will one day be carried to the utmost degree of the pathetic in Pauline and in Sévère, throughout it a language somewhat rude, but artless and strong, ever familiar; at the same time, it is true, an ill-founded taste straying sometimes in the pursuit of grandeur, of delicacies infinite and full of grace, but somewhat critical, and of subtile analyses of passion reasoning upon itself. Such was the hôtel de Rambouillet. It recognized itself in and defended the *Cid* against the all-powerful minister.[1] It was in the noble *salon* that Corneille encountered Balzac, and conversed with him concerning Rome and the Romans. Let the discourses upon the Romans addressed by Balzac to the Marchioness de Rambouillet[2]

---

[1] It is very certain that the author of *Mirame* show some littleness in the ridiculous quarrel raised against *The Cid;* but it must be acknowledged that he had some State reasons not to be despised. He who had brought about the royal edict against duels could not endure verses in their honor; there was also in *The Cid* more than one word unfavorable to the prime ministers. Besides, the cardinal loved Corneille; he gave him a good pension, and even performed the marriage ceremony for him. One day Corneille having presented himself more sad and thoughtful than ordinary before the Cardinal Richelieu, the latter asked him if he was working. Corneille replied that he was far from having the tranquillity necessary for composition, that his head was turned with love. It was necessary to explain the whole matter, and he told the cardinal that he was passionately in love with the daughter of Lieutenant General d'Andely, and that he could not obtain her from her father. The cardinal requested this father, so hard to please, to come to him at Paris. He arrived trembling at receiving such an unexpected order, and returned very glad to get off with giving his daughter to a man in such high credit. See the brothers Parfait, *History of the French Theatre*, vol. v., p. 304.

[2] Works of Balzac, in-fol., vol. ii., p. 419.

be read, and it will be seen whether the conversations of this period were useless. I dare say that France never witnessed a time when politics were more the order of the day. Every one was then occupied with public affairs. It was neither Lucan nor Tacitus who taught Corneille the language of *Cinna* and of the first scene of *La Mort de Pompée.* The true school of Corneille was the spectacle of what passed around him, the story of great contemporaneous events, the conversations of Richelieu and of his familiars, Father Joseph, Mazarin, Lyonne, and those who were every day in the companies which he frequented, where ambassadors, warriors, bishops, councillors of state mingled with men of letters. Corneille read all his pieces at the hôtel de Rambouillet. It was in all its glory, and it declined with him; his masterpiece, the masterpiece also of the French stage, *Polyeucte*, appeared in 1643, that is, during the most brilliant days of the hôtel de Rambouillet, and I may add of France, for it was in this same year, 1643, that one of the youngest disciples of the illustrious hôtel, the most passionate admirer of Corneille, the brother of Mademoiselle de Bourbon, the Duke d'Enghien, gained at the age of twenty-two years, in a manner worthy of Alexander and of Cæsar, one of those battles of which history records but five or six—that battle of Rocroy, in which the designs of Henri IV. and of

Richelieu were justified by victory, and by which France succeeded Spain in the moral and military supremacy of Europe.

Voiture was admired by his most intellectual and fastidious contemporaries. La Fontaine places him in the number of his masters.[1] Madame de Sévigné characterizes his mind as "free, playful, charming."[2] Boileau says that Voiture is, in his eyes, a sort of clown, asking what there is in him to be so much admired.[3] Let us confess it: we all more or less resemble this clown: we are scarcely able at the present day to account for the fame of Voiture. Many reasons may be assigned for it which militate neither against Voiture nor ourselves.

Of all our faculties, wit is that which has most to do with social intercourse, but which leaves the least trace. A sally, a repartee, cannot be separated from the manner in which they are expressed. Sprightly sayings have not all their grace except in the mouth of a man of wit. It is not thus with words proceeding from the heart, and with great thoughts. As they come from the depths of human nature, which changes not, they have infinite perspectives, and they endure as long as the heart and the reason. But wit plays

---

[1] Maitre Vincent, etc.
[2] Letter of November 24, 1676.
[3] Third Satire.

upon the surface; it sparkles and becomes extinguished in an instant. Wit is the offspring of the moment. The effect of an impromptu depends upon a thousand things, which, in disappearing, carry with them what had most charmed us. What, I pray you, is the present value of a pleasantry perpetrated two centuries ago?

Madame de Sévigné, in her enthusiasm for him who had been one of the masters of her youth, exclaims: "So much the worse for those who do not understand him!" But it is easy for the amiable marchioness to speak concerning him; she had an intimate knowledge of the manners, of the things, of the men, of the women, of the adventures, of the little accidents to which the verses and prose of Voiture related. His nephew, Martin Pinchesne, who, a year or two after the death of his uncle, published his works, was foolish or kind enough to suppress the dates of the jokes and the names of most of the persons who had called them forth, so that even in the seventeenth century those who had not been of Voiture's society, had need of a commentator to understand him. Tallemant confesses that there are in his writings many things, the point of which he has not been able to discover. "At some future day," says he, "if it can be done without offending too many people, I will have them printed with notes, and I will add to them such other pieces as I shall be able to find of the society of the hôtel de Rambouillet."[1]

In fact, to relish Voiture, he should have been seen upon the theatre of his success from 1630 to 1648, with those pretty women who sought to be amused, among those young gentlemen who, in the interval of battles, were partaking of the most refined pleasures of the mind. Voiture reigned at the hôtel de Rambouillet. Corneille, timid and proud, neglected and full of himself, was but ill at ease in this great society: he listened almost always in silence, and seldom conversed except with Balzac, his fellow-citizen in the Roman republic. But Voiture was the gayety, the life, the soul of the house. He was always in the proper mood; his inexhaustible flow of spirits mingled in every thing, animated every thing, and, while Corneille was grave in the midst of trifles, and introducing, involuntarily, into the very comedies which he wished to make most diverting, tragic movements, Voiture, in the most serious matters, was lavishing his witticisms. He represents the playful side of the hôtel de Rambouillet, as Corneille did its severe side.

Let us not forget that Voiture wrote only as he was

---

[1] Tallemant, ii., p. 295.

inspired by the occasion—that circumstance was his favorite muse, and that she dictated to him most of those little things, produced in haste, and which he did not even take the trouble to collect. It is then ridiculous to criticise them. They were for the most part songs, intended to be sung, and which were sung. The editor has sometimes indicated the airs, and we have found nearly all of them in a curious collection, belonging to the library of the Arsenal, entitled *Chansons notées.*

But Voiture has not merely a facility full of charm; it seems to me that in his somewhat more studied efforts, he has ideas, philosophy, sensibility, sometimes even passion. I feel obliged to shelter myself behind the authority of Boileau, who, in his letter to Perrault,[1] eulogizes Voiture, and particularly his elegies. For my part, I prefer them to all those which appeared before 1648, the year of the death of Voiture, and of the end, or at least of the decay of the hôtel de Rambouillet, excepting, indeed, the elegies of Corneille, now too much forgotten, and which contain passages vieing with the most touching of his tragedies.[2]

---

[1] Edit. of Saint-Surin, vol. iv., p. 375.

[2] See in the *Œuvres diverses* of Corneille, ed. of Amsterdam, 1740, p. 174, the elegy containing a declaration of love: it is not dated, but must have been written during the youth of Corneille, and even before his glory, for he does not speak of it, whilst later he uses a very dif-

I would call attention to the elegy to a coquette, whom Voiture names Bélise. Is there, indeed, no elevation, no force in the following verses?

Your charms which but the face adorn,
Can ne'er control a soul well born,
Your sway 's too harsh to be secure;
If any one can it endure,

---

ferent tone. The lady to whom his elegy is addressed, must have been of good birth, if the young poet is to be believed. He paints finely the passage from admiration to love:

Mais de ce sentiment la flatteuse imposture
N'empêcha pas le mal pour cacher la blessure,
Et ce soin d'admirer, qui dure plus d'un jour,
S'il n'est amour déjà, devient bientôt amour.
Un je ne sais quel trouble où je me vis réduire
De cette vérité sut assez tôt m'instruire:
Par d'inquiets transports me sentant émouvoir,
J'en connus le sujet quand j'osai vous revoir.
. . . .
Un désordre confus m'expliqua mon martyre:
Je voulus vous parler, mais je ne sus que dire.
Je rougis, je pâlis, et d'un tacite aveu
Je n'aime point, dis-je, hélas! qu'il s'en faut peu! etc.

The piece entitled *Jalousie*, and which is not finished, has parts which seem written by Molière.

Le plus léger chagrin d'une humeur inégale,
Le moindre égarement d'un mauvais intervalle,
Un souris par mégarde à ses yeux dérobé,
Un coup d'œil par hasard sur un autre tombé,
. . . .
Tout cela fait pour lui de grands crimes d'État,
Et plus l'amour est fort, plus il est délicat.

Corneille felt a tender sentiment for the Marchioness de B. A. T. (we are ignorant of the name of the person concealed under these initials). He speaks of himself now in a very different manner from that of his youth, and he turns the honors of his glory to the profit of his love:

Je connais mes défauts, mais après tout je pense
Être pour vous encore un captif d'importance,

With so much scorn, ingratitude,
He must be born for servitude,
Or else some wretch whom gods pursue
In wrath by giving him to you.
For praise and honor vainly moved,
You cannot love, yet would be loved,[1] etc.

We must give almost in full the elegy to a lady whom he had quitted for another, and to whom he returned :

Leaving for me her native pride,
Sweet Iris could no more deride ;
Approved my flame, my hopes allow'd,
Received my love, heard what I vow'd,

Car vous aimez le gloire, et vous savez qu'un roi
Ne vous en peut jamais assurer tant que moi, etc.

Corneille bid adieu to her whose love he despairs of obtaining ; he yields to younger rivals :

Négligez-moi pour eux, mais dites en vous-même :
Moins il me veut aimer, plus il fait voir qu'il m'aime,
Et m'aime d'autant plus que son cœur enflammé
N'ose même aspirer au bonheur d'être aimé.
Je fais tous ses plaisirs, j'ai toutes ses pensées,
Sans que le moindre espoir les ait intéressées.
Puissé-je malgré vous y penser au peu moins,
M'échapper quelque jour vers quelques autres soins,
Trouver quelques plaisirs ailleurs qu'en votre idée,
Et voir toute mon âme un peu moins obsédée ;
Et vous, de qui je n'ose attendre jamais rien,
Ne ressentir jamais un mal pareil au mien !

I will not quote, but indicate the stanzas addressed to the same person, and which express the same sentiments in a different meter :

Marquise, si mon visage
A quelques traits un peu vieux, etc.

[1] Vol. ii., p. 87. The first edition of Voiture is that given by his nephew, Pinchesne, almost immediately after his death, in 1650, in-4°, and which is dedicated to Condé. There was already a seventh edition, in-12, in 1665. The last and most complete is that of 1745, 2 vol., small in-8°. It is this that we shall quote.

Bestow'd those tokens, one by one,
Which lovers hang their hopes upon.
Treatment so mild, 't must be averr'd,
Some feeling in my bosom stirr'd,—
Of love? This perjured soul 'gainst you
Such injury could never do;
Of friendship only, yet so strong,
I thought to love 't would turn ere long.
In her I daily hoped to meet
The traits which render you so sweet,
Those charms divine, by which, at will,
You either make alive or kill;
Your graces perfectly refined,
The native grandeur of your mind,
That discourse sweet, to nature true,
But these I find alone in you.
Of beauty, sooth, she had enough
To move the heart of sternest stuff;
A hundred charms in her I found,
But greater charms in you abound;
None of those looks with which, as darts,
Your eyes transfix the hardest hearts.
How oft, when by your beauty smit,
Or by your grace or sparkling wit,
I've said, and I can quickly prove,
That Philis merits truest love?

We cannot mistake a true sensibility, the accent of passion, or, if you please, of pleasure, in these *stanzas*, addressed to an Aminte who is unknown to us:

When simply with two words you chose
To make my pains forever cease;
When I had felt a martyr's woes,
You oped the skies and gave me peace.
Your charms, which nothing can eclipse,
Conceal'd the rigor of your part,
Love's lures were all upon your lips,
And all his shafts went to my heart.
You took at once a beauty new,
A radiance vieing that above.

Ah! how mine eyes were then on you,
And how your eyes saw me in love!

Here, in a very different style, are some verses, which, twenty years later, Saint-Evremond would not have disavowed. Voiture is writing to the Duke d'Enghien on his recovery from a disease by which it was thought he would be carried off, after the campaign in Germany, in 1645:

I much rejoice, my lord, to know
Your safe return from Allemagne,
From sickness, too, that laid you low,
Just at the close of the campaign;
Spreading a hope throughout all Spain,
That Heaven at last would show it grace
By cutting short your fearful race,
And that undoubted valor stay
Which it so dreads to face.
But, seignior, let me know, I pray,
Does Death, who, on the battle-fields,—
'Mid cries and terrible alarms,
'Mid flames, and swords, and spears, and shields,
The noise and rage of clashing arms,—
Appears for you to have some charms,
And seem'd so very fine before
To you array'd in garb of war:
Does he appear the same, I pray,
When leisurely he takes his way
Towards one too sick to hold his head;
And has he not an ugly grin,
When cold and stiff he saunters in,
To take a man from out his bed? etc.

In justice to Voiture, it must be acknowledged: he is the creator of a particular literature—the literature of society, if the expression may be allowed.

He excelled in playful and light poetry; in that kind of trifling verse in which he has since had so many insipid imitators; which Voltaire carried so far, and which forms the best part, the truest title, to his poetic glory. Voiture was indeed the miniature Voltaire of the hôtel de Rambouillet.

I leave him, after saying to his honor that, though an attendant at the court, he had not the manners of a courtier. Voiture is the first example of a man of letters who preserved his independence among the greatest lords: he had rather the saucy tone and manners of his successors of the end of the eighteenth century. He was very caustic, and therefore much dreaded. Great care was taken not to incur one of his epigrams, for they were sharp swift arrows that flew all over Paris, tearing their poor victim to pieces in a thousand different places at the same time. The Duke d'Enghien, who loved to laugh, and who could appreciate a joke, because he himself had great wit, agreed perfectly with Voiture, saying, however, "He would be insupportable, if he was one of ourselves." Besides, Voiture, still surpassing his disciples of the eighteenth century, had procured an excellent post through his success in society. He was appointed introducer of ambassadors to his Royal Highness, Gaston, Duke of Orleans. He was also appointed an officer of finance, in which capacity he seldom served, although he thence derived a handsome income. He had been intrusted with more than one important mission, principally to the Count-Duke d'Olivares. In person he was well made, and he dressed himself in the best taste. It was his office to be the chevalier, the lover, and, as they then said, the *mourant* (dying man) of all the belles, especially of the pretty Mademoiselle Paulet, whose somewhat bold manners and blond hair had won for her the name of the lioness of the hôtel de Rambouillet.

Such was the society into which, about the year 1635 or 1636—after the great ball which bore off Mademoiselle de Bourbon from the Carmelites—the Princess de Condé introduced her daughter, with her son, the young Duke d'Enghien. They did not enter it unprepared. The hôtel de Condé was also the rendezvous of the best company. Situated in the vast space at present occupied by the Rue de Condé, the street, place, and theatre de l'Odéon, as far as the Rue des Fossés-Monsieur-le-Prince, it was, says Sauval,[1] magnificently built, and Madame the Princess did its honors with a dignity almost royal, tempered with grace and wit. Lenet, to whom we must always refer in regard to every thing connected with the

---

[1] Vol. ii., p. 66. It was the ancient hôtel de Gondi, *the most magnificent of the times*, says again Sauval, *Ibid.*, p. 181. Perelle has engraved the hôtel and the gardens.

Condés, informs us that Madame the Princess had bestowed great pains upon the manners of her children. "Marguerite de Montmorency,[1] who had been the beauty, grace, and majesty of her times, and who was proportionably so in advanced age, even till her death, had always around her a circle of the most agreeable and intellectual ladies of the court. Near her were found all the most gallant, the most *honnête*, and most elevated, both by birth and merit. The young prince became pleased with this society. He frequented it continually, and from it received the first tincture of that noble and gallant civility which he has ever possessed, which he still preserves towards ladies. . . . Mademoiselle de Bourbon, his sister, who was afterwards the Duchess de Longueville, possessed great spirit and extraordinary beauty." We can then easily conceive how the two young people were received at the hôtel de Rambouillet. From the first moment, they gave it the greatest lustre.

Mademoiselle de Bourbon, the person whom we have described, with beautiful blue eyes, light hair, fine form, careless and languishing air, was formed exactly, by the bent of her mind and character, to become an accomplished pupil of the hôtel de Ram-

[1] Lenet, edit. Michaud, pp. 447 and 450.

bouillet. There was in her an innate depth of pride, which slumbered in ordinary life, but, at intervals, was promptly aroused. Her mind was of the finest stamp, but its delicacy often turned to subtilty. Especially the tender, Platonic gallantry, which was the order of the day, was calculated to charm without causing her fear, for her rank protected her; and, besides, she says in the most humble of confessions, the pleasures of sense never attracted her. What touched her, and ended in misleading her, was a desire to be loved, and also the wish to appear, to show, as they then said, the power of her mind and of her eyes.

Her brother, the Duke d'Enghien, had her hauteur, but nothing whatever of her delicacy. In spite of all the efforts of his mother, and the example of his sister, the easy manner of the warrior always marked him; and he often carried freedom of thought and language even to license. Though not handsome, he was well made; and, when elegantly dressed, he presented a fine appearance. His keen eyes, very aqueline nose, somewhat decayed teeth, abundant and usually disordered hair, gave him an eagle-like look when animated.[1] He possessed an

[1] One is deceived in expecting to become acquainted with the great Condé, by seeing the celebrated portrait of Nanteuil. This portrait is of 1662. It represents Condé fatigued and grown old, after the civil war.

agreeable mind, a gayety which was most freely exhibited in the midst of dangers, and which did not abandon him in prison. Whatever may be said of him, he was full of heart. He loved his friends, and he never betrayed one of them. He exacted much from them, but he also gave them much. He lavished their blood, as well as his own, upon the battle-field; but he promoted their interests, and demanded for them more than for himself. Any other person, after the battle of Rocroy, would have been jealous of Gassion, who was said to have advised the manœuvre which decided the day; he himself, from the field of battle, demanded for Gassion the baton of Marshal of France, and the office of Lieutenant-General for Sirot, who, at the head of the reserve, had completed the victory. When, in the fight of the Rue Saint-Antoine, escaping with difficulty from the carnage, harassed with fatigue, defeated, covered with blood, he arrived, sword in hand, at the house of Mademoiselle, his first exclamation, accompanied with a torrent of tears, was, "Ah! madame, you see a man who has lost all his friends!" At Brussels, when negotiating his return to France, he stipulated also for a similar grace to those who had followed him. He wrote very spirited verses, but they were

We must look for the conqueror of Rocroy and of Lens, in the portraits of Haret, of Michel Lasne, and especially of Duret.

satirical and somewhat soldierlike.[1] He once loved, in the Spanish fashion, according to all the rules of the hôtel de Rambouillet. We shall presently make known the object of this touching passion, which does lasting honor to the great Condé; but we may here say that she was a heroine worthy of the hero.

Represent to yourself these two young persons at the hôtel de Rambouillet. There Condé amused himself and laughed freely with Voiture and the wits around him; but his favorite was Corneille. The latter, who was poor, and somewhat fond of money, complained to Segrais, a Normand like himself,[2] that the Prince de Condé, who professed so much admiration for his works, had never made him large presents. Segrais did not then know, that until the death of his father in 1646, the Duke d'Enghien had nothing but his glory, that he was unable to give the least pension; and what pension, I ask, would have been worth so much as the presence of Condé at the first representation of *Cinna*, and the sobs which escaped him at those memorable words:

Let us be friends, *Cinna;* 'tis I who ask thee, etc.

We should remark in passing that this same Condé,

---

[1] See farther on.

[2] *Mémoires anecdotes*, p. 103.

who was the enthusiastic admirer of Corneille, became the friend of Bossuet, and the faithful defender of Molière. He had seen Bossuet almost a child beginning his career as a preacher at the hôtel de Rambouillet; he had been present at, and had thought of taking part in the brilliant struggles of his doctorship: near the close of his life he sought his conversation, and found in him not only the most eloquent, but the most exact historian, the most faithful painter of Rocroy, especially the most worthy interpreter of that great heart, immortal dwelling of the beautiful and good.

Mademoiselle de Bourbon soon became one of the most brilliant ornaments of the hôtel de Rambouillet. She there met the Marchioness de Sablé, still beautiful, and celebrated for her admiration of Spanish manners, and for her loves with Montmorency. Madame de Sablé guided the first steps of her youth, and twenty-five years after, received her at that common rendezvous of noble disabused hearts, religion. But Mademoiselle de Bourbon was then in the morning of life; and, little thinking of the storms that awaited her, she yielded herself, on leaving the Carmelites, to all the pleasures which came before her.

Like her brother, she admired Corneille; but she had a particular taste for Voiture, and this taste never forsook her. She thought, she spoke continually of

Voiture, like Madame de Sévigné. It was not the charm of his wit alone that pleased her; she was, doubtless, touched with the sensibility which we have shown that he possessed, and which places Voiture above all his rivals. In the famous quarrel concerning the two sonnets upon Job, and upon Uranie, which divided the court and the city, the *salons* and the Academy, when every one was for Benserade, Madame de Longueville, then the arbiter of taste and of elegance, took in hand the cause of Voiture, and brought all to her opinion. A whole volume has been written on this quarrel: it is not exhausted, and we shall hereafter take it up by aid of new pieces, which, in showing for the first time the motives of Madame de Longueville, will reveal to us the delicacy of her mind, which belongs to that of her heart.[1]

Mademoiselle de Bourbon became acquainted, also, at the hôtel de Rambouillet, with the cultivated, moderate, discreet Chapelain, the sincere friend of good literature, and who might have become a writer of the third, perhaps, even of the second rank, as well as his friend, Pélisson, if, as was said by Boileau, whose shafts of wit are all serious judgments, he had been contented to write in prose. Mademoiselle de Bourbon conceived a great esteem for Chapelain, and,

---

[1] Farther on, chap. iv.

when she married, she made Monsieur de Longueville give him a pension sufficient to enable him to labor in security upon that famous *Pucelle*, which was to be the Iliad of France, which was applauded in advance in the *salons* of the Rue Saint-Thomas-du-Louvre, and of which the young admirer of Corneille and Voiture was already beginning to grow weary.

Among the mediocre wits whom she met in the illustrious hôtel, was Godeau, the little abbé, who was called in the house the dwarf of Julie, and who during all his life, by turns bishop of Grasse and of Vence, kept up a written correspondence, half devotional, half gallant, with Mademoiselle de Bourbon and Madame de Longueville.[1] There was Esprit, too,

---

[1] Observe the style in which he writes from Grasse, the 18th December, 1637, to Mademoiselle de Bourbon: "Mademoiselle, I am proud to learn that she, who occupies all hearts, should fear that she is not in my memory. Though it were a temple, you should there have a place; judge, then, whether I have no interest in preserving you in it, in order that you may render it precious, poor and unfaithful as it was before. It is principally at the altar, Mademoiselle, that you are present with me. I truly ask God to add other lilies to those of your crown, but I ask him, also, to mingle with them the love of the thorns of his Son, and to strengthen you in the generous contempt of the grandeur in which I have seen (an allusion to the thought entertained by Mademoiselle de Bourbon of becoming a Carmelite)." Elsewhere, May 3, 1641. . . . . . "Our Lord is very good, but he is jealous, and he would prefer that we should never have tasted his spirit, than to become digusted with it, and suffer it to be quenched. Roses have thorns which defend their beauty, but princesses are in the midst of roses which do not secure them against the temptations which the pleasures of the world inspire. . . ." See *Letters of M. Godeau, Bishop of Vence, on different subjects;* Paris, 1713, p. 17 and p. 143.

of the French Academy, who played all sorts of parts: at first, a man of letters and messmate of the chancellor, who placed him in the Academy, then suddenly a priest of l'Oratoire, then a man of the world again, and father of a family, who could not have been devoid of merit, for he had the esteem of the best judges of his times: attached afterwards to the embassy of Munster, one of the pensioners of M. and Madame de Longueville, preceptor of their nephews, the young princes de Conti, holding a prominent place in the *salon* of Madame de Sablé, consulted by La Rochefoucauld, and even passing for one of the authors of the *Maximes*, a reputation which he might have preserved if he had not been so imprudent as to print a work in 1678.[1]

I should be scrupulous, were I to forget Madame Scudéry as one of the frequenters of the hôtel de Rambouillet. She was certainly very homely, yet a person of true talent, writing perhaps too rapidly, but with a correctness and polish which were not common in 1640. She enjoyed and merited great consideration. Leibnitz sought the honor of her correspondence. She wrote verses which were relished in their time, and which still seem to us very agree-

[1] *De la Fausseté des Vertus humaines*, by M. Esprit; in-12, two vol., Paris, 1678.

able. Her romances are so long, and the episodes in them so embarrassing to one another, that it is absolutely impossible to read them at the present day. But those who dare to enter this labyrinth will meet here and there portraits well drawn, and resembling, though somewhat flattered, the illustrious originals, poorly disguised under Greek, Persian, and Roman names; exact descriptions of the finest places, and most magnificent palaces of France and of Paris, transported to Rome or to Armenia; great sentiments then in vogue; tendernesses of a refined Platonism; conversations sometimes a little insipid, sometimes a little refined, but which give a very agreeable idea of the real conversations which Madame Scudéry tried to imitate. Madame de Lafayette will, some day, abridge these pictures and these discourses; she will take from them these insipidities and weaknesses; she will soften these subtilties; but she will preserve the charm of these heroic and gallant manners, and the delicate minds, whose delights are in *Zaïdé*, and *The Princesses de Clèves*, in the *Bérénice* of Racine, the *Psyché* of Molière, and of Corneille, will not read without pleasure, certain chapters of the *Grand Cyrus.* Georges Scudéry himself, insupportable on account of his self-love and bravado style, was a man of honor, reliable as a friend, and who, in the most trying moments, before Mazarin, on whom he depended, preserved proudly his fidelity to Condé and his sister.

It is proper to mention these different persons, because they reappear in the life of Madame de Longueville. At the hôtel de Rambouillet, they attached themselves to Mademoiselle de Bourbon, and began her reputation, which grew rapidly from year to year.

Mademoiselle de Bourbon passed the winters in Paris, at the hôtel de Condé, at the Louvre, at the Palais Cardinal, in some hôtels of the Place-Royal, especially at the hôtel de Rambouillet, amid balls, concerts, comedies, gallant conversations; and everywhere she was brilliant by the graces of her mind and person. In summer she was occupied with other pleasures: she went to Fontainebleau with the court, or to visit her mother at Chantilly, or to see Cardinal Richelieu and the duchess d'Aiguillon at Ruel, or perhaps to Liancourt, to visit the Duchess of Liancourt, Jeanne de Schomberg; or perhaps again, to Labarre, near Paris, to pass some time with the Baroness Du Vigean, who, though of inferior rank, but of great fortune, had the most amiable family,—a son, the Marquis de Fors, one of the bravest comrades of the Duke d'Enghien, and two charming daughters, who were greatly sought by all the young and gallant nobility. Before as well as after her marriage, Mademoiselle de Bourbon divided her time among these different residences, which rivalled each other in magnificence and charms. Naturally, it was to her mother, at Chantilly, that she went most frequently.

We must look in Du Cerceau[1] and in Perelle[2] to know what Chantilly was at the beginning and at the end of the seventeenth century. This vast and beautiful domain had long belonged to the family of Montmorency, and it came into that of Condé, in 1632, through Madame the Princess, on the death of her brother, decapitated at Toulouse. It assembles then the souvenirs of the two greatest military families of ancient France. Anne and Louis de Bourbon pervade it, and their spirits will cover and protect Chantilly so long as there shall remain among us any patriotic piety, any national pride. The Montmorencys transferred the charming chateau to the Condés a little before the *renaissance*, which Du Cerceau has described in all its details. It was the great Condé, during the last fifteen years of his life, who, finding in the vicinity the most beautiful woods, a true forest, with a canal resembling a river, abundant waters and vast gardens, drew from them the wonders which the

---

1 *The most excellent Buildings of France*, in-fol., 1607, vol. ii. Many plates of the castle, none of the garden.

2 *Views of the finest Buildings of France*, by Perelle.—*General view of the Château de Chantilly, of its canals, fountains, and groves*, etc.

graver of Perelle has preserved for us, and which Bossuet could not help praising,—those fountains, those cascades, those grottoes, those pavilions, "those superb avenues, those water-jets which ceased neither day nor night."[1] They have ceased now. The bad taste of the seventeenth century and revolutions have destroyed Chantilly. A prince worthy of his name had undertaken to restore it to its first beauty. He had wished to expend upon it the fortune which the mishaps of the house of Condé had brought to him, and that which he held from his own house. The young captain had dreamed of returning at a future day, after having extended and secured French dominion in Africa, to repose with his lieutenants in the sacred home of the Montmorencys and the Condés, restored and embellished by his own hand. Providence ordered otherwise, and Chantilly still awaits a repairing hand. But let us return to the Chantilly of the middle of the seventeenth century, before the epoch of its great magnificence, between the periods described respectively by Du Cerceau and Perelle.

It was already a delicious abode. Madame the Princess delighted in it, and there passed, with her children, almost every summer. She brought with

---

[1] Bossuet, funeral oration on the great Condé.

her a little court, composed of the friends of her son and daughter, with some of the choicest wits, and particularly Voiture, with whom they could not dispense. In default of Voiture, they had his small change, Montreuil or Sarrazin, attachés of the house of Condé, and who were successively secretaries of Condé, of the Prince de Conti, and of Madame de Longueville. They were men of fine spirit; and Boileau, in his letter to Perrault, names Sarrazin after Voiture. M. the Prince, for whom the country possessed but little charm, remained usually in Paris, to prosecute his designs and his fortune. Madame the Princess did not dislike diversion, and young people devoted themselves to her with ardor. Court was paid to the ladies. During the heat of the day, they amused themselves in reading romances or poetry; in the evening they took long promenades and held long conversations. They lived after the manner of Astrea, in awaiting the adventures of the great Cyrus. Even in 1650, after the death of her husband, during the captivity of her two sons and of her son-in-law and the exile of her daughter, the troubles of the civil war and the noise of arms, Lenet relates to us how the Princess de Condé passed the time at Chantilly:[1] "The promenades were the most agree-

---

[1] Edition Michaud, p. 229.

able in the world. . . . The evenings were not less diverting. The company repaired to the apartment of the princess, where they played at different games. There were often fine voices, and especially agreeable conversations and stories of intrigues, which made life pass as pleasantly as possible. . . . These diversions were interrupted by bad news, occasionally brought or written. It was a very great pleasure to see all the young ladies sad or gay, according to the rare or frequent visits made to them, and according to the nature of the letters which they received; and as the affairs of each were pretty well known, it was easy to enter into them enough in advance to be amused. Every moment some visitors or some messages arrived, which caused great jealousy among those who did not receive them; and all this occasioned songs, sonnets, and elegies, which were not less diverting to the indifferent than to the interested. They made rhymes and enigmas, which occupied spare hours. Some might be seen walking along the banks of the ponds, in the avenues of the garden or park, on the terrace or on the downs, alone or in troops, according to the humor of the moment; while others were singing an air or reciting verses, or reading romances on a balcony, or walking or reclining upon the grass. Never did any one see so beautiful a place, in so beautiful a season, filled with better or more amiable company."

But before 1650, before the Fronde, which divided all French society, Chantilly was a still more agreeable abode. Judge of it by this letter, which Sarrazin wrote from thence, at the commencement of 1648, to Mademoiselle de Rambouillet, at that time Madame de Montausier, who had just set out, with her husband, for their government of Saintonge and d'Angoumois :[1]

Whate'er of that beautiful land they may say,
Where homage devout was paid to Astrée;
However superbly or brightly they may
That mansion enchanted portray,
  Where am'rous Armida and am'rous Alcine
Then captives enamor'd consign'd;
Those gardens, abounding with pleasures refined,
  Which boasted, despite Falerine,
Of holding the proudest Paladins confined:
  How charming soever one might
  The tale of their glories relate,
They match not in beauty the spot whence I date,
  The spot whence to you I now write
A truth whose resemblance to fiction is great.

The hum which the zephyr excites among the leaves of the grove when night is about to cover the earth, was gently agitating the forest of Chantilly,

---

[1] *Œuvres de Sarrazin*, at Paris, in 4°, 1656, p. 281. This first edition was reproduced in two small volumes in 1663, and in 1685. In 1674, appeared the *Nouvelles Œuvres de Sarrazin*, in two parts, containing prose and verse.

when, upon the principal road, three nymphs appeared to the solitary Tircis. They were not those poor wood-nymphs, more worthy of pity than envy, who, for lodging and clothing, have nothing but the bark of the trees. Their equipage was superb, and their clothing brilliant. . . . The majestic air of the oldest impressed all who approached her with profound respect. The one by her side displayed a beauty which neither painting, sculpture, nor poetry have ever realized. The third had that easy air that is given to the Graces.

> Slowly two demigods beside her stroll'd,
> The one of aspect sweet, the other bold;
> The one walk'd like a conq'ror in his might,
> And even Mars would have appall'd;
> The other could with truth enough be call'd
> The earth's delight.

That is to say, Madame, yesterday evening, at twilight, I met, on the great road to Chantilly, Madame the Princess, who was never in better health, accompanied by Madame de Longueville, who never looked more beautiful, and Madame de Saint-Loup,[1] who was never more gay, all three in deshabille and in a calash, followed by the Princes de Condé and de Conti. . . . Madame the Princess, perceiving me,

---

1 Mademoiselle Chateignier de La Rocheposay, one of the prettiest of women, and much courted by the Duke de Candale, the brother of Mademoiselle d'Epernon.

exclaimed: Sarrazin, I wish you to sit down this moment, and write to Madame de Montausier, that Chantilly was never more beautiful, that time there never passed more pleasantly, that her society was never more desired, and that she is making a fool of herself by staying at Saintonge, while we are here:

Tell her what we do each day,
Tell her every thing we say.
In obedience to command,
Lo! I take my pen in hand.
When gay Aurora, on her endless race
In far-off India, shows her smiling face,
And flocks of little birds, roused from their rest,
Sing sweetly 'mong the trees so gayly dress'd,
And tardy serfs go forth to sow or reap,
At Chantilly we're fast asleep.
So, when the night her sombre vestment spreads,
And Cynthia 'mid the stars her radiance sheds,
When now past midnight's goal she onward speeds,
When calm the noise of day succeeds,
When all throughout the world to sleep betake,
At Chantilly we're wide awake.
And oh! between these two extremes,
What careless, happy lives lead we!
And oh! this mansion of Silvie[1]
Gives joys by night, by day sweet dreams!

. . . .

Music we have of every sort,
Of lutes, and violins, and voice;
And in the woods we oft rejoice,
With dogs and horns, to take the hunter's sport.
Sometimes on horseback off we fly,
And at the swiftest speed we try
To catch the ring suspended high.
In tilting, too, we pleasure take,

---

[1] See the pretty engraving of Parelle.

And many handsome tourneys make, etc.

. . . .

And shall I here, too, make you find
The list of good things furnish'd for our mind?
Say Ablancourt, Calprenède, and Corneille,
Or rather, vulgarly to speak,
Say verse, and hist'ry, and romance,
Divert us daily without fail,
And that our joys are never marr'd perchance? etc.

We may by this judge what Chantilly must have been eight or ten years before, when all there were young; when the great Condé was still the Duke d'Enghien; Madame de Longueville, Mademoiselle de Bourbon; Madame de Montausier, Mademoiselle de Rambouillet; when, instead of the civil war, a flourishing peace or glorious victories filled every heart with gladness. The Duke d'Enghien was never there except amid a crowd of brave and gallant gentlemen, who afterwards fought with him at Rocroy, at Fribourg, at Dunkirk, at Lens, but who then shared his pleasures at the hôtel de Condé and at Chantilly—devoted confidants of his designs and of his loves. Among these were the Duke de Nemours, so suddenly slain, and whose brother—inheritor of his title, of his beauty, and his bravery—perished also in a frightful duel in the midst of the Fronde; Coligny, killed also, at an early age, in a duel of another character; his brother, Dandelot, afterwards Duke de Châtillon, one of the heroes of Lens, who promised to be a great warrior, and who perished at the attack of Charenton, during the first days of the Fronde; Laval, the son of the Marquis de Sablé, handsome, brave, and witty, who distinguished himself, and was slain at the siege of Dunkirk; La Moussaye, his aid-de-camp and principal officer in every battle, who, too, died young at Stenay, in 1650; Chabot, who married the beautiful and rich heiress of the Rohans; Pisani, the son of the Marchioness de Rambouillet, who fell sword in hand; the Marquis de Fors Du Vigean, Nangis, Tavannes, Seneçay, and many others, among whom arose the young Montmorency-Boutteville, afterwards Duke Maréchal-de-Luxembourg; all this school of Condé, entirely different from that of Turenne, into which the Duke d'Enghien early breathed his genius and the divine part of art, as Napoleon so well expressed it, the instinct of war, the glance which seized the strategic point of an affair, with audacity and obstinacy in execution; that admirable school, which began at Rocroy, and from which arose twelve marshals, without counting those generals who sustained the honor of France to the very end of the century. These were the youth who amused themselves at Chantilly, preluding glory by gallantry.

Mademoiselle de Bourbon, in selecting companions, was equal to her brother. She formed a connection with the Marchioness de Sablé, who became the friend of her whole life; but she had younger friends, if not more dear, at least with whom she was more familiar; she had formed a little private society, composed chiefly of Mademoiselle de Rambouillet, of Mesdemoiselles Du Vigean, and of her two cousins, Mesdemoiselles de Boutteville. It must be confessed that it was a circle of charming and redoubtable beauties, harmonious in their graceful youth, but destined soon to be separated, and to become rivals or enemies.

Voiture, we may conceive, took great care of these beautiful ladies, and especially of Mademoiselle de Bourbon: he celebrated her in verse and in prose, in every tune, and upon every occasion. Even in his letters written to others, he cannot cease speaking of her mind and beauty: "The mind of Mademoiselle de Bourbon," says he, "is all that can cause one to doubt whether her beauty is the most perfect thing in the world." He is continually comparing her to an angel:

> "Of pearls and stars and flowers of finest shade,
> Bourbon, the heaven hath thy complexion made,
> And 'mid thy charms it hath enshrined
> An angel's mind."

In another place he says:

> "The Bourbon, you might safely swear,
> Seeing her skin so fresh, so fair,
> Had from a lily sprung."

It is to her again that he addresses this agreeable

song, intended, doubtless, to be chanted in a low tone by the side of Mademoiselle de Bourbon, as she lay dozing in one of the groves of Chantilly:

> "Our Aurora 'mid roses
> Now gently reposes;
> Let each keep silence once more,
> And let no one disturb her,
> Unless it be life to restore."[1]

And if these ladies staid too long in the country, when Voiture was not with them, he called them back to Paris, in his burlesque, sentimental complaints."[2]

But they did not spend the whole summer at Chantilly. Madame the Princess possessed several other country-seats in the vicinity: Marlou, La Versine, Méru, l'Isle-Adam, charming places to which she often went. She was also obliged to visit the cardinal and Madame d'Aiguillon in their beautiful summer residence at Ruel, on the borders of the Seine, between Saint-Germain and Paris.[3] The pleasures of these places were very different from those of Chantilly.

---

[1] Edit. of 1745, vol. 1st, etc. *Our Aurora*, hitherto perfectly unknown, is in fact Mademoiselle de Bourbon herself, according to an old tradition preserved by the manuscript collection of songs, called *Recueil de Maurepas*, for opposite to the first couplet this note is found: *For Mademoiselle de Bourbon, sleeping.*

[2] *Ibid.*, p. 170. See also the song to Madame la Princesse, to the air *Des Landriri;* ibid., p. 129.

[3] See the different views of Ruel, by Parelle.

Art reigned at Ruel. Like Paris, it had a theatre, where the cardinal caused the representation of pieces with machinery brought from Italy. He gave great mythological ballets, like those of the Louvre, and feasts of a magnificence almost royal; whilst at Chantilly, much more removed from Paris, there was doubtless grandeur and opulence, but a grandeur full of quiet, and an opulence which placed especially at its service the beauties of nature. Ruel was also quite as lively as the Palais-Cardinal. Richelieu labored there with his ministers: there he received the court, France, Europe. Business was there mingled with diversion. The Duchess d'Aiguillon was worthy of her uncle, ambitious and prudent, devoted to him to whom she owed every thing, sharing his cares as well as his fortune, and governing admirably his house. She was still young enough, of a regular beauty, and not implicated in any affair of gallantry. Calumny or slander had attacked her relations with Richelieu, and even with Madame Du Vigean. She had more sense than wit, and was by no means a *précieuse*, although she frequented the hôtel de Rambouillet. Madame the Princess did not like Richelieu; she could not pardon the death of her brother, Montmorency, whom all her prayers and tears had not been able to save; but she subscribed to the political opinions of her husband. She had been obliged to agree to the marriage of the Duke d'Enghien with Mademoiselle de Brézé, and she was continually with his children at the Palais-Cardinal and at Ruel. She was received there in a manner that was unavoidable, and the poets of the cardinal chanted the praises of both the mother and daughter. Richelieu, as is well known, had five poets whom he employed to labor for his theatre: Bois-Robert, Colletet, l'Etoile, Corneille, and Rotrou. They were called the five authors, and as such, produced in common several pieces: *l'Aveugle de Smyrne*, *La Comédie des Tuileries*, etc. This did not prevent the presence of other poets at the palace of his Eminence: Georges Scudéry, Voiture himself, who paid court to Richelieu and celebrated the Duchess d'Aiguillon. It was at Ruel that, meeting in an avenue Queen Anne, and challenged by her to make some verses on the spot, Voiture improvised that little piece, remarkable especially for the ease and boldness with which he ventured to speak to her of Buckingham. But the two favorites of the cardinal were Desmarets and Bois-Robert; he employed their pens upon every occasion, in what was light as well as in what was serious. It seems that Desmarets had been instructed to do the poetic honors of Ruel to Madame the Princess and to her daughter. We find in fact, in the collection, now rare enough and very little read, of the works of the king's counsellor and minister of war, Desmarets, dedicated to Richelieu, and handsomely printed,[1] a multitude of very agreeable verses, which were sung in the mythological ballets of Ruel, and of which several are addressed to Mademoiselle de Bourbon, and to Madame the Princess. In a *Mascarade of the Graces and the Loves, addressing themselves to Madame the Duchess d'Aiguillon in presence of Madame the Princess and of Mademoiselle de Bourbon*, the Graces say to the latter:

Wonderful beauty! offspring too of royalty,
  Whose charms to own the gods have e'en repined,
We truly thought we were but three,
  Yet now a thousand graces in thee find.

These are but insipid affairs, while the two following pieces have at least the advantage of describing the person of Mademoiselle de Bourbon, as she then was before her marriage, a few years after the portrait of Ducayer. We here see Mademoiselle de Bourbon beginning to fulfil the promise of her youth, and the angelic face described to us by Madame de Motteville, already accompanied by other attractions of true beauty:

To Mademoiselle de Bourbon.

Thou with whose charms naught can compare,
    Pride of a nation's heart,
Whose beauteous tints, whose graces rare
    The strongest love impart,

---

[1] Paris, in-4°, 1641.

To win thee, ah! why should I aim,
Since e'en the purest flame,
Though nurtured in the skies,
Could not deserve a glance from thy bright eyes! etc.

To the same.

Complexion where the rose and lily wed,
Beauty of magic powers,
Charming these souls of ours;
Tresses so lustrous, lips so ruby red;
Who ever could resist, who could resign
Attractions so divine? etc.

A few leagues from Chantilly were the beautiful lands of Liancourt, which Jeanne de Schomberg, at first Duchess de Brissac, then Duchess de Liancourt, had converted into a magnificent abode. She was a person of the greatest merit, and we have received from her pen a very remarkable work,[1] destined for the education of her grand-daughter, Mademoiselle de La Roche-Guyon, who, in 1659, married the son of La Rochefoucauld. She took pleasure in planning and carrying out the arrangements of a sumptuous establishment. She bought Rue de Seine, the ancient hôtel de Bouillon, and erected in its place the hôtel de Liancourt, afterwards called the hôtel de La Rochefoucauld, which extended from the Rue de Seine to the Rue des Augustins, in the space now occupied by the Rue des Beaux Arts. "At Liancourt," says Talle-

[1] *Reglement donné par une dame de haute qualité à madame sa petit-fille*, published first in 1698, reprinted in 1779.

mant,[1] "the duchess had done all that any one could do for avenues and meadows. Every year she added some new beauty." In 1656, Silvestre designed and engraved the *different views of the castle and gardens, fountains, cascades, canals, and parterres of Liancourt.*[2] Madame the Princess often made a visit to this beautiful place. At one time when the small-pox was making fearful ravages in the neighborhood of Chantilly, and in the domains of the princess, Marlou, La Versine, Méru, she sent her children, with all their young friends, to pass some time at Liancourt. The Mesdemoiselles Du Vigean alone were wanting, having been called to Paris by their mother. The only son of the house, La Roche-Guyon, was one of the friends of the Duke d'Enghien; he was slain in 1646, while serving under him at the bloody siege of Mardyk. It was autumn. On All-Saints' Day, these young ladies performed their devotions with accustomed exactitude. They then gave themselves up to quiet diversions, and, for want of better, and sharing the dominant taste for wit, also in the company perhaps of Montreuil or Sarrazin, they employed themselves in making rhymes; so that even on All-Saints' Day they addressed to Marlou,

---

[1] Tallemant, vol. iv., p. 806.

[2] Cotin has made an exact *Déscription de Liancourt* in his *Œuvres galantes*, second edition, 1665, pp. 108-115.

where Madame the Princess was then staying, *The Life and Miracles of Saint Marguerite Charlotte de Montmorency, Princess de Condé, versified at Liancourt.* These verses, says the manuscript from which we borrow these details,[1] were made upon the spot, and the authors appear to have been Mademoiselle de Bourbon, and Mesdemoiselles de Rambouillet, de Boutteville, and de Brienne.

Yet to a living saint, on this Saints' Day,
A charming saint, we ought to pray.

. . . .

As soon as she was born, her matchless eyes
Beam'd like two suns in summer skies:
Her cheeks of lilies made—her lips, when closed,
Were beds whereon the rose reposed;
And then in partly opening them to smile,
Pearls of the East she showed the while, etc.

It was impossible for them to forget the two amiable absentees, Mesdemoiselles Du Vigean, who were fatiguing themselves at Paris, while they were passing the time so agreeably at Liancourt. They wrote to them a very long letter in verse, wherein they regretted their absence, and enumerated their consolations. These unpublished verses, like the preceding, are also very mediocre; but it must not be forgotten that they are the impromptus of young girls and noble-born ladies.[2]

---

[1] Manuscripts of Conrart, in-4°, vol. xi., p. 443. [2] *Ibid.*, p. 851.

Letter of Mademoiselle de Bourbon, and of Mesdemoiselles de Rambouillet, de Boutteville, and de Brienne, sent from Liancourt to Mesdemoiselles Du Vigean at Paris.

Four clever nymphs, perhaps more free
Than even those of wood and sea,
To two who with their hearts in pain
Curse bitterly the prisoner's chain;

We who pretended every wise
That praise for us was always stored,
That by an arrow from our eyes
We might be everywhere adored.

. . . .

Of empire we have been deprived;
We've been forsaken, frown'd upon:
At Méru, scarce had we arrived,
Than to Versine we're forced to run.

. . . .

There, too, that foe to female grace,
That death to all of woman's charms,
Our vanity still to abase,
O'erwhelm'd us with the worst alarms.

At noise of this disease so fell,
Each hurries off with looks forlorn;
For, sooth, to lovers all farewell,
If, of our beauty we are shorn!

Of Love's keen weapons to make sure,
In some place fit for his domains,
We came at last to Liancourt,
Where Flora with sweet Zephyr reigns,

Where full a hundred walks are found,
A hundred fountains and cascades—
A hundred meads where streams abound,
Made for the pleasures of the Naiads.

A place, like which, there are so few,
We hoped some length of time to own,

But here now comes that Richelieu,[1]
And hence, at last, we must be gone.

See us, whom lovers all agreed
The brightest stars of France to call;
But we are wand'ring stars indeed,
Who now possess no power at all.

What was most curious and unexpected was, that the mania for rhyming took possession of Condé himself. As we have said, he had much wit and gayety, and he entered willingly into the society with which he was surrounded. In the midst of the Fronde, when war was also carried on by means of songs, he made more than one, bearing his own peculiar stamp. During the first war of Paris, in which Condé, still faithful to the true interests of his house, sided with the court, one of the most ardent chieftains of the opposing party was the Count de Maure, a cadet of the Duke de Mortemart, uncle of Madame de Montespan, husband of the witty Anne Doni d'Attichy, intimate friend of Madame de Sablé. In the councils of the Fronde, the count always favored the most rash resolutions. The Mazarins turned him into ridicule, and overwhelmed him with a shower of epigrams. Bachaumont, one of the authors of the celebrated *Voyage de Chapelle et Bachaumont*, had

---

[1] The cardinal, now old and sick, was as much dreaded by these young girls as the small-pox, from which they had been flying.

written against him some little verses, which terminated thus:[1]

Oh! a buff-jacket, with black velvet sleeves,
Is worn by the great Count de Maure;
And over this hero, whom well it relieves,
There is a buff-jacket, with black velvet sleeves:
Look out, Sir Condé, one easy perceives
You are destined for food to this hero in war.
Oh! a buff-jacket, with black velvet sleeves,
Is worn by the great Count de Maure.

Condé, according to the testimony of Tallemant, whom we have no reason to discredit, added the following lines:

He's a blood-thirsty tiger, the worst of his kind,
This very same brave Count de Maure;
When to be 'mong the foremost in fight he's a mind,
He's a blood-thirsty tiger, the worst of his kind.
But he's not very oft with the foremost we find,
Thus is it that Condé was not kill'd before.
He's a blood-thirsty tiger, the worst of his kind,
This very same brave Count de Maure.

Among his best lieutenants was the Count de Marsin, father of the marshal, indeed much superior to him, and a veritable warrior. Condé esteemed him highly, but for all that he did not spare him. One day at table, in drinking his health, he improvised to a tune, then very common, this little song,[2] which has

---

[1] Tallemant, vol. ii., p. 337, attributes these couplets to Bachaumont; Madame de Motteville, vol. iii., p. 230, gives them without the author's name, and they are found with many others in a long mazarinade, entitled, *Triolets de Saint-Germain*, in-4°, 1649.

[2] Library of the Arsenal, *Belles-Lettres Françaises*, No. 70, collection in-fol., entitled: *Chansons Notées*, vol. ii., p. 66.

never been published, and which seems to us very piquant:

My dear Marsin, I drink to thee,
Mars truly must thy cousin be,
Bellona sure thy ma,
But who may be thy pa
Is more than I can see.
Tin, tin, trelin, tin, tin, tin.

At Liancourt, having nothing to do, and vexed because his sister and her beautiful friends stayed so long at church on All-Saint's Day, he addressed to them the following epigram:[1]

Impose on others, if you may,
A hundred pater-nosters say,
And mumble o'er to day your prayers.
You're very artful, we believe,
For, if a beau his love declares,
You're ready then your prayers to leave.

Among other friends whom he had with him at Liancourt, was the Marquis de Roussillon, an excellent officer and man of spirit, together with the intrepid La Moussaye, who was faithful to him to the last, and who, during the captivity of Condé, shut himself up with Madame de Longueville in the citadel of Stenay, where he died. Roussillon and La Moussaye, having been compelled to leave Liancourt for Lyons, Condé, in imitation of his sister's letter to the Mesdemoiselles Du Vigean, wrote, or caused to

---

[1] Manuscripts of Conrart, in-4°, vol. xi., p. 848.

be written, one of the same kind to his two absent friends. We give this piece almost entire, because it is written by Condé, or because Condé, at least, had a hand in it, and especially because it describes so naturally the life lead at Liancourt, at Chantilly, and in all the grand abodes of that aristocracy of the seventeenth century, so badly appreciated, and which, during peace, honored and cultivated the arts, which gave to letters a Rochefoucauld, a Retz, a Saint-Evremond, a Saint-Simond, without speaking of Madame de Sévigné and Madame de La Fayette, and which, when war broke out, flew to the battle-field, and lavished its blood in the cause of France. These are the verses of the future hero of Rocroy:

Letter[1] *of Monseigneur the Duke d'Enghien, written from Liancourt to MM. de Roussillon and de La Moussaye at Lyons.*

Since you've been gone, a hundred dear delights
  Have e'er consumed our days and nights;
And to recount these pastimes so diverse,
  We are compell'd to write in verse.

Upon the spot most beautiful of earth,
  To pleasures ever giving birth,
Where Art, with Nature, every charm employs,
  We daily find a thousand joys;

A troop of young and peerless maids,
  More beautiful by virtue's aids,

---

[1] Manuscripts of Conrart, in-4°, vol. xi., p. 848.

In sports commingle with a hundred youth,
Sage, gallant, handsome too forsooth.

Each, in a way to envy, e'er displays
His person and his winning ways;
At every moment, too, he tries his best
To please the one who rules his breast:

Talks of his love 'mid groves and promenades,
While leaning o'er the bright cascades,
And really seems the utmost bliss to gain
When sadly he recounts his pain.

A dozen gallants, blest with stoutest lungs,
In comedies employ their tongues;
Display their forms in garments rich and rare,
And strut with a majestic air.

At night, we list to charming serenades,
Or please ourselves with mascarades;
But still, among the pastimes most in quest,
The *Ballet du Printemps* seems best.

. . . .

The ladies oft, when favor'd by the sky,
Love on their well-train'd nags to fly;
To scare the partridge, give the wolf a chase,
And o'er to Marlou have a race.

And lovers meantime whisper in their ear,
Oh! beauty, to the gods so dear!
Leave birds and beasts, since from your eyes fly darts
That daily pierce the bravest hearts.

These are our pastimes, these the sports we take,
And happiness enough they make.
Did you imagine that you hence could bear
A portion of the joys we share?[1]

---

[1] Writing in verse had become a great amusement with all this young and ingenious society. Vol. xiii. of the Manuscripts of Conrart, in-fol., p. 337, contains an epistle in verse to the Duke d'Enghien, when he was at Dijon, and only twenty years of age.

A very natural feeling leads us to inquire into the destiny of this court of young and brave gentlemen, of gay and charming young women, then surrounding Mademoiselle de Bourbon and her brother. We have told that of the gentlemen: all of them became illustrious warriors; most of them died upon the battle-field. But what became of their amiable companions, that swarm of youthful beauties whom we followed upon the steps of Mademoiselle de Bourbon to Chantilly, to Ruel, to Liancourt,—those five inseparable friends, whose verses, less pleasing than their faces, we have published, Mademoiselle de Rambouillet, Mademoiselle de Brienne, Mademoiselle de Montmorency-Boutteville, Mademoiselle Du Vigean? They had the most dissimilar fortunes, as we shall rapidly indicate.

Marie-Antoinette de Lomélie, daughter of the Count de Brienne, one of the ministers of Queen Anne, married, in 1642, the Marquis de Gamache, who became lieutenant-general. Her portraits, traced by herself, may be seen among the *Portraits* of Mademoiselle, with those of her father and mother. She made no noise; all her life passed on quietly and piously. She died at the age of eighty years, in 1704. She kept up continually, with Madame de Longueville, the most friendly intercourse. She was the least brilliant of the five friends, but she was the most fortunate.

What became of Mademoiselle de Rambouillet is well known. Spirituelle but ambitious, after having married Montausier, in 1645, she sought, as well as her husband, the favors of the court, and obtained them by paying the ransom. It is sad to begin in youth with harshness to one's lovers, as they said at the hôtel de Rambouillet, and to be married only as a sort of favor, like the Armande of the *Fémmes Savantes*, in order to become one of the most obliging of duennas. At first appointed a maid of honor of Queen Marie-Thérèse, she had, in 1664, the courage to take the place of the virtuous Duchess de Navailles, who would not countenance the lòve of the young king, Louis XIV., and Mademoiselle de La Vallière. Hence the well-founded accusations entertained by the benevolent Madame de Motteville herself, and which, at a later period, were confirmed by her weakness, when the king abandoned Mademoiselle de La Vallière for Madame de Montespan.[1]

[1] Mémoires, vol. vi., p. 105. "This lady did not hate the court. She desired general approbation, and especially the approbation of those who had credit, for naturally she had a greediness for all that is called favor."—*Ibid.*, p. 167. "According to what I have said of Madame de Montausier, it is easy to judge that she must have been agreeable to the king, not only because she had fine qualities, but because the merit which she possessed was entirely conformed to the fashion of the world. One day that the queen-mother had unwil-

It was in the midst of all these rumors that her husband was named Governor of the Dauphin. Montausier was certainly a man of merit, and, like his

---

lingly received Mademoiselle de La Vallière, Madame de Montausier applauded this condescension, which had given Queen Maria-Theresa so much pain."—*Ibid.* "I cannot help, in this place, mentioning a circumstance which may show how much the hearts and minds of people of court are ordinarily spoiled. At the moment when the queen had commanded me to go and speak to the queen her mother, I met Madame de Montausier, who was rejoicing over the very matter that had thrown the queen into despair. She said to me with an exclamation of joy: Ah! Madame, the queen-mother has done an admirable act in wishing to see La Vallière. See the tact of a very shrewd woman and of a good politician. But, added this lady, she is so feeble that we cannot hope that she will sustain this act as she should. I was truly astonished to see the operations of different sentiments in different persons, and, unwilling to reply, I quitted her. . . . The Duke de Montausier, who had the reputation of a man of honor, caused in me, about the same time, a similar pain, for, in speaking of the ill-feeling which the queen-mother entertained towards the Countess de Brancas, he said to me these words: Ah! truly the queen is very pleasant to be offended, because Madame de Brancas is so complaisant towards the king as to keep company with Mademoiselle de La Vallière. If she were cunning and wise, she would be very glad that the king was in love with Mademoiselle de Brancas, for, being the daughter of the first officer in her service (the Count de Brancas was chevalier d'honneur of the queen-mother), he, his wife and his daughter, would be of great advantage to her with the king." When the amours of the king with Madame de Montespan commenced, Madame de Montausier was not more severe, *Mémoires de Mademoiselle*, vol. v., p. 254: "Madame de Montespan took up her quarters in the room belonging to Madame de Montausier, near that of the king; and it was observed that a sentinel, who had been placed in the passage communicating with the lodging of the king and that of Madame de Montespan, had been removed. . . . I am told, said the queen, that it is Madame de Montausier who conducts this intrigue, that she deceives me, that the king visits Madame de Montespan in her room. Madame de Montausier said to the queen: Since your Majesty would be made to believe that I give mistresses to the king, what injury may

wife, he had great qualities, which he spoiled by great defects. He made a great show of virtue, under which was hidden much that was pitiful. He was very free in censuring every one, and suffered no one to fail in rendering him his due. He was abrupt, headstrong, of an insupportable haughtiness and pride.[1] Charged provisionally and by commission with the government of Normandy, at the death of M. de Longueville, in 1663, he assumed the dignity of a prince of the blood, and exacted all the honor that was rendered to M. de Longueville him-

---

any one expect to escape? The queen replied to her in equivocal terms: I know more than you think; I am not the dupe of any one." Appearances were all against Madame de Montausier. Also, at a later period, Montespan, who was evil-minded enough to misinterpret the honor done by the king to his wife, made for Madame Montausier a most disagreeable scene. Madame de Montausier complained to the king, who sent for Montespan, for the purpose of putting him in prison. See *Mademoiselle*, vol. vi., 82: "This affair made a great noise in the world, because it was an extraordinary outrage upon a woman who had thus far sustained an excellent reputation. M. de Montausier was at Rambouillet; he did not know of the affair; they even said that it was concealed from him; others imagined that he knew it, but that it was for his advantage to seem ignorant. A little while after he was made tutor of the Dauphin, etc."

1 If it is true, as several contemporaries assure us, and among others, Segrais, that Montausier had served as a model for the *Misanthrope*, it was because Molière, who did not search things closely, has taken a difficult virtue for reality. But Molière told his secret to no one, and probably there is no secret here except that of genius. The *Misanthrope* is not the copy of any original. Many originals have been before the great observer, and furnished him with a thousand particular traits; but the entire and complete character of the *Misanthrope* is his own creation.

self. Hard towards his inferiors, difficult with his equals, he knew perfectly how to manage his credit and push his fortune. Born a Protestant, he became converted for the sake of his wife, as well as for political purposes.[1] Madame de Montausier was more amiable, but quite as careful of her own interests. She was of that same school of which Madame de Maintenon was the consummate mistress,—that school which seeks the appearance of good rather than good itself, which accommodates itself to meanness, skilfully concealed, and bestows all its care, all its study upon not compromising itself; whilst proud and truly honest souls, whom passion misleads, take no pains to hide their faults, being careless of reputation when virtue is lost. Madame de Montausier was especially occupied with herself. She had the confidence of the king. She became a duchess. Her career was brilliant, but was she happy? She became embroiled and reconciled more than once with Madame de Longueville. She died in 1671, after her mother, the noble marchioness, who died in 1665, and, like her, she was buried in that convent of the Carmelites of the Rue Saint-Jacques, which

---

[1] Tallemant, vol. ii., p. 243: "Our marquis, seeing that his religion was an obstacle to his designs, changed it. He said that salvation could be obtained in either; but in the change he seems to have consulted his interest."

most of the friends of Mademoiselle de Bourbon seem to have made a place of rendezvous during life and after death.

Mademoiselle de Montmorency-Boutteville, Isabelle Angélique,[1] possessed at an early age a beauty which she preserved to the end. Her younger sister, Marie Louise, yielded to her, says Lenet,[2] not as to the more beautiful, but as to the elder. She married the Marquis de Valency, and disappeared ten years before her sister, in 1684. Isabelle de Montmorency had much mind, and to the brilliancy of her charms united at first great coquetry, and afterwards the most shameful artifices. The first pages of her life are a romance—the last, a vulgar story. Protected, as well as her sister and brother, by Madame the Princess, and placed almost upon an equality with

---

[1] Every one called her Elizabeth, and she is thus named in the most authentic printed documents; but in all our manuscripts she never signs herself Elizabeth, but almost always Isabelle. See several of her autograph letters among the papers of Lenet in the National Library. A manuscript piece, the judicial evidence given by Madame de Châtillon before an ecclesiastical commission delegated by the Pope, in the matter of the canonization of the Mother Madeleine de Saint-Joseph, can leave no doubt; Madame de Châtillon deposes thus: "My name is Isabelle Angélique de Montmorency; I am a native of the city of Paris; I am thirty-two years of age, daughter of Henry François de Montmorency, Count de Boutteville and other places, and of Isabelle Angélique de Vienne, his lawful wife; I am widow of Gaspard de Coligny, Duke de Châtillon . . ." and she signs: "Moy, Isabelle Angélique de Montmorency."

[2] Lenet, ed. Mich., p. 437.

Mademoiselle de Bourbon and the Duke d'Enghien, she made, or seemed to make, some impression upon the latter; but she inflamed especially the handsome and the brave Dandelot. Madame de Boutteville refused to give him her daughter, because he was a Protestant and simply a younger brother, his elder brother, Coligny, being heir to the fortune and title of the Châtillons. But, after the death of Coligny, Dandelot who took his name, feeling himself upheld by the Duke d'Enghien and by his sister, carried off Mademoiselle de Boutteville, with her own consent of course, and after that it became necessary to marry the two fugitives.[1] Voiture wrote some very lively verses upon this elopement,[2] and Sarrazin made a ballad upon the method of conducting such matters.[3] It would be supposed that a marriage so passionately desired on both sides would result in continued happiness to both parties. It was not, however, so. Coligny having become Duke de Châtillon, thought much more of war than of his wife: he covered himself with glory at Lens; but, as we have said, he perished in a miserable combat at Charenton in 1649. It must be confessed that he was the first to do wrong, and in

---

[1] See long details on this subject in Madame de Motteville, vol. 1st., p. 292, etc.

[2] *Œuvres de Voiture*, vol. ii., p. 174, Epistle to M. de Coligny.

[3] *Œuvres de Sarrazin*, in-4°; Poésies, p. 74.

dying he asked pardon of her whose pride he had especially wounded.[1] The young and beautiful widow soon found consolation; she got possession of the heart of Condé, which had been for some time unoccupied, and exerted herself to keep it without bestowing her own, or even giving it to another, skilful in the art of promoting her interests and her pleasures. The memoirs of the times, and particularly those of La Rochefoucauld, describe her as managing at once the imperious Condé, from whom she drew great advantages, and the suspicious Nemours, whom she preferred, striving to conciliate them, and to win them both to the court with which she had a secret treaty. A little while after she plunges into the most diverse intrigues, connecting herself with the Marshal d'Hoquincourt and with the Abbé Fouquet, retaining over the absent Condé the power of her charms, trying this power upon the young king Louis XIV., marrying in 1664 the Duke de Meklembourg in the hope of a crown in Germany, and leaving after her the reputation of having been as beautiful and as selfish as the Duchess de Montbazon. The latter doubtless possessed beauty of a superior style, but the other, less imposing, was a thousand times more agreeable. They were by turns the two most dangerous

---

[1] Madame de Motteville, vol. iii., p. 183, etc.

rivals and mortal enemies of Madame de Longueville.[1]

But we now present a very different person, whose destiny, like her character, forms a perfect contrast with that of Madame de Châtillon; very beautiful also, but less dazzling and more touching; a person who had not perhaps the mind and the finesse of the seductive friend of her childhood, but who knew none of her artifices and intrigues; who glittered a moment only to be quickly extinguished, but who has left a virtuous and sweet memory; a person superior perhaps to Mademoiselle de La Vallière herself, for she also loved and was able to resist her heart, and, without falling, deceived in her affections, she determined to finish her life like the sister Louise de la Miséricorde. Let us not pity her too much: she tasted in this world an inexpressible happiness; she felt beating for her the heart of a hero, that of the conqueror of Rocroy and of Fribourg, of the ardent and impetuous Duke d'Enghien, who could not quit her without shedding tears and without fainting. Sensible to a passion so true, and which promised to be so durable, but disarmed in some measure by the charm of a modest and sincere virtue, she made Condé know, at least once in his life, what was true love.

---

[1] See on Madame de Montbazon, the chapter which follows, and, on Madame de Châtillon, the INTRODUCTION.

After that he knew nothing but the transient intoxication of the senses, especially the passion of war, for which he was born—his true passion indeed, his mistress, his part, his country, his king, the true object of all his life, and by turns his shame and his glory.

This charming creature, who for several years was the idol of Condé, was the young Mademoiselle Du Vigean. Her destiny was so touching, and it was so intimately connected with that of Mademoiselle de Bourbon and of Madame de Longueville, that we shall be pardoned for dwelling a few moments upon it.

Mademoiselle Du Vigean was the youngest daughter of François Poussart de Fors, at first Baron, then Marquis Du Vigean, a man of little importance,[1] and of Anne de Neubourg, who was a very great character under Louis XIII., thanks to the friendship of the Duchess d'Aiguillon, niece of Richelieu. Admitted into the first society, the letters and poesy of Voiture show that Madame Du Vigean held well her place.[2]

---

[1] We are not very well acquainted with the origin and history of the Du Vigeans. We find a Protestant Vigean in the States-General in 1615, where he performed an active part.—*Journal historique et anecdotes de la cour et de Paris*, among the manuscript papers of Conrart; in-4°, vol. xi., p. 238.

[2] Letter of Voiture to Madame Du Vigean, in sending him an elegy which he had made and which she had asked, vol. i., p. 27. It is also Madame Du Vigean whom he designates by the name of the *Belle*

This success, and the connection which was the occasion of it, could not fail to make her the subject of envy, and various rumors were spread concerning her and Madame d'Aiguillon, equally injurious to both, and of which we find no feeble echo in the scandalous chronicle of Tallemant and in the songs of the times.[1] She possessed at La Barre, near Paris, above Saint-Denis and d'Enghien, and quite near to Montmorency, a charming residence which Voiture has described, and where she received magnificently the best and choicest society, even to Madame the Princess and Mademoiselle de Bourbon.[2]

Madame Du Vigean had two sons and two daughters. The eldest of the sons, the Marquis de Fors, was an officer of the greatest promise, who was killed at the age of twenty years at the siege of Arras, where the Duke d'Enghien served as a volunteer. He had been made a prisoner twice, but he perished finally, after prodigies of valor. He was wept by the Duke d'Enghien and by all his comrades. Magnificent funeral ceremonies were performed over him, and Desmarets, one of the poets of Richelieu, consecrated to him a

---

Baronne, in two couplets, at page 120 and 127 of vol. ii. It seems that the Du Vigeans resided at first in the quarter Saint-Germain, as well as Madame d'Aiguillon, and that she afterwards resided in the Rue Saint-Thomas-du-Louvre.

1 Tallemant, vol. ii., p. 32, and Library of the Arsenal, *Collection of Historical Songs*, vol. i., p. 149.

2 *Œuvres*, vol. i., pp. 20-25; letter tenth to the Cardinal de La Valette.

long elegy.[1] His young brother, who also served, finished his career still more sadly: he was assassinated under circumstances which could never be discovered.

As to the two sisters, their eulogy is found in all the gallant poems of this epoch. They are praised equally with Mademoiselle de Boutteville and Mademoiselle de Bourbon, in a piece in the manuscript collection of Maurepas,[2] and Voiture places them in a review of the beauties of the court of Chantilly, addressed to Madame the Princess.[3] He is pleased to celebrate the mother and the two daughters, and particularly the young Du Vigean:

Baroness so sweet, so fair too,
The mother, or the sister, are you
Of these two gentle belles whom all
Your daughters call?

. . . .

Upon her face, (De Fors, Du Vigean's eldest sister) beneath her feet,
Spring flowers beautiful and sweet,
Which elsewhere no one sees, etc.

A rising sun this Vigean (the younger) glows,
A bud just ready to unclose, etc.

Of love though ignorant indeed,
Yet in her eyes one may love read,
And everywhere she sets it free
Unconsciously.[4]

---

[1] Desmarets, *Œuvres poétique*, in-4°, 1641, pp. 18-21.
[2] Vol. ii., fol. 301. [3] Vol. i., p. 131. [4] *Ibid.*, p. 136.

Here again are a few words of Voiture, hitherto unintelligible, and which now have a certain application :

> Our Aurora, de La Barre,
> Is now a glowing sun.
> . . . .
> These matchless charms, in truth,
> Revive my long lost youth.

Evidently the poet speaks of Mademoiselle Du Vigean the younger, who, after having been a rising sun, an aurora, became, in a few years, a sun in full splendor. She was called the Aurora of La Barre, from the name of the house of which she was the most amiable ornament.

In writing all these verses in honor of Mesdemoiselles Du Vigean, Voiture had doubtless under his eyes the devices which had been made for them and for their mother, and which are preserved in the papers of Conrart:[1] " For Madame Du Vigean, who

---

[1] Library of the Arsenal, manuscripts of Conrart, in-4°, vol. xi., p. 855.—Devices were then in fashion; at a later period Mademoiselle placed portraits in them, and Madame Sablé maxims and thoughts. These devices had nothing official in them, and in that they resembled what are now called fancy seals, which must not be confounded with family arms. Individuals made devices for themselves and others; they had them printed, and they are regarded as true works of art. There is in the Arsenal, *Belles-Lettres Françaises*, No. 348, a collection, in-folio, upon vellum, of great beauty. It had been made for the Duchess de La Trémouille, whose portrait is found among those of Mademoiselle. Each device occupies an entire leaf. We find here those of Anne of Austria, of Madame the Princess, of Mademoiselle de

had lost her eldest son, an orange-tree, having at its foot its topmost branch cut off, covered with flowers and fruit: *Quis dolor.*" "For Mademoiselle de Fors, her eldest daughter, a rose among several flowers: *Dat decor imperium.*" "For Mademoiselle Du Vigean, her second daughter, a lighted taper, surrounded with moths: *Oblecto sed uro.*" Let us add these two devices, which describe so well the character, and already the reputation of those who were the subject of them: "For Mademoiselle de Rambouillet, a crown with this inscription: *Me quieren todos.*" "For Mademoiselle de Bourbon, an ermine: *Intus candidior.*"

In 1635, at the great ball given at the Louvre by Louis XIII., tò which Mademoiselle de Bourbon consented to go with so much difficulty, and which proved the ruin of her religious ardor, among the ladies who danced with her, Andrè d'Ormesson[1] mentions Mesdemoiselles Du Vigean. The eldest, Anne Fors Du Vigean, was pretty, sweet, insinuating,[2] and, says Madame de Motteville, ambitious and

---

Montpensier, and of many other illustrious females of the seventeenth century. We limit ourselves to giving the device of Madame de Longueville. It is very different from that of Mademoiselle de Bourbon. It is a bunch of lilies upon a nest of serpents, with these words: *Meo moriuntur odore.*

[1] Fol., 332, verso.

[2] *Mémoires*, vol. iii., p. 393. See also vol. iv., p. 39.

prone to flattery. She was married to M. de Pons, who had not much property, but who pretended to be connected with the illustrious house d'Albredt. Becoming a widow in 1648, and the confidant of the Duchess d'Aiguillon, intimate friend of her mother, she succeeded in obtaining the love of the nephew, the young Duke de Richelieu, and in marrying him, notwithstanding the duchess and notwithstanding the queen, thanks to the protection of Condé and of Madame de Longueville. For this fortunate protection she was indebted to the remembrances of childhood, especially to the tender and profound sentiment which Condé and his sister had early felt and ever preserved for her younger sister, the young, beautiful, virtuous, and unfortunate Mademoiselle Du Vigean.

Contemporaneous memoirs give neither the particular name, nor the precise date of the birth of this amiable person. But, thanks to the unpublished documents which have been placed in our hands, we know that the young Du Vigean was born in 1622, and that she was called Martha,[1] a modest name, and answering well to her character and destiny. She was then almost of the same age as Mademoiselle

[1] Deposition in the affair of the beatification of the Mother Madeleine de Saint-Joseph: "I, Sister Marthe Poussar du Vigean, called de Jésus, aged 28 years. . . November 17, 1650."

de Bourbon. She had been brought up with her, and, when they appeared together, it was almost with the same éclat. It is impossible to find any portrait or engraving of her which can be relied upon. Her charms were greatly heightened by a modesty full of grace, and the verses which we have quoted from Voiture, show her still young, in the innocence of a beauty of which she was ignorant, and which excited passions which she herself did not share.

Let us say, in the first place, in order to justify Condé and her who received his first homage, that the inclination of the Duke d'Enghien for the young Du Vigean, preceded his marriage with Mademoiselle de Brézé, niece of the cardinal, and continued till the year 1640, when the young duke was leading, at Paris, at the hôtel de Condé, at Chantilly, and elsewhere, the innocent life which we have described, surrounded by his comrades in arms, and among the charming and dangerous companions of Mademoiselle de Bourbon. It was then that he met Madame Du Vigean and her two daughters, and that he began, says Lenet, "to feel for Mademoiselle Du Vigean an esteem and a friendship which became, by degrees, a strong and tender love."[1]

Indeed, the Duke d'Enghien might have imagined

---

[1] *Mémoires de Lenet*, edit. Michaud, p. 550.

that it would not be impossible for him to obtain from his father and from the king, that is, from the Cardinal de Richelieu, their consent to a marriage, disproportionate, without doubt, but in no wise degrading to him. Mademoiselle Du Vigean was very rich, and her family was in great credit; Richelieu favored her; and it would not have been displeasing to him to see a prince of the blood descending somewhat from his own rank. The marriage which was imposed upon Condé some time after, was not much above what this might have been. A little delusion was permitted to the age and impetuosity of the young duke, and, once the affections engaged, they yielded only to time and necessity.

With such a sentiment in the heart, one can imagine how much the Duke d'Enghien must have suffered from the marriage to which he was condemned in 1641. It is to his chagrin upon this occasion, that the sickness with which he was then attacked is attributed. Although his young wife, Claire-Clémence Maillé de Brézé, was very agreeable, he did not live with her, and formed, from the moment of his marriage, the design of repudiating her as soon as he could. He protested against the violence which had been done to him. He made this protestation in the shape of a national deed, clothed with all legal forms, and signed by himself, by the president of

Vernon, superintendent of his house, and by Perrault, at that time his secretary.[1]

We have related how, notwithstanding his disorder, as soon as he learned that the campaign was about to open, nothing could retain him, neither the prayers of his family, nor the tears of his mistress; he set out hardly convalescent, and returned covered with glory. On his return, he "continued to give to Mademoiselle Du Vigean all the marks of a tender and respectful passion."[2]

In 1642, being at the waters of Bourbon with the Cardinal de Richelieu, the Duke d'Enghien, at a most critical period, seized a pretext for going to Paris, "where the passion which he felt for Mademoiselle Du Vigean called him."[3]

It was especially after the death of the cardinal, in the years 1643 and 1644, that the amours of Condé were chiefly observable. Gallantry being then fashionable, these amours were neither a mystery nor a scandal. The National Library possesses more than one manuscript history of the regency of Anne of Austria, the author of which declares that he was the witness of every thing that he relates, and, in a letter addressed to the Prince de Condé, dedicates these memoirs to him.[4] The tenderness of the two young

---

1 Lenet, edit. Michaud, p. 550. 2 Lenet, *ibid.* 3 *Ibid.*

4 *Supplement Français*, No. 925. The author seems to be called Mau-

people is here several times alluded to. After the campaign of Flanders, in which the Duke d'Orleans had taken Gravelines, and in which Condé had taken Fribourg, "these illustrious conquerors," says our manuscript, "having carried their laurels to the feet of the regent, who was then at Fontainebleau, retired, the first to Paris, and the other to Chantilly. If the court of Fontainebleau surpassed that of Chantilly in number, the latter did not yield to it in gallantry and in pleasures. The Princess de Condé, the Duchesses d'Anguyen and de Longueville, were there, accompanied by a dozen of the most agreeable persons of quality in France. In addition to the beauty of the place, games and promenades, music and the chase, and every thing generally that can make a place agreeable, were to be found here. The young Du Vigean was there, for whom the Duke d'Anguyen had then much esteem and friendship. She, on her side, responded to it, and every one favored them."

It is necessary to look into the memoirs of the times for the details of this curious episode of the youth of Condé, the vicissitudes of this connection, as tender as it was pure, the hopes, the fears, the

passant. "It is the custom," says he, in commencing, "of all those who write history, to wish to appear faithful, disinterested, and exempt from all passion. For my part, I do not pretend to persuade any one of my sincerity, but I dare to declare that I have seen most of the things which I undertake to write about."

jealousies, all the troubles which accompany love. Mademoiselle Du Vigean had besought[1] Condé to conceal his sentiments in public; she had engaged him, in joke, perhaps, to make believe that he loved Mademoiselle de Boutteville; but the latter was so beautiful, and the game was so dangerous, that Mademoiselle Du Vigean hastened to countermand her order, and to forbid the duke to see Mademoiselle de Boutteville and to speak to her. Condé again obeyed her; he discontinued all intercourse with his cousin, and yielded his place to Dandelot, whose projects he was the more eager to favor, as he felt some anxiety in regard to his own; for Mademoiselle Du Vigean had warned him that her father was thinking of marrying her to this same Dandelot, and that he had offered the Marshal de Châtillon a very

---

[1] Mémoires de Madame de Motteville, vol. i., p. 295: "The Duke d'Enghien had so strong a passion for Mademoiselle Du Vigean, that I have heard Madame Du Vigean, her mother, say that he had often wished to break his marriage, having been forced to espouse the Duchess d'Enghien, in order that he might marry her daughter, and that he had even labored to this end. I have heard Madame de Montausier, who knew these intrigues, say that this prince had pretended to love Mademoiselle de Boutteville, by the express order of Mademoiselle Du Vigean, in order to conceal in public the friendship which he had for her, but that the beauty of Mademoiselle de Boutteville having frightened Mademoiselle Du Vigean, she had forbidden him, a little after, to see her and to speak to her, and that he had obeyed her so promptly, that all at once he ceased all intercourse with her, and that, to show that he had no affection for her, he caused her to marry Dandelot."

considerable dower to have his son as a son-in-law.[1] "This news," says Madame de Motteville, "gave the prince the utmost alarm: he often faced the enemies of the State, but his heart was not so valiant against love as against them."[2] He took fright therefore, and, to parry the blow, he entered so earnestly into the cause of Dandelot, that he counselled him to elope with Mademoiselle de Boutteville.

In the mean time he continued all his efforts to break his own marriage; he labored for it with ardor and perseverance. The Duchess d'Enghien falling sick, he anticipated the accomplishment of his wishes; but she recovered; it was therefore necessary to obtain a judicial dissolution of his marriage. The thing was almost impossible, for the Duchess d'Enghien was then, at least, perfectly irreproachable, and moreover he had by her a son. Such, however, was the passion of Condé, that he addressed himself to Cardinal Mazarin,[3] who, not being very scrupulous, would have permitted the rupture, if he had not feared that Condé, once at liberty, might aspire to Mademoiselle, and become much too powerful.

Thus we are enabled to judge of the depth of

---

[1] Mémoires de Madame de Motteville, p. 294. [2] *Ibid.*
[3] *Mémoires de Mademoiselle*, vol. 1st, p. 84.

Condé's feelings. These feelings were inspired not only by the beauty of Mademoiselle Du Vigean, but by her candor and her modesty, by that tenderness at once devoted and virtuous, which led her far enough to be compromised somewhat in the eyes of the world, while it suffered her to do nothing which might mar in the mind of Condé the ideal of angelic purity which she represented to him. Hence that passion mingled with respect and ardor which he burned to satisfy in despite of all obstacles, and which was never gratified. Madame de Motteville, who was informed of the least details of this amorous intrigue by Madame de Montausier, its witness and almost confidant, says expressly, as "a thing to be believed by every one,"[1] that Mademoiselle Du Vigean "is the only one whom Condé truly loved." Mademoiselle, who from different motives did not love those whom Condé loved, and who was very severe upon Madame de Châtillon, expresses herself thus in regard to the loves of Condé and of Mademoiselle Du Vigean: "She was very beautiful; this illustrious lover was also deeply moved. When he set out for the army, the desire of glory did not prevent him from feeling the grief of separation, and he could not bid adieu without shedding tears; and when he departed on his last journey

[1] Mémoires, vol. i., p. 302.

to Germany (where he achieved the victory of Nortlingen), he fainted when he left her."

Such a passion was too violent to continue for a great length of time; it was prolonged even beyond ordinary bounds. Mademoiselle Du Vigean would consent to be the wife alone of Condé, and the marriage of the latter could not be broken: things advanced on neither side, and every one grew weary.

It may be imagined that the interest which Condé manifested for Mademoiselle Du Vigean intimidated those who would have aspired to her hand. Two marriages were proposed to her. Among her admirers was the Marquis d'Huxelles, who afterwards married Marie de Bailleul, daughter of the Superintendent of Finances. D'Huxelles was a very distinguished military man, who expected to become Marshal of France, and whose services and premature death in consequence of his wounds,[1] enabled his son to obtain that honor. He thought very seriously of marrying Mademoiselle Du Vigean.[2] He hesitated on account of the reports which did not fail to find circulation. "Although," says Lenet, from whom we obtain these facts, "I know with all the certainty that

[1] The Marquis d'Huxelles died in 1658, of his wounds, and of his chagrin on account of not receiving the appointment of Marshal. The office was conferred upon his son in 1703. Mademoiselle d'Huxelles was amiable and sprightly. She died at an advanced age in 1712.

[2] *Mémoires de Lenet*, part i., p. 207.

one can have in regard to matters of this kind, that love was never more passionate than that on the part of the prince, nor listened to with more discretion and modesty, than was exhibited on the part of Mademoiselle Du Vigean." And in this Madame de Motteville and Mademoiselle agree perfectly with Lenet.

Mademoiselle Du Vigean had been also sought by another amiable and brave gentleman, the Marquis Jacques Stuart de Saint-Mégrin, brother of the beautiful Saint-Mégrin of whom the Duke d'Orleans was so fond. Saint-Mégrin continued for a long time his affection for Mademoiselle Du Vigean;[1] but he dared not come in competition with Condé. At a later period he learned with extreme joy that his suit might be heard; and he addressed himself at once to the parents of Mademoiselle Du Vigean. The marriage did not take place: a passion such as that which we have just described was destined to have a very different dénoûement.

It is known that after the German campaign of 1645, and the disputed victory of Nortlingen, Condé was seized with a violent sickness. It was then that, despairing of a dissolution of his marriage, and of conquering the virtuous scruples of Mademoiselle Du

[1] *Mémoires de Mademoiselle*, vol. i., p. 84.

Vigean, he resolved to turn his thoughts in another direction. Mademoiselle Du Vigean did not complain; she closed her ears to all propositions, resisted the counsels and even the orders of her family, and in the full splendor of her beauty and her youth she cast herself among the Carmelites of the Rue Saint-Jacques.[1] Condé did not attempt to see her again, but he always preserved for her, says Lenet, a remembrance full of respect.[2] The love of Condé was not, then, a transient caprice. It began before his marriage; it continued four long years; it remained ardent and pure in the midst of camps, and was extinguished only in the despair of bringing it to a

---

[1] As every thing then was the subject of songs, the two following couplets, which we find among the *Chansons Notées* of the Arsenal, were written upon this occasion:

Sur L'Air: *Laire lan lère.*

Lorsque Vigean quitta la cour,
Les Jeux, les Graces, les Amours
Entrèrent dans le Monastère.
    Laire la laire lan lère,
    Laire la laire lan la.

Les Jeux pleurèrent ce jour-là;
Ce jour la Beauté se voila,
Et fit vœu d'être solitaire.
    Laire la laire, etc.

[2] *Ibid.* The remembrance which Condé preserved for Mademoiselle Du Vigean was such, that Mademoiselle asserts, vol. i., p. 88, that if Condé favored Chabot in his designs upon Mademoiselle de Rohan, it was because Chabot had been his confidant with Mademoiselle Du Vigean. "So," says she, "after having been served during one of the most important periods of his life, it is not wonderful that he took care to promote the marriage so desired by Chabot."

happy conclusion, and after a long and critical disorder, from which the hero of Nortlingen arose ever to renounce love for glory and ambition.

It would be gratifying to follow Mademoiselle Du Vigean to the convent of the Carmelites, to know at what time precisely she entered it, what occupied her there, and when she died. These are points upon which no contemporaries enlighten us, and all that we are now able to assert with certainty is, that Mademoiselle Du Vigean made a profession in 1649. Thus, she must have joined the Carmelites in 1647, since the vows can be taken only after a service of one or two years as a candidate and a novice. She took the name of sister Marthe de Jésus;[1] she died in 1665; she was never prioress; she was sub-prioress in 1659, and ceased to be so in 1662. According to custom, she must have held this situation six years, and consequently her term of service was between the years 1656 and 1662; whence it follows that all the letters of Madame de Longueville, addressed to sister Marthe and to the Mother Sub-prioress, between 1656 and 1662, are to the same nun, and that this nun was Mademoiselle Du Vigean, which accounts for the particularly affectionate tone

---

[1] It was customary to take in religion one's baptismal name, as Louise de La Vallière was called Louise de La Miséricorde, and Anne Marie d'Epernon, Anne Marie de Jésus, etc.

of these letters. In fact, we have found in the National Library, in the collection of Doctor Vallant[1] and in those of Gaignières,[2] two billets from Mademoiselle Du Vigean, then sister Marthe, to Madame de Sablé, and another to that very Marchioness d'Huxelles whose place she might have occupied. These billets are the only relics which remain to us of this interesting person, who, because she was too pleasing to a prince, was compelled to bury her beauty and her virtue in a cloister.

Such is often the end of the pleasures of youth, the inclinations of the most generous, the feasts of the heart and of life. Mademoiselle de Bourbon witnessed the birth, growth, and death of the loves of Condé and of Mademoiselle Du Vigean. Villefore says that she thwarted them, but he produces no proof of this. It is at least very certain that she strove to repair, as much as she could, the injury which her brother had done to her young and charming friend. For her sake, she loaded her sister with benefits, and, when the poor forlorn creature sought an asylum among the Carmelites, she maintained with her an affectionate intercourse; she visited her, wrote to her often, and, even to the end of life, retained for her a place in her heart by the side of Madame de Sablé.

---

[1] Vol. v. [2] *Lettres originales*, vol. iv.

But let us not anticipate the future. We are still amid the illusions of youth, still in the season of pleasures and love. Whilst around her, at the hôtel de Rambouillet and at the hôtel de Condé, at Chantilly, at Ruel, at Liancourt, all was heroism and gallantry, whilst surrounded by young and brilliant cavaliers, destined to become great captains; with agreeable female friends who drew after them all hearts, what did Mademoiselle de Bourbon do with her own? Did she bestow it as did Mademoiselle Du Vigean and Mademoiselle de Boutteville? Among so many adorers who crowded around her, did she distinguish none? Tender and somewhat coquettish, with the soul and the eyes of Chimène, what Rodrigue among the heroes of her brother's court found her sensible? At the age of nineteen, she had been promised to the Prince de Joinville, son of Henri de Lorraine, Duke de Guise. A powerful alliance would this have been, which had united the Montmorencys, the Condés, and the Guises; but the Prince de Joinville died in Italy, where he went to meet his father, in the violent and obstinate persecution which the implacable avenger and indefatigable promoter of royal authority, Cardinal de Richelieu, did not cease to exercise against the Guises in remembrance of the League. It is said that a marriage was also contemplated between her and d'Armand, Marquis de Brézé, nephew of Cardinal

Richelieu, brother of her who was forced upon the Duke d'Enghien, the intrepid sailor who twice beat the fleets of Spain, and perished at the age of twenty-seven, from a cannon shot, at the siege of Orbitello, in 1646. This marriage would have placed in the hands of the house of Condé, by means of the two heroic brothers-in-law, all the forces of France, both by sea and land; but this marriage was defeated, for reasons in regard to which there are various opinions.[1]

Mademoiselle de Bourbon attracted whilst she discouraged. There was not a gentleman who would not have given his life for her favor; but no one was rash enough to aspire to her hand. Many then sighed for her, and some even paid her the most marked homage. Mention is made, among others, of the Duke de Beaufort, more brave than witty, loyal and chivalrous enough, who, being politely rejected, fell at the feet of Madame de Montbazon, and served her till death. Especial notice is taken of Maurice de Coligny, the son of Marshal de Châtillon. In 1642 M. the Prince and Madame the Princess, not finding a single young lord in all the kingdom to whom policy permitted them to give Mademoiselle de Bourbon, proposed to her the greatest lord of France, after the princes of the blood, the Duke de Longue-

---

Villefore, pp. 37, 38.

ville. He was the widower of Louise de Bourbon, daughter of the Count de Soissons, by whom he had Marie d'Orleans, who was already seventeen or eighteen years of age: he was forty-seven, and even at this age was said to be still attached to Madame de Montbazon. Mademoiselle de Bourbon resisted, or at least testified at first a great repugnance; it was, however, necessary to yield; herein she displayed the resolution which she testified on all great occasions. She married then on the 2d of June, 1642, at the age of twenty-three years, her heart and mind filled with poetry and gallantry, a man much older than herself, and who was not even sufficiently touched with her charms to renounce his old mistress.

The fêtes on the occasion of this marriage were still more brilliant than those which took place at the marriage of the Duke d'Enghien. Mademoiselle de Bourbon walked to the altar with a sort of intrepidity, and she seemed almost gay at the hôtel de Longueville, occupying the spectators so much with her dazzling beauty that they did not remark the violence which she did to her feelings. It is her historian, the Jansenist Villefore, who has preserved for us this tradition. Scarcely a year had flown by, when, without even giving her heart, for a long time yet unoccupied, she was the involuntary cause of a most tragic quarrel, in which Coligny, who had sighed for her, perished in the flower of youth, and perhaps under her own eyes, by the hand of one of those Guises to whom she had been for a moment destined. Sinister prelude of the storms that awaited her first adventure, which consecrated her beauty in so sad a manner, and which won for her, at the age of twenty-four years, in the world of gallantry, a renown, a popularity even, almost equal to that which victory had achieved for her brother, the Duke d'Enghien.

CHAPTER III.

1642 to 1644.

Poetry and gallantry—State of affairs in 1643—Battle of Rocroy—Mazarin and the *Importants*—Madame de Montbazon—Letter attributed to Madame de Longueville—Duel between Coligny and De Guise.—An unpublished novel of the seventeenth century.

We find Mademoiselle de Bourbon married then on the 2d of June, 1642. "For her it was a cruel destiny; M. de Longueville was old, she was young and beautiful as an angel." Thus, in relation to this marriage, speaks Mademoiselle, the faithful interpreter of the opinions of that period.[1]

Henri II., Duke de Longueville, descended from that famous Count de Dunois whose name is connected with that of Jeanne d'Arc, in the great wars of the independence under Charles VII. He was the son of Henri d'Orleans, first of the name, sovereign prince of Neuchâtel and Vallengin, a warrior worthy of his ancestors, and who gave the League a mortal blow by the victory of Senlis. His mother was Catherine de Gonzague, sister of the Duke de Ne-

[1] *Mémoires*, edition of Amsterdam, 1735; vol. i., p. 45.

vers, who was father of the two celebrated princesses, Marie, Queen of Poland, and Anne, the Palatine. Born in 1595, Henri II. had first married Louise de Bourbon, daughter of the Count de Soissons, high steward of France, who died in 1637, and by whom he had Marie d'Orleans, Mademoiselle de Longueville, who, in 1650, played a conspicuous part in the Fronde, and at length married the Duke de Nemours, brother of him who was slain by the Duke de Beaufort. Thus, when the Duke de Longueville took a second wife in 1642, he was forty-seven years of age, and to this wife he brought a daughter-in-law nearly as old, but of a very different character,—beautiful, intellectual, but deprived of all sensibility, who soon became the censor of her mother-in-law and her enemy in the family circle, and even with posterity by means of the memoirs which she has left of the Fronde.

The Duke de Longueville was truly a great lord He was gallant and brave,[1] liberal even to magnificence, of a noble and generous character, but feeble; willing to engage in an enterprise, and ready tc abandon it; without passion, and without ambition; and possessing all that was necessary to make him

---

[1] A fine portrait of M. de Longueville, painted by Champagne, and engraved by Nanteuil, forms the frontispiece of *The Pucelle* of Chapelain, in-fol., 1656.

shine in the second rank, but incapable of holding the first. He began by making some opposition to Richelieu, but he yielded soon enough; afterwards he engaged in the Fronde; he shared the captivity of his two brothers-in-law, but scarcely did he leave the prison, than he made peace with the court. Nature had fitted him to follow the path which his fathers had traced for him, and to serve the crown in great military and civil offices, which he would have worthily filled. The misfortune of his life was to be continually engaged, through his own fault and through that of others, in enterprises and adventures for which he was unfitted, and in which his good qualities were less prominent than his defects.

Let us add that M. de Longueville, whose morals were not the best, had, in early youth, by Jacqueline d'Illiers, afterwards abbess of Saint-Avit, a natural daughter, Catherine Angélique d'Orleans, who was successively a nun in several religious houses, and who died abbess of Maubuisson, in 1664, at the age of forty-seven years. Already in the decline of life, he became smitten with the Duchess de Montbazon, who rejoiced at this useful conquest, and maintained it, as is said, even after the second marriage of M. de Longueville, notwithstanding the displeasure of Madame the Princess, and the very bitter reproaches which she cast upon her son-in-law.

It must be confessed that there was little in such a person to captivate the heart and the imagination of a young woman such as we have described Mademoiselle de Bourbon. With her instincts of pride and heroism, her refinements of spirit and heart, her principles and habits as a *précieuse*, she could not admire M. de Longueville, and, formed as she was, admiration was for her the road to love. She was destined, with all her advantages, to be wounded by a rival; and what made this wound more painful was, that this rival, so little worthy of being compared with her in character, was the greatest beauty of the day, so that the apparent infidelity of M. de Longueville seemed an offensive preference for this rival's charms; and, as we have said, Mademoiselle de Bourbon was not only tender, she was vain-glorious, and somewhat coquettish. However, as she did not love her husband, her gentleness, easily sustained by her indifference, saved her from irritation. She considered herself at liberty to be admired, and she continued to live at the hôtel de Longueville, as she had done at the hôtel de Condé, with the same court of young and agreeable female friends, of young and brilliant cavaliers.[1]

---

[1] The hôtel of the Dukes de Longueville is not at all the one which, after the death of her husband, Madame de Longueville bought of the Epernons, on the Rue Saint Thomas-du-Louvre, near the hôtel de Ram-

The marriage fêtes had hardly ended when Madame de Longueville was seized with sickness. The small-pox, then so dreaded, which had driven her away from Chantilly, and against which she had made, at Liancourt, such bad verses, caught her in the autumn of 1642, and placed her charming face in peril. All Rambouillet was moved. The Marchioness de Sablé, too faithful to this fear of contagion, which was the ridicule of her life, could not

---

bouillet, where she resided with her children, and which bore her name from 1664 till the close of the seventeenth century. The dwelling of the Longuevilles was the old hôtel d'Alençon. (See Sauval, vol. i., pp. 65 and 70, especially p. 119.) It was situated on the Rue des Poulies, among the rich hôtels which line the right side of that street from the Rue Saint Honoré to the Seine, and which, with their dependencies and their gardens, extend to the Louvre. It was almost opposite to the Rue des Fossés-Saint-Germain-l'Auxerrois. Upon its right, towards the Seine, was the Petit-Bourbon, which, having served as a residence and a stronghold in Paris to the eldest of the house of Bourbon, became a royal building, a sort of appendage to the Louvre, where the young king, Louis XIV., gave several great balls, and the theatre of which was lent to Molière, for the performance of his comedies, upon his arrival in Paris. Upon the left, on the same line, after the hôtel de Longueville, came the hôtels de Villequier and d'Aumont; and a little nearer to the church and house of l'Oratoire, the hôtels de La Force and de Créqui. When, in 1663, Louis XIV., having entered into full possession of royal authority, and wishing to signalize his reign by great monuments, undertook to finish the Louvre and to give it a façade worthy of the rest of the edifice, it was necessary for him to pull down, with the Petit-Bourbon, a part of the hôtels of the Rue des Poulies, and among others that of Longueville. This was the most ancient and most considerable. It was composed of a large front building, of a vast court, of the hôtel proper, with immense gardens. Those of our readers who desire to be sure of the correctness of these details, have only to cast their eyes upon the excellent plan of Gomboust, which gives an admirable view of Paris in the seventeenth century, in 1652.

persuade herself, notwithstanding the most sincere tenderness, to take care of the interesting sufferer; but Mademoiselle de Rambouillet did not abandon her,[1] and there was a sort of public rejoicing when it was known that Madame de Longueville had been spared, and that, if she had lost the first freshness of her beauty, she had preserved all its brilliancy. These are the very words of Retz,[2] and the gallant Bishop de Grasse, Godeau, confirms them by compliments which, in a sermon-like manner, he addresses to Madame de Longueville.[3]

During this sickness, M. de Longueville did not come near his wife. The Cardinal de Richelieu had

---

[1] It is truly inconceivable that a woman of so much mind as Madame de Sablé, could have carried her fear of sickness and contagion so far as all contemporary writers, Voiture, Tallemant, Mademoiselle, etc., testify. Her weakness upon this occasion, and the fidelity of Mademoiselle de Rambouillet, are attested to us by several unpublished letters of those ladies, which we find in the Library of the Arsenal, among the papers of Conrart, in-4°, vol. xiv.

[2] It is in vain that Mademoiselle says, vol. 1st, p. 47, that Madame de Longueville remained marked with the small-pox. Retz affirms the contrary. Edit. of Amsterdam, 1731, vol. i., p. 185: "The small-pox had taken away the first flower of her beauty, but left her all its brilliancy."

[3] *Letters de Monseigneur Godeau sur divers sujets*, Paris, 1713, lettei 76, p. 243: "Degrasse, December 13, 1642. . . . As to your face, another will rejoice, with much more propriety, that it will not be spoiled. Mademoiselle Paulet tells me so. I have so good an opinion of your sense, that I believe you would have been easily consoled if your disease had left its marks. Scars are often given by Divine Mercy to make persons, who have loved too well their complexions, see that it is a flower liable to fade even as it begins to bloom."

just sent for him to take command of the army of Italy in the place of the Duke de Bouillon, the elder brother of Turenne, who, compromised in the affair of Cinq-Mars, had been arrested, by order of the cardinal, at the head of his army, conducted from Cazal to Lyons, to the Château de Pièrre-Encise, and who was fortunate enough to be able to purchase his life by abandoning his stronghold of Sedan.

The winter of 1643 passed away for Madame de Longueville in the agreeable occupations which had delighted her youth. She was constantly at the Louvre, at the hôtel de Condé, at the Place-Royal, or at the hôtel de Rambouillet, whose éclat was every day increasing. It was about the time of the *Guirlande de Julie.* Tallemant had proposed to add to the collection of poems, by Voiture, many other productions of the hôtel de Rambouillet. In truth, we might furnish it by aid of the manuscripts of Conrart, who was also one of the inmates of the illustrious hôtel. We might draw continually from these inexhaustible manuscripts, and we should only be embarrassed as to choice. But if all these verses describe admirably the society of the seventeenth century—fond of wit as well as of bravery, intoxicated with heroism and gallantry—they would charm, perhaps moderately, the society of the present day, and we have already put our readers to a test which we should not dare to repeat. Let us simply say that Madame de Longueville was still more surrounded than Mademoiselle de Bourbon with that poetic incense, somewhat tiresome it is true, but which has rarely been displeasing to beauties the most spirituelle. We have before us poems of every kind, and from every hand, which describe her sometimes at the balls of the Louvre and of the Luxembourg, sometimes at court with her two beautiful friends, Mesdemoiselles Du Vigean, sometimes following her husband into his government of Normandy, and called back by the hôtel de Rambouillet, everywhere pursued with assiduous cares and homages, and displaying everywhere a gentleness full of charm, with a carelessness which seldom abandoned her when her heart was not occupied. And it was not yet occupied, or, if at all, only at the surface. She did not love, but she had distinguished, in the crowd of her adorers, Maurice, Count de Coligny, elder brother of Dandelot, son of Marshal de Châtillon, who had sighed for her before her marriage, and had not yet yielded to a husband of forty-seven years, but little jealous, and even still in the chains of another.

"I do not know," says Lenet,[1] "whether Coligny was attached to Mademoiselle de Bourbon by reason

---

[1] Edit. Michaud, p. 450.

of her beauty, her wit, or the respect which he owed her; but I know well, that although he saw her only in the midst of company, in presence of the princess or of the duke, it was said in the end that he had sentiments of love for her." In addition to this, there is not a word in regard to Coligny, his character, his mind, or his person. All that we know is, that he was one of the particular friends of La Rochefoucauld, and especially of the Duke d'Enghien,[1] who employed him in more than one delicate negotiation. We confess that such silence is but little in his favor; but let us bear in mind that Coligny was young, that he had not had time to make himself known, and that he was naturally eclipsed by his younger brother, Dandelot, who inherited his title and took his place near Condé. In the absence of every other document, a manuscript of the National Library, to which we have already had recourse, furnishes us some other details, the correctness of which we do not guaranty, but which, for want of better, we are not permitted to neglect. This manuscript represents Coligny to us as very well made, without, however, a very elegant form; intellectual and ambitious, but in merit below his ambition. The author, taking appearance for reality, supposes also that Madame de Longueville

---

[1] *Mémoires de La Rochefoucauld*, collection Petitot, vol. li., pp. 370 and 386.

shared the sentiments of Coligny, because she did not repress them; and he paints, in a very romantic manner, the beginning of their pretended loves. We give the entire passage, leaving it to the judgment of the reader.[1]

"Anne de Bourbon, Duchess de Longueville, was then one of the most pleasing persons in the world, as well on account of the charms of her mind, as on account of those of her beauty. Coligny, eldest son of the Marshal de Châtillon, loved her passionately, and it is said that he was beloved by her. He was a young man of very fine form, but he looked more like a German than a Frenchman. He had infinite spirits and great thoughts, but it was believed that his valor[2] did not equal his ambition. Even before the marriage of this princess, he was on the best terms with her. It is said that he adopted a very excellent and very singular plan for declaring to her his passion. The romance of *Polexandre*[3] was very fashionable and much in vogue, but especially at the hôtel de Condé, which was then regarded as the tem-

---

[1] Bibliothèque Nationale, *Supplement français*, No. 925.

[2] There can be no doubt in this case as to courage; a Coligny, a friend of Condé, having never been suspected of wanting it.

[3] The *Polexandre* of Gomberville appeared in 1637. This romance had great success, and in a short time went through several editions; the best and the most complete is that of 1645, in five parts, forming eight volumes.

ple of gallantry and of wit. The Duke d'Enghien read this book continually, and, finding in it a tender and passionate letter, he showed it to Coligny, from whom he had nothing to conceal. The latter saw how he might profit by so favorable an occasion, and proposed to the Duke d'Enghien to make a copy, and place it adroitly in the pocket of the duchess. Scarcely a day passed that some fête did not occur at the hôtel de Condé, and there was dancing almost every evening. The proposition was accepted, and Coligny, having volunteered to copy this letter, gave it to the Duke d'Enghien. Upon this day every one was in the gayest attire, and the duchess shone with a thousand rays. The ball began early, and the duke, having taken the hand of his sister, executed easily their design. I know no more of the affair, but apparently the letter was read without giving any offence to the duchess."

Whilst the young people thus gave themselves up to the pleasures of gallantry, grave events were changing the face of the court and of France.

Richelieu had died on the 2d of December, 1642, after having seen Cinq-Mars ascend the scaffold, the Count de Soissons buried in his victory of Marfée, and the Duke de Bouillon compelled to surrender the principality of Sedan to the royal power. Scarcely had he closed his eyes than his enemies renewed their designs and their hopes. Faithful to his minister even after his death, Louis XIII. kept them within bounds for some time. He employed Mazarin, whom the cardinal had given to him, and continued his policy by softening it; but it did not survive him even for a single year. The 14th of May, 1643, he went to join him, leaving a king four years of age, the regency in the hands of a woman, our northern frontier menaced, factions chafing, and, to sustain the burden of affairs, the Duke d'Orleans and the Prince de Condé fortunately united in the council of the regency, Mazarin at the head of the cabinet, and the Duke d'Enghien at the head of the army. This was all that was needed for the safety of France.

The Duke d'Enghien received in Flanders, publicly, by the hands of a courier extraordinary, the news of the king's death. He feared that this news might increase the courage of the Spaniards, and diminish that of the French; he determined to conceal it, and to hasten the inevitable battle which was to decide the destiny of his country. Lost, it would introduce the enemy into the heart of the kingdom; but, gained, it would impress upon Spain and all Europe a terror necessary to the beginning of a new reign; it would strengthen the regency of Anne of Austria; it would place royalty above all factions, without taking into consideration the high elevation which it would give to the house of Condé. The Duke d'Enghien submitted the affair to the council of generals, but only for form's sake, declaring that he took upon himself the event; and the next day, May 19th, whilst the body of Louis XIII. was on its way to Saint-Denis, he hazarded the battle of Rocroy. It continued a whole day. Compromised for a short time by the Marshal de l'Hôpital, who had been intrusted with conducting it, it was gained by Condé himself, not yet twenty-two years of age—thanks to a manœuvre which first revealed the great captain, and inaugurated a new school of warfare.[1] Condé, with Gassion, was charged with the command of the right wing. He had confided his left to La Ferté-Seneterre, as well as to the Marshal de l'Hôpital, who represented the old school. He had placed Espenan in the centre with the infantry, and the reserve in the hands of Sirot,[2] an officer of tried bravery, like Gassion. Directed by Condé in person, the right French wing overthrew every thing that opposed it, and pushed the enemy vigorously. During this time the

---

[1] I rely upon the report given by Lenet, which is almost the same as that sent at the time, by order of the Duke d'Enghien, to his father, the Prince de Condé. Lenet, edit. Michaud, p. 479, etc. See commencement of chap. iv.

[2] Claude de Letouf de Pradines, Baron de Sirot, a Burgundian gentleman, born near 1600, mortally wounded in 1652, at the bridge de Gergeau, in the wars of the Fronde.

left wing, under La Ferté-Seneterre and Marshal de l'Hôpital, was very badly treated, and its two commanders placed *hors de combat;* in giving way it threatened to draw with it the centre, where Espenan was maintaining a firm ground, but earnestly calling for reinforcements. Any other than Condé would doubtless have turned upon his steps and retraced, in an equivocal attitude, the space gloriously run over, and, thus affording aid to his left and his centre, contrive, by means of his reserve, to achieve the victory, or cover and repair the defeat. Condé took a very different course: instead of giving way, he advanced still more; then, having arrived at the extreme of the enemy's lines, where the Italian infantry were located, he turned to the left, threw himself upon this infantry, passed it furiously, and went thundering down upon the rear of the victorious wing, after telling Sirot to march, with all his reserve, to the help of Espenan and of l'Hôpital. Thus caught between two fires, the enemy yielded on the left as well as on the right, and the day was won. But it was not enough to have delivered France from present danger, it was necessary at the same time to secure the future by removing the terror connected with the name of Spanish arms—the name of that old Spanish infantry which formed the reserve, and, according to the rules of ancient strategy and the policy of the court of Madrid, had been carefully preserved, that is, had remained useless. Nothing remained but to destroy this infantry. Condé assailed it on all sides with his victorious squadrons, with all that he could pick up of his own infantry, especially with his artillery, and, after a memorable resistance, he succeeded in demolishing it, root and branch:[1] it perished almost to a man at Rocroy.

At the report of this battle, in which every thing was wonderful—the youth of the general, the boldness and the novelty of the manœuvres, and the grandeur of the results—the court and all Paris went into transports of enthusiasm. The greatest disasters had been anticipated, but the army was safe, it was victorious, and the future seemed crowded with similar achievements. From the time of Henri IV., France had doubtless had excellent generals, who were well acquainted with their profession, and who had met

---

[1] Bossuet, in his admirable narrative of the battle of Rocroy, has perfectly painted its close—the destruction of the Spanish infantry; but he has not even indicated the manœuvre which decided the day. It is to be regretted that Napoleon did not pay the same attention to the campaigns of Condé as he did to those of Turenne and of Frederic, and that after having incidentally judged, with the superiority of a master, and worthily relieved the judicious boldness which achieved the battle of Nortlingen, in which Condé did not fear to engage his only remaining wing for re-establishing the combat, instead of employing it to make a very difficult retreat before the cavalry of Jean de Vert, he did not devote a chapter to the examination of the battle of Rocroy, which opens a new military school.

with great success in Germany and in Italy; but here was a general, of twenty-two years, who eclipsed them all, and who created a new mode of warfare, wherein boldness was at the service of calculation, just as Descartes and Corneille—pardon me the comparison—had created a new philosophy and a new poesy, to serve as a solid foundation or brilliant interpreter to sublime sentiments and thoughts. Rocroy answers to the *Cid*, to *Cinna*, and to *Polyeucte*, so also to the *Discours de La Méthode* in the history of French greatness: incomparable epoch, which no other has ever equalled, and which not even that of the Consulate, after Marengo, approaches, because, amid all its splendors, it had neither a Descartes nor a Corneille!

We may easily imagine the intoxication of the hôtel de Condé, when La Moussaye, one of the companions of the Duke d'Enghien in the amusements of Chantilly and Liancourt, and who had served him faithfully during the eventful day, brought the triumphant news. All the muses of Rambouillet, great and small, sang the exploits of their brilliant pupil. The Spanish flags taken at Rocroy were displayed for several days in the great halls of the hôtel de Condé, before being transported to Nôtre-Dame. The people hastened to behold them. While all hearts were beating with patriotic pride, all eyes were also moved to tears when it was known that the young captain, as humane and pious as he was brave, had, before all his army, knelt upon the battle-field in thanksgiving to God; that he had immediately taken care of the wounded, conquerors and conquered, as if they had been of his own household, consoling them, encouraging them, distributing every thing abundantly among them without ever humiliating them; that he had asked for his lieutenants every recompense, wishing, like the Cid, Polexandre, and Cyrus, those heroes of tragedy and romance, glory alone. In a short time it was known, that after a few days devoted to religion and to humanity, the Duke d'Enghien had resumed the pursuit of the enemy, and that he was already under the walls of Thionville.

The house of Condé needed the éclat and the strength which it received from the victory of Rocroy in order to face its own enemies, and to obtain satisfaction of the insult which it had just received in the person of Madame de Longueville.

It is necessary to have a just idea of the situation of affairs, as well as of the situation of the parties who disputed the government, in order to see the importance of an adventure which in itself seems to be of little consequence.

Soon after the death of Richelieu, there sprang up

a powerful faction, composed of all those whom the imperious cardinal had sacrificed to his designs, whom he had had exiled from the court or from France, and who, their terrible adversary being dead, burned to take possession of his spoils. They expected the support of Queen Anne, for she also had been oppressed, and it was in her service that they had incurred persecution. The favor of the regent appeared to them a debt, and they claimed it in a manner which, little by little, wounded the queen and turned her against them. In proportion as they lost ground with her, Mazarin gained it. He was still young, handsome, mild, insinuating, faithful to the policy of Richelieu, his master, but practising it differently; of a mind less elevated, less extensive—not uniting, like his incomparable predecessor, the genius of administration in all its branches to that of politics in general; especially a diplomatist, but a diplomatist of the first order, with his name attached to two of the greatest treaties of the seventeenth century, the treaty of Westphalia and that of the Pyrenees; inexhaustible in resources and in expedients; always preferring artifice to violence; managing every one, treating with all parties, choosing rather to corrupt than to exterminate them; aiming, especially in 1643, to penetrate into the heart of the queen, as had been attempted by Richelieu, but possessing many other means for succeeding in his design. The handsome cardinal[1] then gained his end. Once master of the heart,[2] he directed easily the mind of the queen, and taught her the difficult art of pursuing steadily the same aim, the supremacy of royal authority, by means of the most contrary conduct, according to the change of circumstances. In the beginning, all his efforts were used in supporting himself and in avoiding the *Importants.* Such was the name applied to the chiefs of the malcontents, on account of the air of importance which they assumed, blaming inconsiderately every measure of government, affecting a sort of melancholy, of profundity, and of refined sublimity, which separated them from other men. They ruled in the *salons*, and they exercised considerable authority at court and throughout all the kingdom, because they had at their head the two great houses of Vendôme and of Lorraine.

The Duke de Beaufort, second son of the Duke César de Vendôme, bore proudly the name of grand-

---

[1] There is not, we believe, or at least we do not know that there is, any portrait painted or engraved of Mazarin in his youth. He was but forty-one years of age in 1643, and a portrait by M. Lasne represents him then with a face still handsome, in which delicacy is united with grandeur.

[2] See, upon this delicate point, M. Walkenær, *Mémoires sur Madame de Sévigné*, vol. i., p. 213, especially the somewhat decided letter of Anne to Mazarin, vol. iii., *Supplement*, p. 471.

son of Henry IV.: he was possessed of bravery and of honor. During the evil times, he had shown a chivalrous fidelity to the queen, who, before having appreciated Mazarin, was much inclined to his side; and he would have perhaps succeeded, if he had not spoiled his affairs by excessive pretensions and by a haughtiness of little efficacy with a Spanish woman, who must be a long time flattered before she can be governed. He had, moreover, no genius, and he would have made a miserable figure in the highest rank: he was made only for the part which he afterwards played, that of a theatrical hero.

The exhausted house of Guise did not possess at this time a single superior man. Long exiled, it had, in 1640, lost in Italy its chief, Charles de Lorraine, and, in 1639, the Prince de Joinville, to whom Mademoiselle de Bourbon had once been destined. The brother who followed this prince was that Henri de Guise, at first archbishop of Rheims, then Duke de Guise, so celebrated for his adventures, his bravery, and his fickleness; who had all kinds of ambition, formed all sorts of enterprises, and succeeded in nothing, not even in being a hero of romance, whatever may be said of him. See, I pray, if this is the life of a chevalier, of an ancient paladin, as Madame de Motteville calls him;[1] and if, according to the pretensions of Mademoiselle,[2] he made love after the manner of romances. After the death of his father and of his elder brother, he made his peace with Richelieu, and returned to the court: a year had scarcely passed by, when he conspired against Richelieu with the Count de Soissons, and was compelled to quit France. Whilst archbishop of Rheims, he was smitten with the beautiful Anne de Gonzague, afterwards Princess Palatine; he was engaged to her by an explicit promise of marriage, and when Anne de Gonzague, relying upon his word, commits the folly of going, under the name of Madame de Guise, to rejoin him at Brussels, she finds him married to the Countess de Bossu, of whom he soon grows weary and abandons, in order to return to Paris, when Richelieu and Louis XIII. are no more. There he pays a very easy court to Madame de Montbazon. A little while after he falls madly in love with Mademoiselle de Pons, one of the maids of honor of Queen Anne, very pretty and very coquettish: he wishes to marry her; he goes to Rome to solicit the dissolution of his first marriage, and by the way, in order to conquer a crown for his new mistress, he places himself at the head of the insurrection of Na-

[1] Vol. ii., p. 108. [2] *Mémoires*, vol. i., p. 231.

ples. He arrives through a thousand hazards, displays the most brilliant valor, without any political or military talent, is made prisoner by the Spaniards, begs Condé, unfortunately then all-powerful in Spain, to obtain his deliverance, promising to him eternal devotion; and after recovering his liberty, thanks to the intervention of Condé, instead of serving him as he had publicly sworn, he abandons him, passes over to Mazarin, takes part in every thing opposed to his liberator, commences a lawsuit against this same Mademoiselle de Pons, whom he wished to make queen of Naples, for the recovery of the furniture and jewels which he had given her, becomes high chamberlain, and is fit only to parade in fêtes and tourneys of the court, and to call forth the speech, when seen in the company of Condé: "There goes the hero of fable by the side of the hero of history:" carrying with him to the tomb, in 1664, that illustrious house of Guise which merited a very different end. In 1643, on his arrival in Paris, he fell into the party of the *Importants*, and he was marvellously formed for one of the chiefs of this party, for he was vain, brilliant, and incapable.

The women occupied a prominent place in this anticipated Fronde of the beginning of the regency. Queen Anne had formerly had for her friends the celebrated Duchess de Chevreuse and Mademoiselle d'Hautefort, afterwards Duchess de Schomberg. These ladies shared equally great beauty, ambition, and a courageously supported disgrace. Marie d'Hautefort[1] was, with Madame de Sablé, one of the models of a true *précieuse*, whose conduct equalled her maxims. Maid of honor to the queen, Louis XIII. had entertained for her that Platonic love, then in fashion, which he also showed for Mademoiselle de La Fayette. Richelieu, after having vainly endeavored to obtain her, had embroiled her with her royal lover, and exiled her from the court. Queen Anne had loved her almost as much as the king; and, as soon as she was free and mistress of herself, she wrote to her with her own hand: "Come, my dear friend, I am dying with impatience to embrace you." Mademoiselle d'Hautefort eagerly obeyed the summons; but when she wished to speak of Mazarin as she formerly did of Richelieu, she found a less favorable audience, and, not knowing how to accommodate herself to the new situation, her stately ten-

---

1 Madame de Motteville has thus painted her, vol. i., p. 47: "Her eyes were blue, large, and full of fire; her teeth white and even, and her complexion had the white and incarnation necessary to a light beauty." Her *Nom de Précieuse* was Hermione, *Grand Dictionnaire des Pretieuses*, vol. i., p. 218. Scarron has greatly celebrated her. Married in 1646 to the Marshal Charles de Schomberg, she followed him into his government of Trois Evechés, encountered Metz, the young Bossuet, and encouraged his first efforts. After the death of the marshal she lived in retirement, and died in 1691.

derness became wearisome. Madame de Chevreuse had possessed the beauty[1] of Mademoiselle d'Hautefort, but not her virtues. Marie de Rohan Montbazon, daughter of the Duke Hercule de Montbazon by a former marriage, was first married to the High Constable de Luynes, early became a widow, and then entered the house of Lorraine by marrying the Duke de Chevreuse. A victim of her fidelity to the queen, banished by Richelieu, she had long wandered in Europe, and returned to France with the pretensions of an emigrant. Occupied with gallantry, devoted to the lover of the moment, she moved heaven and earth to overturn Mazarin and to put in his place Châteauneuf, the old keeper of the seals, who, in the party, passed for a man of superior capacity, and in the State for being the most important minister. She exacted also a high situation for La Rochefoucauld, who had been more or less tenderly attached to her, and who still possessed that romantic

[1] To judge of her beauty, she should not be seen as Retz saw her at fifty years of age, nor as most of her portraits show her at the approach of age, with the widow's cap which she wore after the death of her second husband; she should be seen when young and brilliant, if not during the life of the High Constable De Luynes, at least at the period of her second marriage. Born in 1604, married in 1617, a widow in 1619, remarried in 1622, at the age of eighteen, she had from fifteen to twenty years of the greatest splendor. Her form was charming. She had blue eyes, light chestnut hair, and a most beautiful bosom. Thus she is represented by several of the portraits of the times possessed by the Duke de Luynes, also by a charming portrait engraved by Daret.

sentimentality, in the fashion of the Duke de Guise, whose foundation is almost always a vanity, shameful in itself, and whose climax must, in this case, be the book of *maxims*.

Mazarin defended himself, as we have said, by gaining, little by little, the heart of the queen; and to the attacks of the houses of Vendôme and of Lorraine he opposed the weight of the old partisans of Richelieu, still numerous and influential, especially the house of Condé, with its alliances and its friendships, the Montmorencys, the Longuevilles, the Brézés, the Ventadours, the Châtillons. Mazarin would have been undone in these difficult beginnings, if the Prince de Condé had not remained firmly attached to royal authority. He supported the uncertain Duke d'Orleans, who, after having engaged in more than one intrigue against Richelieu, and saved himself by betraying his friends, had attempted again to lay his snares. The prince was too good a politician not to understand that it was better for him to be the powerful protector, rather than the unequal adversary of royalty; that in this case it was necessary to defend it with energy, and that his rank would always raise him above a minister, when this minister was not Richelieu; and if no one contested the capacity of Mazarin, no one would suspect all his power. As chief of the council and governor of Paris, M. the Prince applied himself, in concert with M. the Lieutenant-General of the kingdom, to baffle all the designs of the *Importants*, and in this way he made bitter enemies.

Their hatred for the house of Condé, hardly fell upon Madame de Longueville. Her gentleness in every thing in which her heart was not seriously engaged, her perfect indifference in regard to politics at this period of her life, with the graces of her mind and of her person, rendered her pleasing to every one, and protected her against the injustice of parties. But aside from the affairs of State, she had an enemy, and a fearful enemy, in the Duchess de Montbazon. We have said that Madame de Montbazon had been the mistress of M. de Longueville; it is necessary that she should be a little better known, for she is one of the principal personages of the drama which we are about to relate.

Marie de Bretagne, who was born about 1612, and who died in 1657, at the age of forty-five, was the eldest daughter of that famous Countess de Vertus, whose father was La Varenne Fouquet, chief of the household, and very obliging servant of Henry IV. The Count de Vertus, of the illustrious house of Bretagne, had married Mademoiselle de La Varenne on account of her extreme beauty, and he had hastened to withdraw her from Paris, and to take her to his own house. He gained nothing by this, and Tallemant[1] has told us, concerning the beautiful and foolish countess, a story of the most tragic nature. In beauty the daughter was worthy of the mother, but in vices she left her far behind. Married, in 1628, to the old Duke de Montbazon, father of Madame de Chevreuse, she soon placed herself at ease. Her mind was not her most brilliant side, and the little that she had was turned to intrigue and perfidy. "Her mind," says the indulgent Madame de Motteville,[2] "was not so fine as her person; her brilliancy was limited to her eyes, which commanded love. She claimed universal admiration." In regard to her character, all are unanimous. Retz, who knew her well, speaks of her in these terms:[3] "Madame de Montbazon was a very great beauty. Modesty was wanting in her air. Her jargon might, in a dull time, have supplied the defects of her mind. She showed but little faith in gallantry, none in business. She loved her own pleasure alone, and above her pleasure her interest. I never saw a person who, in vice, preserved so little respect for virtue." Su-

---

[1] Tallemant, vol. iii., p. 407. [2] *Mémoires*, vol. i., p. 46.

[3] Vol. i., p. 221. He cites, as well as Tallemant and even Madame de Motteville, incredible things. The collections of songs of the times abound in outrageous epigrams against her. See the *Collection of Maurepas*, in the National Library, and the collections of *Chanson's historiques*, of the Library of the Arsenal.

premely vain and passionately fond of money, it was by aid of her beauty that she sought influence and fortune. She therefore took infinite care of it, as of her idol, as of her resources, her treasure. She kept it in repair, heightened it by all kinds of artifices, and preserved it almost uninjured till her death. Madame de Motteville asserts that, during the latter part of her life, she was as full of vanity as if she were but twenty-five years of age;[1] that she had the same desire to please, and that she wore her mourning garb in so charming a manner, that "the order of nature seemed changed, since years and beauty could be found united." Ten years before, in 1647, at the age of thirty-five, when Mazarin gave a comedy in the Italian style, that is, an opera, there was in the evening a great ball, and the Duchess de Montbazon was present, adorned with pearls, with a red feather on her head, and so dazzling in her appearance that the whole company was completely ravished. We can imagine what she was in 1643, at the age of thirty-one years.

Of the two conditions of perfect beauty, strength and grace,[2] Madame de Montbazon possessed the first in the highest degree; but this quality being almost alone, or entirely dominant, left something to be de-

---

[1] Vol. v., p. 246.

[2] See Introduction.

sired—that precisely which makes the charm of beauty. She was tall and majestic, to such a point indeed that Tallemant, who always exaggerates, and seldom lies, says: "She was a Colossus."[1] She possessed all the charms of embonpoint. Her throat reminded one of the fulness, in this particular, of the antique statues, exceeding them perhaps somewhat. What struck the beholder most were her eyes and hair of intense blackness, upon a groundwork of the most dazzling white. Her defect was a nose somewhat too prominent, with a mouth so large as to give her face an appearance of severity.[2] It was plain enough that she was the very opposite of Madame de Longueville. The latter was tall, but not to excess. The richness of her form did not diminish its delicacy. A moderate embonpoint exhibited, in full and exquisite measure, the beauty of the female form. Her eyes were of the softest blue; her hair of the most beautiful blonde. She had the most majestic

---

[1] Vol. iii., p. 410.

[2] In regard to the beauty of Madame de Montbazon, we have united what is said by Tallemant, vol. iii., p. 411, and by Madame de Motteville, vol. i., p. 146. The reader may judge of the truth of our description by going to see, at Versailles, in the curious gallery of the northern attic, under No. 2030, a small picture, representing Madame de Montbazon, at the age of thirty-five to forty years, with a collar of pearls, a beautiful forehead, fine black eyes, a magnificent throat; but all somewhat strong and without much distinction. This picture seems the original of the portrait engraved by Le Blond.

air, and yet her peculiar characteristic was grace. To these add the great difference of manners and tone. Madame de Longueville was, in her deportment, dignity, politeness, modesty, sweetness itself, with a languor and a nonchalance which formed not her least charm. Her words were few, as well as her gestures; the inflexions of her voice were a perfect music.[1] The excess, into which she never fell, might have been a sort of fastidiousness. Every thing in her was wit, sentiment, charm. Madame de Montbazon, on the contrary, was free of speech, bold and easy in her tone, full of stateliness and pride.

She was nevertheless a very attractive creature, when she wished to be so, and she had a great number of adorers, and of happy adorers, from Gaston, Duke of Orleans, and the Count de Soissons, slain at Marfée, to Rancé, the young and gallant editor of Anacreon, and the future founder of La Trappe. M. de Longueville had been for some time her lover by title, and he afforded her considerable advantages. When he married Mademoiselle de Bourbon, Madame the Princess exacted, without however being very faithfully obeyed, the discontinuance of all intercourse with his old mistress. Hence, in that interested soul, an irritation, which wounded vanity

---

[1] Villefore, p. 32.

redoubled, when she saw this young woman, with her great name, her marvellous mind, her undefinable charms, advance into the world of gallantry, without the least effort draw after her all hearts, and take possession of, or at least share that empire of beauty of which she was so proud, and which was to her so precious. On the other hand, the Duke de Beaufort had not been able to restrain a passionate admiration for Madame de Longueville, which had been very coldly received. He was wounded by it, and his wound bled for a long time, as his friend, La Châtre, informs us,[1] even after he had transferred his homage to Madame de Montbazon. The latter, as may be easily imagined, was again exasperated. Finally, the Duke de Guise, recently from Paris, placed himself in the party of the *Importants*, and at the service of Madame de Montbazon, who received him very well, at the same time that she was striving to keep or to recall M. de Longueville, and that she was ruling Beaufort, whose office near her was that, somewhat, of an attending cavalier. Thus we see that Madame de Montbazon disposed, through Beaufort and through Guise, as also through her daughter-in-law, Madame de Chevreuse, of the house of Vendôme, and of the house of Lorraine, and she employed all this credit

---

1 *Mémoires* of La Châtre in the collection Petitot, vol. li., p. 280.

to the profit of her hatred against Madame de Longueville. She burned to injure her; she found an opportunity to do it.

One day when a large company was assembled at her house, some person picked up two letters, having no signatures, but in the handwriting of a female, and of a somewhat equivocal style. They were read; a thousand jokes were perpetrated concerning them, and some effort made to discover the author. Madame de Montbazon pretended that they had fallen from the pocket of Maurice de Coligny, who had just gone out, and that they were in the handwriting of Madame de Longueville. The word of command thus once given, all the echoes of the party of the *Importants* spread it, and this adventure became the entertainment of the court. The following are the two letters, found at the house of Madame de Montbazon: a frivolous curiosity has preserved them very faithfully:[1]

I.

"I should much more regret the change in your conduct if I thought myself less worthy of a continuation of your affection. I confess to you that so long as I believed it to be true and warm, mine gave

[1] Mademoiselle, vol. 1st, pp. 62 and 68.

you all the advantages which you could desire. Now, hope nothing more from me than the esteem which I owe to your discretion. I have too much pride to share the passion which you have so often sworn to me, and I desire to punish your negligence in seeing me, in no other way than by depriving you entirely of my society. I request that you will visit me no more, since I have no more the power of commanding your presence."

II.

"To what conclusion have you come after so long a silence? Do you not know that the same pride which rendered me sensible to your past affection forbids me to endure the false appearances of its continuation! You say that my suspicions and my inequalities render you the most unhappy person in the world: I assure you that I believe no such thing, although I cannot deny that you have perfectly loved me, as you must confess that my esteem has worthily recompensed you. So far we have done each other justice, and I am determined not to have in the end less goodness, if your conduct responds to my intentions. You would find them less unreasonable if you had more passion, and the difficulties of seeing me would only augment instead of diminishing it. I suffer for not loving enough, and you for loving too much.[1] If I must believe you, let us exchange humors: I shall find repose in doing my duty, and you in doing yours must fail, in order to obtain liberty. I do not perceive that I forget the manner in which I passed the winter with you, and that I speak to you as frankly as I have heretofore done. I hope that you will make as good use of it, and that I shall not regret being overcome in the resolution which I have made to return to it no more. I shall remain in my lodgings three or four days in succession, and will be seen only in the evening: you know the reason."

These letters were not forged. They had been really written by Madame de Fouquerolles to the handsome and elegant Marquis de Maulevrier,[2] who had been foolish enough to drop them in the *salon* of Madame de Montbazon. Maulevrier, trembling at being discovered, and at having compromised Madame de Fouquerolles, ran to one of the chiefs of the *Importants*, La Rochefoucauld, who was his friend, confided to him his secret, and begged him to undertake to hush up the affair. La Rochefoucauld made

---

[1] It seems to me that it would be better to say: "I suffer for loving too much, and you for not loving enough."

[2] See Mademoiselle, Madame de Motteville, and La Rochefoucauld.

Madame de Montbazon understand that it was for her interest to be generous on this occasion, for the error or fraud would be easily recognized as soon as the writing should be compared with that of Madame de Longueville. Madame de Montbazon placed the original letters in the hands of La Rochefoucauld, who showed them to M. the Prince, and to Madame the Princess, to Madame de Rambouillet, and to Madame Sablé, particular friends of Madame de Longueville, and, the truth being well established, burned them in the presence of the queen, delivering Maulevrier and Madame de Fouquerolles from the terrible uneasiness into which they had been for some time thrown.[1]

It had perhaps been wise to have dropped the matter here. This was the somewhat interested opinion of the weak and prudent M. de Longueville, who wished to manage Madame de Montbazon, and who did not believe that the honor of his wife would gain much by farther disclosures. Madame de Longueville was not very much irritated; but Madame the Princess, impelled by her high spirit, and still intoxicated by the success of her son, exacted a reparation equal to the offence, and declared loudly that, if the queen and the government did not defend the honor

[1] Mémoires de La Rochefoucauld, Collection Petitot, vol. li., p. 387.

of her house, she and all her family would withdraw from the court. She was indignant at the mere idea of placing her daughter in the scales with the grand-daughter of a cook, as she called La Varenne, father of the Countess de Vertus, who had been chief of the hôtel of Henri IV. In vain did the whole party of the *Importants*, with Beaufort and Guise at their head, agitate and threaten; in vain did Madame de Chevreuse, who had not yet lost all her credit with the queen, strive earnestly in behalf of her mother-in-law. Mazarin was too wise to take two enemies upon his arms at once, and to become embroiled with the Condés, without any hope of gaining or disarming the Lorraines and the Vendômes. He inclined the queen without difficulty to the side of Madame the Princess. Madame de Longueville had gone to pass the first moments of this disagreeable adventure at La Barre, with her dear friends, Mesdemoiselles Du Vigean. The queen herself went to see her there, and promised her protection. It was decided that the Duchess de Montbazon should repair to Madame the Princess at the hôtel de Condé, and make to her a public reparation. Madame de Motteville tells, in a very pleasant way, how much diplomacy was necessary in order to arrange the speech of Madame de Montbazon and the reply of Madame the Princess. The queen was in her cabinet, and Madame the

Princess, terribly excited, was with her, endeavoring to make the affair one of high-treason. Madame de Chevreuse, engaged for a thousand reasons in the quarrel of her mother-in-law, was with Cardinal Mazarin, composing the speech necessary to be made upon the occasion. Every word of it occasioned an hour's discussion. The cardinal, greatly embarrassed, went from one side to the other to accommodate their differences, as if this peace was necessary to the happiness of France, and to his own in particular. It was concluded that the criminal should go, the next day, to Madame the Princess, and say that the expressions used in regard to the letters were false, invented by evil-disposed persons, and that she herself had never entertained them, knowing too well the virtue of Madame de Longueville and the respect that was due to her. This harangue was written upon a small piece of paper and attached to her fan, in order that she might repeat it word for word to Madame the Princess. She did it in the most haughty manner possible, putting on an air which seemed to say: I jest in every word I utter.

Mademoiselle[1] gives us the two speeches made upon the occasion: "Madame, I come here to protest to you that I am innocent of the wickedness of

[1] Vol. i., p. 65.

which I have been accused: no person of honor can utter a calumny like this. If I had committed a fault like this, I should have submitted to any punishment which it might have pleased the queen to inflict upon me; I should have never shown myself in the world, and would have asked your pardon. I beg you to believe that I shall never fail in the respect which I owe to you and in the opinion which I have of the virtue and of the merit of Madame de Longueville." Madame the Princess replied: "Madame, I receive very willingly the assurance which you give me that you have had no part in the wicked things that have been circulated; I have too much respect for the commands of the queen."

We find in the manuscript journal of Olivier d'Ormesson some details which add to the piquancy of this comical scene. It took place on the 8th of August. The Cardinal Mazarin was present, as a witness on the part of the queen. Madame de Montbazon having begun her speech without saying *Madame*, the princess complained, and she was obliged to recommence with the respectful addition. Such a reconciliation amounted to nothing, and a few days after war recommenced.

Besides the satisfaction which she had just received, Madame the Princess had asked and had been permitted the privilege of never associating with the

Duchess de Montbazon. Some time after, Madame de Chevreuse invited the queen to a collation in the garden of Renard. This garden was the rendezvous of the best society. It was at the termination of the Tuileries, near the Porte de la Conférence, which conducted to the Cours-la-Reine; that is, at the left angle of the Place Louis XV., upon the ground since occupied by two of those ditches which even to this day have spoiled that magnificent place which might so easily be rendered the most beautiful in Europe. In the summer, on returning from the Cours, which was the promenade of the nobility, and the spot where the beauties of the day exercised their powers, it was customary to stop at the garden Renard, for the purpose of taking refreshments, and to listen to the serenades performed after the Spanish fashion. The queen took great pleasure in visiting this place during the fine summer evenings. She desired Madame the Princess to partake with her the collation offered by Madame de Chevreuse, assuring her at the same time that Madame de Montbazon would not be present; but the latter person was really there, and even pretended to do the honors of the collation as mother-in-law of the lady who gave it. Madame the Princess wished to withdraw, in order that the entertainment might not be disturbed: the queen had no right whatever to detain her. She therefore begged Madame de Montbazon to pretend sickness, and by leaving the company, to relieve her from embarrassment. The haughty duchess would not consent to fly before her enemy, and kept her place. The queen, offended, refused the collation, and quitted the promenade. On the morrow, an order from the king enjoined upon Madame de Montbazon to leave Paris. This disgrace irritated the *Importants*. They thought themselves humiliated and enfeebled, and there were no violent or extreme measures which they did not contemplate. The Duke de Beaufort, smitten at once in his credit and in his love, raised loud cries, and it was reported that a plot had been formed against the life of Mazarin.[1] In this conjuncture the cardinal showed himself the worthy heir of Richelieu. Although he may have lacked his patience, his cunning, and his intrigue, he was not deprived of courage, and he knew how to take his part. He was already on very good terms with the queen, and began to seem necessary, or at least very useful to her. He represented to her mildly, but forcibly, what she owed to the State and to the royal authority now menaced; that it was necessary to prefer the interests of her son and of his crown to friendships which were perhaps at one time

---

[1] See the *Mémoires* of the times, and especially those of Campion.

well enough, but which were now becoming dangerous. He won her, and the ruin of the *Importants* was decided. On the 2d of September, the Duke de Beaufort was arrested within the very walls of the Louvre, and he was conducted to Vincennes. The command of the Swiss was taken from his friend, La Châtre. The Bishop de Beauvais, who for a short time enjoyed the favor of the queen, and was thought of as the successor of Richelieu, was sent to his church; the Duke de Vendôme, as well as the Duke de Mercœur, his eldest son, were exiled, and Madame de Chevreuse banished to Tours. These measures, seasonably executed, broke up the party of the *Importants*. The intestine disorders which menaced the new reign were destined to await more favorable days. Mazarin, soon without a rival with the queen, continued at home and especially abroad the policy of his predecessor, and royalty, as well as France, anticipated a succession of glorious years, thanks to the union of the princes of the blood with the crown, to the skilful management of the prime minister, to the prudence of Condé, and to the military genius of the Duke d'Enghien.

The latter had returned to Paris at the close of the campaign, after having taken Thionville and several other places, and brought his victorious army over the Rhine. The queen had received him as the deliverer of France. Mazarin, who thought more of the reality than of the appearance of power, told him that his greatest ambition was to be his chaplain and his business man with the queen. At a distance the Duke d'Enghien had applauded all that had been done, and he returned still burning for Mademoiselle Du Vigean, and furious on account of the insult which had been offered to his sister. He adored his sister, and he loved Coligny. He was acquainted with, and he had favored his passion. Burning himself with a love as ardent as it was chaste, he knew that his sister could not have been insensible to the passion of Maurice; but he revolted at the thought of attributing to her the letters of one Madame de Fouquerolles, and he took it in a manner which intimidated the most insolent.

Among the friends of the Duke de Beaufort and of Madame de Montbazon, was the Duke de Guise, afterwards chief of the house of Lorraine in France. He had been secured, as well as all his family, on account of Gaston, Duke of Orleans, who had taken, as a second wife, a princess of this house, the beautiful Marguerite.[1] The Duke de Guise was such as we have described him. He had committed more than one folly, but he had not yet shamefully failed

[1] Second daughter of Duke François. This marriage, contracted in 1632, is a romance, which may be read in all the memoirs of the times.

in all his enterprises; his incapacity was not declared. He had all the prestige of his name, of youth, of beauty, and of a bravery bordering upon temerity. The avowed servant of Madame de Montbazon, he had espoused her quarrel, without entering into the violence of Beaufort, and he stood boldly up before the victorious Condés.

Coligny had been prudent enough to withdraw during the storm, for fear of still more compromising Madame de Longueville by becoming openly her defender; but some months having passed, he thought that he might show himself, and, as we are informed by the unpublished work upon the regency, which we have several times quoted,[1] "the prison of the Duke de Beaufort not affording him an opportunity to draw his sword, he addressed himself to the Duke de Guise." La Rochefoucauld states it thus:[2] "The Duke d'Enghien, not being able to testify to the Duke de Beaufort, who was in prison, the resentment which he felt on account of what had happened between Madame de Longueville and Madame de Montbazon, suffered Coligny to fight with the Duke de Guise, who had taken part in this affair." The Duke d'Enghien knew, then, and approved what Coligny did. As for Madame de Longueville, it is

---

[1] Royal Library, *Supplément Français*, No. 925, fol. 11.
[2] *Mémoires*, p. 391.

absurd to suppóse that she, wishing to be avenged, drove on Coligny, for every one attributes to her a conduct very moderate compared with that of Madame the Princess. Far from encouraging the quarrel, she sought to appease it, and Madame de Motteville herself refutes the report which she relates by saying: "Her jealousy of the Duchess de Montbazon, being proportioned to her love for her husband, did not carry her away so far as to prevent her from finding her advantage in dissembling this outrage."

La Rochefoucauld gives us a piece of information which explains what follows: Coligny had just risen from a long sickness; he was still feeble, and he was not very skilful in fencing.[1] It was in this condition that he attacked the Duke de Guise, who, like all fancy heroes, possessed great skill in this kind of exercise.

Let us say a few words in regard to the seconds whom they chose; they are in all respects worthy of the trouble. The seconds were then witnesses who fought. Coligny took for his second and for the bearer of his challenge, Godefroi, Count d'Estrades, a man of cool and well-tried courage. D'Estrades had served in Holland, under Maurice de Nassau. He had distinguished himself in several such encoun-

---

Mémoires, p. 391.

ters. One day, as Tallemant relates, fighting with a bully who placed himself on the border of a little ditch, saying to Estrades : "I will not pass over this ditch." "And I," said Estrades, making a mark behind him with his sword, "I will not pass over this mark." They fought ; Estrades slew him. He was employed, by turns and with equal success, in war and in diplomacy, and became Marshal of France in 1675. The second of the Duke de Guise was the Marquis de Bridieu, a gentleman of Limosin, a brave officer, and friend of the house of Lorraine, who, in 1650, made an admirable defence of an important stronghold on the frontiers of Flanders, against the Spanish army and against Turenne, for which he was created lieutenant-general.[1]

---

[1] The Place-Royale and its environs were then the quarters of the upper classes. Begun in 1604 (*Antiquities and most remarkable things of Paris*, 1608, by Bonfons and by Du Breuil, p. 430), on the ruins of the Palais des Tournelles, by Henri IV., it was finished in 1612. (*Theatre of the Antiquities of Paris*, by Father Du Breuil, in-4°, 1613, p. 1050.) It is, as is known, a great square, or rather a rectangle, bordered on all sides by thirty-seven pavilions, supported by pillars forming a gallery, which extends entirely around the place. In the midst was a vast yard, divided into six beautiful grass-plots. In the centre was the equestrian statue of Louis XIII. The statue was by Biard, and the horse by Daniel de Volterre. On one of the faces of the pedestal of white marble, was the following inscription: "To the glorious and immortal memory of the great and invincible Louis the Just, thirteenth of the name, King of France and of Navarre, Armand, Cardinal de Richelieu, his principal minister, has raised this statue as an eternal mark of his zeal, of his fidelity, and of his gratitude, in 1639." Under Louis XIV. this beautiful square was surrounded with a rail-

It was agreed that the affair should take place at the Place-Royale—the usual theatre of these combats, and which they had a thousand times stained with

---

ing of excellent workmanship. Lemaire, said in 1685, vol. iii., p. 807: "They are now making a balustrade of iron, which will extend entirely around it and inclose a very agreeable garden, in which there will be four great reservoirs of water in the four corners. Private persons having their residences here, will contribute to the expense of this, each the sum of one thousand livres. The city will furnish the rest." Germain Brice, in the first edition of his curious work, which appeared in 1685, as did that of Lemaire, says the same thing, adding that the inhabitants alone of the place will have the right of enjoying the garden which is to be laid out. "No one will enter except those belonging to the houses which have been furnished with keys." In the second edition of Brice, of 1687, the beautiful railing was not erected; it is in the edition which follows, of 1701; it is seen in La Caille, in 1714; and in the engraving of Defer, in 1716. As to the garden and the four reservoirs, they are not even yet in the plan of Turgot, in 1740. It was the Restoration which accomplished the designs of the administration of Louis XIV. How many public and domestic events has this place witnessed during the seventeenth century, how many noble tourneys, how many atrocious duels, how many amiable rendezvous! What conversations, worthy of those of Décaméron, it has heard,—conversations which Corneille has collected in one of his first comedies, and in several acts of the *Menteur!* What graceful creatures have inhabited these pavilions! What sumptuous furniture, what treasures of taste have been assembled here! How many illustrious personages, of every kind, have mounted these beautiful staircases! Richelieu and Condé, Corneille and Molière, have trod them a thousand times. It was while walking under this gallery that Descartes, conversing with Pascal, suggested to him the idea of his beautiful experiments upon the weight of the air. It was there also that, while going one evening from the house of Madame de Guimenée, the melancholy De Thou received from Cinq-Mars the involuntary confidence of the conspiracy which was to lead them both to the scaffold. It was there, in short, that Madame de Sévigné was born, and close by it she lived. On reaching the Place-Royale by its true entrance, the Rue-Royale, beside the Rue Saint-Antoine, we find at the

the best blood. The Place-Royale was also the residence of the greatest ladies, the flower of gallantry, Marguerite de Rohan, Madame de Guimenée, Ma-

---

right angle the hôtel de Rohan, long occupied by the old Duchess Dowager, widow of that great Duke de Rohan, one of the first generals, and the greatest military writers of his age. In the left angle was the hôtel de Chaulnes, whose magnificent apartments have been celebrated by Bois-Robert, and which, at a later period, passed to Nicolaï. At the other two corners of the place were, to the right, on the side of the Rue des Tournelles and of the Boulevard, the vast and sumptuous hôtel of Saint-Géran; and to the left, on the side of the street Saint-Louis, the hôtel which was occupied by Richelieu before he had built and finished Palais-Cardinal. The four galleries were filled with hôtels not unworthy of those already mentioned. There was the hôtel of the Marshal de Lavardin, that of M. de Nouveau, that of Villequier, captain of the guards, who sold it to M. de Hameaux, by whom it was resold, in 1680, to the Rohan-Chabots, and from them this hôtel, even in passing through other hands, retained the name of hôtel Chabot. M. Wolckenær, in his *La Bruyère*, p. 743, says that the Count de Montgomery and the unfortunate Marquis de Langlade, so celebrated in the history of unjust condemnations, lived together at the Place-Royale. Brice, in 1685, indicates the hôtel of the Marquis de Dangeau, and in 1713, on the right, in entering by the Rue Saint-Antoine, the hôtel of the Baron de Breteuil, and on the other side the house of the President Carrel. We know certainly that Madame de Sablé resided at the Place-Royale, as well as the Countess de Maure, with Mademoiselle de Vaudy; but the difficulty would be to discover the inhabitants of all the other pavilions, and thus to make an exact and complete history of the Place-Royale until the close of the seventeenth century. We suggest this subject of study to some pupil of the *Ecole des Chartes*, or to some young artist; they would find in it matter of the most interesting investigation, as well as descriptions the most charming, and a modest glory would not fail to follow after a few years of the most attractive labor. We take the liberty of pointing out to them, besides Felibien, vol. ii., Sauval, vol. ii., p. 624, the plan of Gomboust, from 1652, and the after plans, the following works: 1st, *The Paris Guide*, etc., by the Sieur de Schayes, 1647; 2d, *The Convenient Book, containing the addresses of the city of Paris, by Abraham Pradel, philosopher and math-*

dame de Chaulnes, Madame de Saint-Géran, Madame de Sablé, the Countess de Maure, and many others, under whose eyes these thoughtless and valiant gentlemen delighted to cross their swords. Many had there breathed their last. In the first quarter of the seventeenth century, duelling was a custom at once useful and disastrous; it encouraged the warlike spirit of the nobility, but it was almost as destructive as war, and for more frivolous causes. To draw the sword for a trifle had become a part of genteel manners, and, as gallantry had its elegancies, so the duel had its refinements. During the period of a few short years, nine hundred gentlemen had perished in private combats. To arrest this scourge, Richelieu procured the terrible decree which punished the surviving combatant with death, and sent the abettors from the Place-Royale to the Place de Grève. Richelieu was inflexible, and the example

---

ematician, Paris, small in 8°; 3d, *The Royal Almanac*, of 1699; 4th, the sequel to the different editions of G. Brice, from 1685 to 1725; 5th, the verses by Scarron, *Adieu au Marais et à la Place-Royale*, edit. of Amsterdam, of 1752, vol. vii., pp. 29–35; 6th, a Manuscript of the National Library, No. 7905, wherein is a *Supplement of the Antiquities of Paris, with all the most remarkable transactions from* 1610 *until the present time, by D. H. J., lawyer.* "*Until the present time,*" is up to 1640. Let us conclude with this remark: there is but one hôtel of the Place-Royale which has remained in the same family from 1612 till our own day, namely, the hôtel which bears the No. 25, and which, from father to son, has come down to its present proprietor, M. the Count de l'Escalopier.

of Montmorency-Boutteville—decapitated, with his second, the Count Deschapelles, for having provoked Beuvron, and for fighting with him on the Place-Royale in full day—impressed a salutary terror, and rendered infractions of the edict rare enough. Coligny braved every thing; he challenged Guise, and, upon the appointed day, the two noble adversaries, assisted by their seconds, d'Estrades and Bridieu, met upon the Place-Royale.

We have it in our power to give the most minute details of the combat, thanks to different contemporary memoirs, and especially to two new documents, the manuscript already quoted in regard to the Regency, and the unpublished journal of Olivier d'Ormesson.

It was on the morning of the 12th of December[1] that d'Estrades carried to the Duke de Guise the challenge of Coligny. The meeting was fixed for the same day, at the Place-Royale, at three[2] o'clock. The two adversaries exhibited nothing unusual during the whole morning, and at three o'clock they were at the rendezvous. A speech[3] is attributed to the Duke de Guise, which gives to this scene an unexpected

[1] It is d'Ormesson who gives this date.

[2] D'Ormesson, manuscript on the Regency, whose author seems to be one Maupassant.

[3] La Rochefoucauld.

grandeur, which exhibits upon the Place-Royale and places in hostility for the last time the two most illustrious combatants of the wars of the League in the persons of their descendants. On receiving his sword, Guise said to Coligny: "We are now going to decide the ancient quarrels of our two houses, and the world shall soon see what difference there is between the blood of the Guise and that of Coligny." Coligny aimed at his adversary a prodigious thrust, says the journal of d'Ormesson,[1] but, still weak on account of his recent sickness, his foot failed him, and he fell upon his knee. Guise, closing with him, placed his foot upon the sword of the fallen man. Coligny, though thus disarmed, would not ask his life. Guise said to him:[2] "I will not kill you, but treat you as you deserve, for having addressed, without any provocation, a prince of my birth;" and thereupon he struck him with the flat of his sword.[3] Coligny, indignant, summoned all his strength, threw himself backwards, disengaged his sword, and renewed the struggle.[4] In this second encounter, Guise was slightly wounded in the shoulder,[5] and Coligny in the hand; but Guise, closing with Coligny a sec-

---

[1] Fol. 28, verso.

[2] D'Ormesson.

[3] D'Ormesson, Maupassant, and La Rochefoucauld.

[4] D'Ormesson.

[5] D'Ormesson; Maupassant says in the right side.

ond time, seized his sword, by which he cut his hand somewhat, and, taking it away, disabled him by a terrible cut upon the arm. At the same time d'Estrades and Bridieu were sorely wounded.[1]

Such was the issue of this duel, the last, I believe, of the celebrated duels of the Place-Royale. It was referred to Parliament, agreeably to the edict of Richelieu; but the course of justice was stayed by the influence of Condé, and especially by the deplorable condition[2] into which Coligny, the most guilty party, had been thrown. The proof that an understanding existed between Condé and Coligny is based upon the fact that the latter found an asylum in his house of Saint-Maur. There he languished some time,[3] and died of the mortification occasioned by

---

[1] D'Ormesson, Maupassant, La Rochefoucauld, Motteville.

[2] Maupassant says that the Duke de Guise and Coligny appeared before the court and justified themselves, the Duke de Guise with the greatest success and Coligny with very bad grace; but D'Ormesson, so well informed in regard to all that was going on in the Council of State and in the Parliament, says not a word of the matter—and nothing is more improbable, Coligny having immediately fallen into a desperate condition.

[3] La Rochefoucauld says that Coligny died four or five months after: it should be four or five days. In fact, we find in the journal of Olivier d'Ormesson, fol. 29, as follows: "Tuesday, December 29, the Marquis de Pardaillan came to see me, and told me that M. de Coligny was at Saint-Maur, and was likely to die of gangrene of his arm." . . . "Wednesday, December 30 (D'Ormesson has, through mistake, made it January), M. de Coligny was beyond hope, his wound making neither flesh nor matter, on account of his naturally bad constitution. M. the Duke d'Enghien had resolved to have his arm taken off."

his poor defence of the cause of his own house and of that of Madame de Longueville.

This affair, with its dramatic circumstances and its tragic denoument, caused an extraordinary and painful sensation throughout Paris and all France. It renewed, for a moment, the differences of parties, and suspended the diversions and fêtes of the winter of 1644;[1] it did not occupy the families interested and the court alone—it touched every individual of the higher ranks, and continued for some time to be the subject of conversation for the *salons*. We easily imagine that, as the story spread, it was gradually lengthened by imaginary incidents. At first, it was supposed that Madame de Longueville loved Coligny. Then, that the tale might not lack interest, it was asserted that she did. Hence the other invention, that she herself had placed the sword in the hand of Coligny, and that d'Estrades, commissioned to challenge the Duke de Guise, having told Coligny that the duke would disavow the injurious words that had been attributed to him, and thus satisfy honor, Coligny had replied to him: "This has nothing to do with the matter; I have promised Madame de Longueville to fight him at the Place-Royale, and I cannot fail to do it."[2] It would not do to spoil so fine a

[1] Mademoiselle, *Mémoires*, vol. i., p. 74.
[2] Madame de Motteville, vol. i., p. 201.

tale, and Madame de Longueville would not have been the sister of the conqueror of Rocroy, a heroine worthy of being compared with those of Spain, who saw their lovers dying at their feet in tourneys, if she had not been present at the combat of Guise and Coligny. We are assured then that on the 12th of December she was in a hôtel of the Place-Royale, at the Duchess de Rohan's, and that there, concealed by a window-curtain, she witnessed the terrible encounter.

Then, as at the present day, it was poetry, that is, song, which placed the seal upon the popularity of an event. When the event was sad, the song was a complaint full of burlesque pathos, and always ridiculous. Such was that which, upon this occasion, ran through every circle, and was really sung, for we find it in the *Collection of noted Songs* of the Arsenal:[1]

Dry now your beauteous eyes,
Sweet Madame de Longueville;
Dry now your beauteous eyes,
Coligny's getting well.
If death he's seem'd to flee,
Oh blame him not therefore;
For as your lover, he
Would live forevermore.

After the song came the romance: Madame de Longueville had hers also. A wit of the times,

---

[1] It is also in Madame de Motteville, vol. i., p. 201.

whose name is unknown to us, composed on this occasion a novel, in which, under fictitious names, and mingling falsehood with truth, he relates the touching adventure which then occupied all Paris. We have discovered this novel of the middle of the seventeenth century in the library of the Arsenal and in the National Library.[1] Its title is: *Story of Agésilan and Isménie;* that is, the story of Coligny and Madame de Longueville. It has the advantage of being very short. Not daring to give it entire, we will partially exhibit this little monument of the growing celebrity of Madame de Longueville.

It must be understood that Isménie loved Agésilan in the most tender manner possible, and she loved him before being married to Amilcar, the Duke de Longueville, by order of her father and of her mother, Antenor and Simiane, M. the Prince and Madame the Princess. Isménie has for an enemy Roxane, Madame de Montbazon, jealous of her beauty, and then follow two portraits of Isménie and Roxane,

---

[1] Library of the Arsenal, small in-4o, lettered on the back, *Fr. Jurisprudence*, 19 (B). "It contains: 1st, Proposals for the reform of Abbeys and Priories; 2d, Fable of the Lion and of the Fox; 3d, Story of M. de Coligny and of Madame de Longueville."—National Library, *Mélanges*, vol. cclxi., in-12°, comprising a collection of songs, letters of Madame de Courcelles, pretended letters of different ladies to Fouquet, and in the midst the history of Agésilan and Isménie. In comparing the two manuscripts, we find but little difference between them.

which are historically exact. "Roxane was wounded by the praises bestowed upon Isménie on account of her beauty, which was truly wonderful. Her hair of a pale yellow, her eyes blue; the whiteness of her complexion and her form were incomparable; her spirit gentle, insinuating, and even pleasing, gave her the approbation of all the world. Roxane, possessed of a beauty and disposition very different, had not so many admirers of her grace as Isménie, although many preferred her beauty. Her hair was of a light brown; her eyes black and well formed, emitting a fire which penetrated the most insensible hearts; her aspect, proud and haughty, inspired fear rather than love; her spirit was cruel, full of violence. It would not do to be at variance with her."

The following is one of the conversations of the two lovers, not so long, fortunately, as those of Astrée and of the great Cyrus, but which possesses their agreeable insipidity, their melancholy sentimentality: "Isménie was walking pensively along a stream which watered the woods of Mirabelle (Chantilly). Suddenly she saw a man emerge from among the thick trees, who, pale and dejected, came and cast himself at her feet. She at once recognized Agésilan, who said to her: 'What! my princess, will you abandon me after so many promises of firmness? In refusing the match which is offered to you, will you not show to the world that my princess has as much fidelity as beauty, and that her word is not to be shaken when she has given it? If you have still any remembrance of the unhappy Agésilan, and of the tenderness which you have had for him, give him one more month before you consent to this marriage. The term is short for an affection which will cost me my life.' 'Agésilan,' said Isménie, 'God knows, if my own feelings were consulted, whether I would belong to any other than to you! For this I have done more than duty demanded: I have long resisted the orders of Antenor and Simiane. I have passed days and nights in weeping the loss of my dear Agésilan. All that I can do is to preserve for him continually my esteem and my friendship.' She embraced him for the last time, and entered the château without waiting for his reply."

Agésilan, in despair, set out to rejoin the army, commanded by the brother of Isménie, Marcomir, Duke d'Enghien, and we are presented with a narrative of the battle of Rocroy, correct enough, except in two particulars. The author does not seem to have been acquainted with the bold and skilful manœuvre which decided the victory, and which we have endeavored to describe. He has also given to Coligny, upon this great occasion, a part which he did not perform. In the novel, Agésilan takes the place of

Gassion, and commands the right wing, whilst Gassion commands the left in place of La Ferté-Seneterre and the Marshal de l'Hôpital; for it is doubtless Gassion who is spoken of under the name of Hilla or Hillarius, "an old colonel of horse, now[1] major-general, a soldier of fortune, but who had occupied every post, having great courage and firmness." Marcomir had confided the right wing to Agésilan, "being sure of his fidelity and of his great courage." Agésilan seeks death, and, according to the rules of romance, he finds only glory, with many wounds, it is true, which will afterwards explain his languor and his weakness. Among other exploits, he has an encounter with Alaric, king of the Goths. Marcomir, on his part, performs extraordinary actions, and kills, with his own hand, the chief of the hostile army. As Agésilan, Coligny is here put in the place of Gassion, so d'Estrades, friend of Coligny, is substituted, under the name of Théodate, for the brave Sirot, who commanded the reserve, and contributed so much to the success of the battle.

The novel describes faithfully the conduct of d'Enghien, Marcomir, after the victory. "After having rendered thanks to God for so great a victory, Mar-

---

[1] The word *now* shows that the novel was composed before the death of Gassion, who was slain before Lens in 1647.

comir returned to his camp. He was slightly wounded, had two horses killed under him, and did in this action all that a good general and a great captain can do: he took great care of the wounded, and he visited them every day." He could not fail to take particular care of Agésilan, his kinsman, and of Théodate; he took them with him to Lutétie, where they received all the praises which their fine actions merited.

In the novel, as well as in some memoirs, it is Roxane, Madame de Montbazon, who invents and counterfeits the two famous letters, in order to dishonor and destroy Isménie. She tries to compel her lover, Florizel, the Duke de Guise, to maintain that these letters are veritable; and not being able to get his consent to such an unworthy action, she asks him to express himself at least with some doubt as to the matter. Florizel has the weakness to please her in this; his words are promptly exaggerated and envenomed, and it is everywhere reported that Florizel defends loudly the truth of these letters, and declares himself ready to maintain it against Agésilan himself, "in whatever manner he may choose." Then comes the indignation of Queen Amalasonte, Anne of Austria, against Isménie, whom she believes guilty; the great wrath of Antenor and of Simiane, M. the Prince and Madame the Princess, against their daughter, and the despair of the latter, for the two imaginary letters by Roxane are much stronger than those which were written by Madame de Fouquerolles to Maulevrier, and which were attributed to Madame de Longueville. First letter: "I cannot suffer you to remain any longer in the sadness into which you are plunged. Your constancy has entirely gained me. Come this evening to the avenue of the Sicamores, near the baths of Diane. I will tell you what I wish you to do." The other letter: "I believe that you are pleased with me, dear Agésilan; but if the walk in the avenue of the Sicamores has pleased you more, the one which I now invite you to take will not please you less. Come, alone, at ten o'clock this evening, through the garden gate; you will find Lydie, who will show you where I am. Adieu."

These two rendezvous are well enough imagined to explain the irritation of Isménie, and to account for the manner in which she drove Agésilan to avenge her, as well for her success in procuring for him a skilful second in Théodate. The duel had been decided upon "in a council held at the house of Isménie, at which Marcomir and Agésilan were present." The preparations for the encounter and the details are less striking and less romantic in the tale than in the history. The scene in it is faithfully related, but much abridged in regard to the two principal adversaries; the intervention of the Duke d'Enghien is more marked.

"It was agreed that the meeting should take place at two o'clock in the afternoon, at the Place des Nymphes (Place-Royale). Florizel was to come with a second, a page, and a lackey; Agésilan and Théodate were to do the same; the two carriages were to meet before the house of Caliste, and the coachmen were to beat each other with their whips in order to pretend that it was a chance fight. Things were conducted according to arrangement, and the balconies and the windows of the houses were filled with ladies. Chrysante and Théodate (Bridieu and d'Estrades) were the first to seize their swords. Chrysante is a gentleman of merit, brave, and one of the strongest men in the world. He is governor of a considerable stronghold on the frontier of Belgium. Théodate, in the first place, gives him a thrust in the body; he at the same time receives one in the arm. Chrysante, feeling incommoded by the loss of blood, wished to make use of his strength and to engage closely with Théodate; he embraced him with both arms, and pressed him with so much violence that, notwithstanding his great wound, he would have strangled Théodate, if the latter had not made an effort to withdraw himself from his hands. It was so great that they both fell to the ground, without a victory on either side, and were separated immediately by persons of quality who arrived upon the spot. In the mean time Florizel and Agésilan were both engaged. Théodate thought it was time to separate them, when he saw the poor Agésilan stretched upon the ground, disarmed. Florizel leaves him in order to meet Théodate, and to embrace him and seek his friendship. He says to him: "I am sorry for the sad condition in which you will find Agésilan. He has quarrelled with me wantonly; I protest to you, with truth, that I have never offended him. Théodate replied briefly enough to this compliment, being in haste to reach Agésilan, whom he finds unconscious, by reason of the dissatisfaction occasioned by his ill-luck,—a dissatisfaction which, in the end, carried him to his grave. At this moment, Marcomir, and several princes and nobles of the court, arrived in the Place des Nymphes. Marcomir placed Agésilan and Théodate in one of his carriages, and gave them an apartment in his hôtel for the safety of their persons."

"Not many days before, the senate had issued a decree against duels, which condemned to death all those who engaged in them. Amalasonte, wishing the decree to be executed according to its tenor, ordered the arrest of Agésilan and Théodate as aggressors, but the proceedings were less rigorous against Florizel and Chrysante. Marcomir complained loudly, and the apprehensions which Amalasonte had lest the matter might produce a civil war—all the court having arranged themselves upon one side or the other—occasioned a command that the affair should pass for an accidental encounter, and that the king should issue letters of pardon; which was done to the satisfaction of all concerned."

Here the romance resumes its rights, and, carrying Madame de Longueville to the bed of the dying Coligny, places in the mouths of both of them those pathetic speeches which never fail to produce an effect upon readers less sensible to true art, than to what is touching in situations of this kind.

"The wounds which Agésilan had received, grew worse every day. The surgeons considered them mortal. Théodate did not care for his own. He was continually by the side of Agésilan, who, feeling his strength diminishing, said to Théodate: I have one request to make of you, and that is, that you will compel Isménie to come and see me for the last time, and that you will be the sole witness to what I have to say to her. Théodate having been assured by the physicians and surgeons that Agésilan could not survive the day, hastened to find Isménie, and to persuade her to come and say adieu to Agésilan, which she did with extreme grief. As soon as Agésilan saw her, the color returned to his face, and the emotion occasioned by beholding her whom he loved dearly, gave him the strength to say: 'Madame, since I have lost you, I have desired nothing more than to die in your service. God has heard my prayers. I cannot be happy so long as I cannot possess you. My passion was too strong to remain contented in the world. I render you thanks for the goodness with which you permit me to tell you that I die for you, and glad that I can no longer trouble your repose.' And, stretching out his hand to her, he said, 'Adieu, my dear Isménie,' and immediately breathed his last. After the final adieu of Agésilan which accompanied his last sigh, Isménie remained some time motionless. Then suddenly she threw herself upon his body, embraced him, took his hands in hers, moistened them with her tears, and, in a clear voice, said: 'Must I survive the most faithful and sincere lover that the world ever saw! Is this, my dear Agésilan, the recompense that you should expect from the ungrateful Isménie? Her alone thou hast loved, and when she abandoned thee, thy despair drove thee to seek death upon the battle-field, where thy great courage, thy reputation, and thy great actions rendered thee immortal; and after that thou comest to breathe thy last before my eyes, and to tell me that thou hast never known joy since losing me, and that thou dost die contented since thou canst not possess me! . . . . Receive, dear and faithful friend, these tears and this endless regret for thy loss, which will pierce my heart a thousand times each day. Receive the atonement which I make thee for all my severity and for all the pains which I have caused thee. Ah! miserable me! what will become of me? Where shall I go? Let me die of regret and of love. I will quit thee no more; I will remain beside thee.' And, embracing him, she kissed his eyes and his face with transports of tenderness, sufficient to break the heart of any one."

But let us bear in mind that all these tender sentiments are poetical inventions of the author of the novel. To render Madame de Longueville more touching, she has been represented as sharing the passion which she inspired. But nothing authorizes us to suppose that she was in love with Coligny. She loved him as one of the companions of her infancy, as one of the comrades of her brother, as a gentleman of nearly her own rank, whose homage she had no reason to reject, and who pleased her by a persevering and devoted tenderness. She permitted him to sigh for her, and to declare himself her loyal knight after the Spanish fashion, according to the principles of Madame de Sablé and of the *précieuses* of the hôtel de Rambouillet, who did not forbid men to serve and to adore them, but in the most respectful fashion. Such were the manners of this epoch. A gentleman did not pass for a well-bred man if he had not a mistress, that is, a lady to whom he paid particular homage, and whose colors he wore at fêtes and on the battle-field. There was not a beauty, however virtuous, who had not lovers, that is, gentlemen who sighed for her in truth and honorably. The Duchess d'Aiguillon, presenting her young nephew, the Duke de Richelieu, to the elder Mademoiselle Du Vigean, begged her to make an *honnête* man of him; and to this end she exhorted the young man seriously to fall in love with the beautiful lady.[1] Madame de Longueville suffered thus the assiduous attentions of Coligny. Her coquetry was flattered by them, while neither her virtue nor even her reputation were sullied. Let us add that she was surrounded by the best examples. The young Du Vigean, her dearest friend, resisted the conqueror of Rocroy; Mademoiselle de Brienne was wholly devoted to her husband, M. de Gamache; Julie de Rambouillet did not hastily yield to the long passion of Montausier, and Isabelle de Montmorency herself did no more than listen to the tender proposi-

[1] Madame de Motteville, vol. iv., p. 42.

tions of Dandelot. Retz affirms that the love was all on the side of Coligny, and he says that he was thus informed by Condé himself; but who is not acquainted with the frivolity of Retz? Who would wish to rely on his testimony when he is alone, and in relation to matters in which he has not personally mingled? In 1643, Retz had hardly the secret of his own intrigues. The well-informed Madame de Motteville, who, at a later period, will not conceal the fall of Madame de Longueville, may be believed when she affirms that in 1643,[1] "she had still a great reputation for virtue and prudence," and that "she erred only in not hating adoration and praise." Finally, we have a decisive testimony, that of La Rochefoucauld. He was at once the friend of Maulevrier and of Coligny; he was therefore well acquainted with the whole affair. Now, he who, at a future day, will turn against Madame de Longueville,—will reveal her weakness, will enlarge her faults, will strive to blacken her character,—declares that, until a certain period—at which we have not yet arrived—all those who attempted to please the sister of Condé, *strove in vain.*[2] After Coligny, the brave and presumptuous Miossens, afterwards Marshal

---

[1] Madame de Motteville, vol. i., pp. 174–197.

[2] *Mémoires* de La Rochefoucauld, Coll. Petitot, vol. li., p. 393.

d'Albret, paid very assiduous court to Madame de Longueville, and he failed like the others. She was too young still, and too recently drawn from the habits of her pure and pious youth; she had not yet reached the age so fatal to the most virtuous intentions: her hour had not yet come. It came at a later period, when Madame de Longueville had become better acquainted with the world and life, and had longer breathed the air of her times; when her brother had forgotten the chaste grandeur of his first loves; when the friend who could sustain her, the beautiful and noble Mademoiselle Du Vigean, was no more beside her; when her husband was at a distance; when, finally, weary of combating, and more than ever carried away by wit and heroic appearances, she met a person, still young and handsome, of great bravery, who passed for a model of chivalrous devotion, who could skilfully interest her self-love in his ambitious projects, and seduce her by the attractions of glory. La Rochefoucauld was the first who touched the soul of Madame de Longueville; he says so, and we believe him. Their connection commenced a little before or a little after the embassy of Munster, their intimacy at the close of 1647 or at the beginning of 1648, and the fulness of their love continued between 1648 and 1652. In 1643, Madame de Longueville was still occupied with the noble and graceful gallantry which she saw everywhere in honor, which she heard celebrated at the hôtel de Rambouillet as well as at the hôtel de Condé, in the great verses of Corneille and in the trifling verses of Voiture. She delighted in exhibiting the power of her charms. A thousand adorers pressed around her. Coligny was perhaps nearest to her heart, but had not, however, entered it. But one cannot, with impunity, trifle with love. It will some day cost Madame de Longueville many tears. Its victim at this time was the eldest of the Châtillons, who perished, in the flower of his youth, by the hand of the eldest of the Guises, to avenge her whom he loved. This tragic adventure, quickly spread by all the echoes of the *salons*, by song and romance, cast a gloom upon the destiny of Madame de Longueville, and gave her, at an early period, a fame at once aristocratic and popular, which prepared her wonderfully to play a great part in that other tragi-comedy, heroic and gallant, called the Fronde.

CHAPTER IV.

1644 to 1649.

Campaigns of Condé in Flanders and on the Rhine—Congress and peace of Munster—Madame de Longueville at Munster—Her portrait by Van Hull—Her return to France—Her brother, the Prince de Conti—Sonnets of Voiture and of Benserade—La Rochefoucauld—Commencement of his connection with Madame de Longueville—The first Fronde—Noble conduct of Condé—Madame de Longueville at the hôtel de Ville—Birth of Charles de Paris, Count de Saint-Paul—Peace of 1649.

We have passed over the most truly beautiful period of the youth of Madame de Longueville, that wherein the splendor of her success was not at the expense of her virtue. The time approaches in which she is about to yield to the manners of her age, and to the long combated wants of her heart. The love which she inspired in others, she is, in turn, about to feel herself, and to engage her, at the age of twenty-eight or twenty-nine years, in a fatal connection, which will make her forget all her duties, and turn her most brilliant qualities against herself, against her family, and against France.

In order to measure the fault of Madame de Longueville, it is necessary to know to what grandeur the house of Condé had reached by its faithful service of king and country.

In the history of France, there are no more glorious years than the first six of the Regency of Anne of Austria and of the government of Mazarin,—tranquil at home after the defeat of the party of the Importants, triumphant upon every battle-field, from 1643 to 1649, from the victory of Rocroy to that of Lens, connected by so many other victories, and crowned by the treaty of Westphalia. It is the house of Condé which occupies nearly the whole of this memorable epoch, or therein, at least, plays the most conspicuous part. In the council, M. the Prince seconds Mazarin, as he had done Richelieu, and shares with him the government. The intrepid Brézé, opening the list of the great admirals of the seventeenth century, holds in check or disperses, in the Mediterranean, the fleets of Spain. M. de Longueville, charged with the greatest embassy of the times, places in the diplomatic balance the weight of his name, of his moderation, and of his magnificence. As to the young Condé,—who has not read, at least in Bossuet, his campaigns in Flanders and upon the Rhine? We have shown how valuable to France was the victory of Rocroy, in 1643; those which followed were not less necessary.

We have for some time been permitted to speak of

Condé as of a young hero, who owed all his success to the ascendency of an irresistible courage. Let us beware of making him a paladin of the middle age, or a brilliant grenadier like such or such a marshal of the empire, or a captain of the family of Alexander, of Cæsar, and of Napoleon. Like them, Condé had doubtless a genius for war, and, as well as Alexander, he excelled especially in execution, and fearlessly exposed his person; but it seems that the splendor of his bravery had concealed the grandeur and originality of his conceptions, as his extreme youth, at Rocroy, had caused a forgetfulness of the fact that for many years he had studied war with passion, and had already made three campaigns under the most renowned masters. If this were the proper place, and if I dared to encounter ridicule by setting myself up as a military man, I would like to compare the campaigns of Condé, in Flanders and upon the Rhine, with those of General Bonaparte in Italy. They have many things in common: the youth of the two generals,[1] that of their principal lieutenants, the political grandeur of the results, the novelty of the manœuvres, the same strategy, the

---

[1] Napoleon was twenty-six years of age at the time of his first battle, that of Montenotte, and thirty at the time of that of Marengo. Condé was not quite twenty-two years of age at Rocroy, and he was twenty-seven at Lens.

same calculations served by the same audacity, by the same activity, by the same obstinacy. It is degrading the art of war to measure military success by the number of combatants, for we should thus make Tamerlane and Gengis-Khan the two greatest captains of the world.

The general of the army of Italy, like Condé, had little more than twenty or twenty-five thousand men drawn up in his greatest battles.[1] I can say to the honor of Condé, that he always had before him the best troops and the best generals of his times, among others, Mercy, the first captain of Germany during the seventeenth century.[2] At one time he had under his command only an army composed of different nations, whose jealousies, and even defections, be-

[1] General Bonaparte entered Italy in 1796, with 30,000 men under arms. He had at most from 15,000 to 20,000 at Montenotte; 20,000 at Castiglione; 13,000 only at Arcola; 16,000, at most, at Rivoli. It is true that at Marengo he had 28,000; but, for conception and execution, who would compare Marengo with Arcola and Rivoli? These were the most scientific and boldest campaigns of Italy, the most resembling those of Rocroy and of Fribourg.

[2] General Bonaparte had no adversaries like Mercy. Beaulieu, apparently thinking himself too strong, had so scattered his troops, that at Montenotte he fought with but half of his army. Wurmser, at Castiglione, committed the same error. D'Alvinzy was superior to them, and at Arcola and at Rivoli he yielded only to the unexpected grandeur of the manœuvres of the French general. Melas fought well at Marengo, as did also General Bonaparte, but neither of them performed any remarkable manœuvre; and this battle would have been lost but for the arrival of Desaix, as Waterloo was lost because Grouchy was not Desaix.

trayed his greatest designs. At another time he was at the head of fatigued and discouraged troops, whose whole strength was in himself alone. And then —which is, in my eyes, the most certain evidence of a great man—he founded an immense school: he left to France many great generals formed by his lessons, prepared by his hands, and who, at a great distance from him and after him, gained victories. To him are we, in a great measure, indebted for Turenne, who, by seeing his actions at Fribourg and at Nortlingen, added more and more activity and audacity to his other qualities. We are indebted to him for Luxembourg and Conti. We are also indebted to him for many others, who might perhaps have equalled those already mentioned, but whose bright hopes were too suddenly extinguished, Gèvres, Laval, La Moussaye, Châtillon. To all this add that magnanimity of a high-born man, who, instead of attributing the honor of success to himself alone, shared it with all those who served him well, and took pleasure in praising Gassion and Sirot after the victory of Rocroy, Turenne after Fribourg and Nortlingen, and Châtillon after Lens.[1]

---

[1] I know nothing more noble than the dispatches of Condé, announcing his different victories. He says very little in them of himself, and much of others. During his retirement at Chantilly, his friends urged him to write his military memoirs; he refused, saying that he would

Condé conquered at Rocroy by the very simple manœuvre which we have pointed out.[1] The problem was, to arrive in the shortest time and with the greatest force upon the point which was to decide the day. It was evident that, the left wing of the enemy being dispersed, but his right wing victorious and threatening to crush all in its way, it was necessary, at every hazard, to arrest and destroy it. To reach this in the speediest manner possible, from the height of the battle-field where Condé was, the most direct road was to make a passage through the Spanish army, by forcing his last line, and falling afterwards like a thunderbolt upon the rear of his triumphing wing. If the infantry, whose overthrow was sought, had been that of the Count de Fontaine,

---

be obliged to blame sometimes estimable generals, and to speak well of himself. Never was any one less a charlatan. In this respect, Turenne resembled Condé. What injures somewhat in my estimation the memoirs of Napoleon, is that ardent and continual self-preoccupation, which sees himself only everywhere, refers every thing to himself, confesses no fault, enlarges the least actions, praises none but mediocre men, depreciates eminent merit, treats Moreau and Kleber as he would have done some of his marshals, and prepares for himself everywhere a pedestal. But we must not forget that Napoleon was writing in exile and in misfortune, and that he was reduced to defend his own glory. See in Lenet, edit. Michaud, several letters of Condé to Mazarin, after Fribourg, after Lerida, after the taking of Ipres and the retaking of Furnes, especially after the battle of Lens. In giving an account of this affair, the secretary of the prince had written: *our victory*. Condé effaced the last word, and substituted *combat*. (Unpublished part of Memoirs of Lenet, pp. 499–515.)

[1] See chapter iii.

it would have remained firm, checked Condé, and achieved his destruction; but he knew that this infantry was a mixture of Italians, Walloons, and Germans: he hoped, therefore, to succeed by dint of energy. For this reason he led the charge himself, and performed prodigies of valor with the most severe calculation. Afterwards, when he was complimented on his courage, he replied that he had never shown any except when it was necessary. It is true that heroes alone have audacity at will. He conducted himself almost in the same manner during the following year, 1644, in his great combats with Mercy, near Fribourg. Finding it impossible to separate any of the divisions of the imperial army, which were protected by formidable intrenchments, he attacked them himself with that French fury to which every thing yields;[1] at the same time he sent Turenne, during the night, to a great distance, through frightful gorges, as did Bonaparte in the marshes of Arcola,[2] to take in flank and rear the hostile army,

---

1 It was at the attack of the lines of Fribourg that he threw into the enemy's intrenchments his baton of command, indicating thereby his resolution to conquer or perish.

2 Napoleon's manœuvre of quitting Verona, in order to go around Caldiero, whom he could not attack in front, and to surprise Alvinzy in the marshes, where valor could make up for numbers, has been, and cannot be too much praised. There was prudence and audacity in it. General Bonaparte, knowing that he would be lost if he did not pass the bridge of Arcola, allowed the destruction of his best lieutenants,

which would have been destroyed, if Mercy, warned in season and confounded by such a manœuvre, had not hastily escaped. In the second battle of Fribourg, Condé renewed this same manœuvre, sending Turenne to a still greater distance than before, in order to cut off all retreat for Mercy, whilst he attacked him in front, and to crush him in his camp or force him to capitulate. The vigilant Mercy escaped a second time; but his retreat, admirable as it was, resembled no less a defeat, for he lost not only the honor of his arms and of the field of battle, but all of his artillery and a part of his troops.

In 1645, Mercy and Condé met again. Mercy had just fought with Turenne at Mariendal. This victory had inflated the courage of the Imperialists, and the emperor and the King of Bavaria were unwilling to make peace. Condé, in again taking command of a defeated army, found it, as in the preceding year, composed of 5000 Weimarians, survivors of the battle of Mariendal, 4000 Swedes, 6000 Hessians, and 8000 Frenchmen, which he had with him. With these 23,000 he conceived the plan of the campaign which was afterwards partly executed by Moreau

---

and barely escaped death himself. On this occasion, he showed himself great by the genius which conceives and by the heroism which executes; and he showed himself the equal of the Alexanders and Condés.

and completed by Napoleon. He resolved to risk a great battle with Mercy, and after having routed him, to march upon Munich and Vienna, and to dictate peace to the emperor in his capital. This plan failed because Condé was at the head of a combined army; because the Swedes and the Hessians refused to follow the French general to such a distance, and because the Swedes even withdrew. Condé could not expect any aid from France, which was exhausted in order to send five armies into Spain, into Italy, into Lorraine, into Flanders, and upon the Rhine. He abandoned therefore his greatest military conception with sorrow and rage, as did Hannibal when he was compelled to quit Italy: it was his wish to exterminate the army of Mercy. The latter, who knew the man with whom he had to deal, had taken a position quite as strong as that of Fribourg—a position which protected him against the favorite manœuvres of Condé—to cut off the enemy or surprise him at a distance in flank or rear. Turenne declared that to attack an enemy thus intrenched was ruinous; and Napoleon, whom no one will accuse of timidity, was of the same opinion.[1] Condé replied as a politician rather than as a military man, that it was in vain to undertake by any manœuvre to drive Mercy from a position wisely

[1] *Mémoires*, vol. v., p. 20.

chosen; that it was necessary, therefore, either to attack him or to retreat, and that to retreat would shake the confidence of all our allies, after the defeat of Mariendal and the defection of the Swedes. France was in need of a victory. Condé gained that of Nortlingen, but he gained it, thanks to two accidents upon which he had no right to count—thanks also to the inspiration of a great character. It must be confessed that in execution Condé was never greater. He saw at once that every thing depended upon Mercy's centre. He made it his own business to attack it. He had one horse slain under him, two wounded, and twenty cuts upon his arms and clothes. Marsin, who under him commanded the French centre, was dangerously wounded, and the intrepid La Moussaye was disabled. The French and the Imperialists, by turns conquerors and conquered, performed prodigies of valor. It was a frightful butchery. Mercy perished in it. In the mean time, Jean de Wert, who commanded the left wing, descended from the height which he occupied, crushed the right wing of the French, and dispersed our reserve, notwithstanding the efforts of his two chiefs, Chabot and Arnauld.[1] It would have been fatal to the whole

[1] This is the same Arnauld from whom we have so many pretty verses in the style of Voiture, and on account of whose absence Madame de Rambouillet regrets that she cannot reply to Godeau. See chap. ii.

army, if, instead of amusing himself with pursuing the flying and pillaging the baggage, Jean de Wert had thrown himself upon the rear of our half-destroyed centre, and pressed our left wing between his victorious squadrons and the still entire division of General Gleen. This error, and the death of Mercy, saved Condé, because he knew how to profit by them with incomparable promptitude. He saw that, after having lost his right wing, his reserve, and a great part of his centre, to try to retreat with his left wing was an operation apparently prudent, but really rash, before an enemy which had still great masses of infantry, much artillery, and a redoubtable cavalry; he saw that it was better to maintain the combat, and that by exposing himself to peril, he might possibly conquer. This rapid glance of a strong mind, which seizes and embraces the only means of safety, however perilous it may be, is the characteristic of the genius of Condé. All wounded as he was, harassed with fatigue, but drawing new vigor from the grandeur of his resolution, he places himself at the head of the left wing of Turenne, dashes, as if in the very beginning of the battle, upon the right wing of the enemy, plunges into its midst, and makes prisoner of its commander; then, turning to the right, he throws himself upon the centre of the Imperialists, rescues his own, rallies it, leads it anew to the combat, and, master of the battle-field, prepares himself to meet Jean de Wert, who, returning from his useless pursuit, learning the death of Mercy[1] and the capture of Gleen, amazed at the disaster produced by his absence, dares neither to attack nor to await Condé, but gathers together his shattered army, and flies to Donauwerth. Condé had, in this second combat, another horse killed under him; he also received a pistol-shot, and indeed barely survived his victory. It was at this time that he suffered from that severe sickness, on recovery from which he found that he had lost with his blood and his strength all his passion for Mademoiselle Du Vigean.[2]

Condé is one of the small number of captains who have no less excelled in the art of besieging than in that of combating.[3] After Rocroy, in 1643, he took Thionville, one of the first fortified places of the times. In 1644, he took Philipsbourg, which commanded the upper Rhine. In 1646, having had the wisdom to consent to serve under the Duke d'Orleans, in order to quiet the distrust and please the vanity of this prince; and although placed in command of

---

[1] Allow me to repeat here that Mercy, whom the Spaniards created Count de Fuentes, and Fontaine, were two French gentlemen, one of Lorraine, the other of Burgundy.

[2] See close of chap. ii.

[3] In Italy, Napoleon never undertook a siege properly so called.

the army only at the close of the campaign, he terminated it by a memorable siege, in which he covered himself with glory: he took Dunkirk on the 11th of October,[1] 1646.

---

[1] The Prince de Condé has left a name in the science of fortification. He studied while at Bourges under the engineer Sarrazin, who rendered Montrond a very difficult place to be taken. When he went to Burgundy, he paid great attention to this part of the military art. There is preserved in the depot of fortifications an atlas of the strongholds of Burgundy, drawn by the hand of Condé: *Plan of the capital cities and frontiers of the Duchy of Burgundy, Bresse, and Gex, made at Dijon, January* 7, 1640, with this dedication:

To MY FATHER.

SIR—This work which I present belongs to you, since all that is mine is yours. I have never been able to see you in the command of armies without thinking of war myself; and I could not believe that my study of fortifications would be agreeable to you, unless continued. If you deign to think well of these efforts of my mind and hand, I desire no other approbation of my labor, as I shall never have any other wish than to live and die in the obedience and respect due to you from him who is, sir,

Your very humble and very obedient son and servant,

LOUIS DE BOURBON.

Following this are eleven plans upon vellum of the strongholds of Burgundy, with remarks.

The great sieges which Condé undertook so successfully, particularly those of Thionville and of Dunkirk, are the admiration of military men. After his return to France in 1660, he was continually consulted upon all projects of fortification, and his name, as well as his opinions, appear in the official correspondence of the department of war, especially during 1664, 1670, and 1673, until 1675, when he retired from the service, and left Vauban to act alone. Fontenelle, in his eulogy of Sauveur, says, that it was in his frequent visits to Chantilly and in his conversations with Condé, that Sauveur conceived the idea of his treatise upon fortification.

Accustomed to repair the errors of others, Condé went, in 1647, to take the place of Count d'Harcourt, who had just made a failure before Lerida. Mazarin had wished, several times, to send Condé to Catalonia; his father, M. the Prince, had always opposed it, and all his friends dissuaded him from accepting this command. He certainly showed great deference for Mazarin, by quitting the ordinary theatre of his exploits for a country where it was necessary to engage in a petty war, with an army incapable of giving battle, and, at most, fit only to sustain itself before the enemy. When every one was making sport of the Count d'Harcourt, who had been unable to take Lerida, Condé had the good sense and generosity to defend this excellent general: he thus in advance defended himself. In fact, having arrived in his turn before Lerida, and receiving from France neither the troops which had been promised to him, nor the munitions and artillery, of which he was in absolute need, and not having sufficient force to meet the Spanish army, and not being able to think of assaulting Lerida with a handful of half-dead soldiers, he had the courage to raise the siege and to make a good retreat, preferring the safety of the army to his own reputation. This conduct, sustained by his accustomed hauteur, did him the greatest honor, and proved that he was master of himself and knew how

23*

to employ by turns prudence or audacity according as circumstances demanded.

Thus, at Lens in 1648, finding the Archduke Léopold in a position as formidable as that of Mercy at Nortlingen, he saw that it would be highly imprudent to tempt fortune a second time; and, knowing that he had not now to deal with Mercy, he undertook to draw the Archduke Léopold and General Beck upon more favorable ground, in a plain where the principal force of the French army, the gendarmery, commanded by Châtillon, might have a great advantage. Numbers, abundance, and discipline were on the side of the Spaniards; misery and audacity on that of the French. Behind the centre of the archduke were towns and hamlets, forming natural intrenchments. His right, composed of all that remained of the old national bands, rested upon the city of Lens. His left wing was posted upon an eminence, which could not be reached except through the most narrow paths. It was necessary to manœuvre with infinite art to induce an enemy to abandon such an impregnable position. Condé commanded a false retreat, which explained perfectly the weakness of the French army. Beck, deceived, detached the Lorraine cavalry to disturb, and, if possible, to cut in pieces our rear guard, which was promptly enough broken and thrown into confusion.

Châtillon marched to their aid with his gendarmery; he drove back the Lorraine troops, and threatened them with slaughter. They could not be abandoned. The archduke sent all his cavalry to their assistance. The combat began; the whole of the hostile army moved and descended into the plain. This was precisely what Condé desired. The very same manœuvre that had failed at Nortlingen, succeeded at Lens. The imperial army had still the immense disadvantage of being obliged to form as it advanced, while the French army had been since morning arranged in good order at the extremity of the plain, upon well-chosen ground. Condé relied especially upon the gendarmery of Châtillon; he had recalled it soon after the first engagement, and had placed it in the second line to give it time to refresh; afterwards, when the two contending bodies had become closely engaged, he let it loose again with its intrepid general, and, after being so useful at the beginning of the fight, it finally decided it by overthrowing every thing in its way. The Spanish infantry remained; it did not show the same obstinacy as at Rocroy, but it cried for life. Old General Beck conducted himself like Fontaine and Mercy: he fought like a lion, was wounded and taken, and he died of despair. The Archduke Léopold, after conducting himself well, escaped into the Pays-Bas with the Count de Fuensaldaigne.

The victory of Lens was as important and as useful as that of Rocroy: to it is due the recommencement of the negotiations of Munster and the conclusion of the treaty of Westphalia. This treaty was the result of the five great campaigns of Condé in Flanders and on the Rhine. Condé was there an armed negotiator, as we might say; M. de Longueville was, at Munster, a pacific negotiator.

Father Bougeant, in his estimable history of the treaty of Westphalia,[1] supposes that Mazarin sent the

[1] *History of the Wars and of the Negotiations which preceded the Treaty of Westphalia*, vol. iii., in-4o. To this work we must add the *Secret Negotiations touching the Peace of Munster and of Osnaburg, or General Collection of Preliminaries, Instructions, Letters, Memoirs, concerning these negotiations, from their commencement until their conclusion, in* 1648, 2 vol., in-fol., Hague, 1725. In vol. xxx. of the *Mélanges de Clerambault*, in the National Library, may be found a summary of all the correspondence of the French cabinet and of the embassy. We give a few extracts:

Year 1645.—June 3, Mazarin to M. de Longueville, complimenting him upon the interesting condition of his wife, and urging him to hasten his departure for Munster. Scarcely arrived, M. de Longueville writes to Mazarin, July 2, telling him that he has reconciled d'Avaux and Servien.

Year 1646.—June 22, Mazarin announces to M. de Longueville the departure of Madame de Longueville. July 24, M. de Longueville notifies Mazarin that he is going to meet Madame de Longueville. October 23, M. de Longueville thanks Mazarin for promising him the office of General of the Swiss.

Year 1647.—January 16, Mazarin to M. de Longueville: The king sends to him a gentleman, as well as to Madame de Longueville, announcing the death of M. the Prince. March 15, Mazarin to M. de

Duke de Longueville to Munster, "in order to remove from the court a prince capable of exciting troubles in it." But, in 1645, Mazarin had no more

---

Longueville, informing him that he cannot have the office of General of the Swiss, and offering him in lieu thereof the Château de Caen. March 25, M. de Longueville to the queen, in regard to the office of General of the Swiss. *Idem*, to Mazarin on the same subject. Dissatisfaction of M. de Longueville; he asks for his discharge; it is granted to him. May 17, M. de Longueville thanks Mazarin for the discharge which he has procured for him; he will not leave until the proper time. June 22, Mazarin complains to M. de Longueville of his last letter, in which he is charged with not desiring peace; he claims the contrary, and shows his resentment of the manner in which the Spaniards have acted. "France wishes peace, and will make it glorious." July 1, M. de Longueville assures his Eminence that his letter is far from bearing the interpretation which he has placed upon it; that he does not know him, which compels him to desire leave to return to France. Same day, d'Avaux writes to Mazarin that he had no part in the letter of M. de Longueville. July 13, Mazarin to M. de Longueville: he is very glad that the intention of his letter is such as he claims; he desires nothing in the world more ardently than peace, and wishes that Pegnaranda (the Spanish ambassador) would leave Munster, that he might have an opportunity to take a trip to Paris. Same day, Mazarin testifies to d'Avaux the pleasure which he experiences in having an understanding with his friends. Same day, important dispatch from Mazarin to Servien, in which he discovers all his thoughts: Treaty with Germany, or, at least, a grant of a truce in the Low Countries. "If nothing was to be done in Flanders and in Germany, war could be easily carried on in Spain and in Italy." July 22, M. de Longueville to Mazarin: The Swedes cannot be satisfied without giving them positive assurances of the establishment of Lutheranism. The Protestants propose to conclude without France. The departure of the Count de Trautmansdorf (imperial ambassador) with liberty to retire, of which he will avail himself as soon as possible. July 29, Mazarin begs M. de Longueville to defer his departure. August 9, Mazarin to M. de Longueville: How to treat with the Swedes. A gentleman of M. de Vandosme, carrying letters to the archduke, was arrested and conducted to Nancy. The Spaniards are far from peace. The King of Spain changes his manner of acting with the emperor. Trautmansdorf might have concluded something

troubles to fear, and the Duke de Longueville was not a man to create them: he suffered himself to be guided at that time, as well as the rest of his family,

---

advantageous for Sweden at the expense of France. August 19, M. de Longueville to Mazarin: The Neapolitans have driven off the Spaniards. Pegnaranda will do nothing until the close of the campaign. He will take this time to visit his Eminence. August 30, Mazarin expresses to M. de Longueville some apprehensions as to the design of his journey. August 30, confidential letter from Lyonne to Servien: he begs him to discover the cabals that M. d'Avaux has made against his Eminence. Orders are given to M. de Turenne to abolish the name of Weimarians. The conclusion of peace must not be deferred on account of the absence of M. de Longueville. M. d'Avaux seeks the protection of M. the Prince and of M. the Duke d'Orleans. September 6, Mazarin to M. de Longueville: Good effects apparently produced by the delay of his journey. September 16, M. de Longueville complains of the delay of business; he recommends to Mazarin the Marshal de La Mothe (who has just been arrested). October 7, renewed solicitations of M. de Longueville in behalf of the Marshal de La Mothe. October 15, M. de Longueville to Mazarin: He fears that the Hollanders may conclude their treaty without France. The enemies have received, with singular joy, the news of the death of M. de Gassion (killed at Lens). October 18, Mazarin informs M. de Longueville of the promotion of seven cardinals, among whom is his brother, the Cardinal de Sainte-Cecile. October 29, M. de Longueville recommends the Prince de Conti for the siege of Trèves or of Liége. November 1, Mazarin informs M. de Longueville that all their dispatches have fallen into the hands of the Spaniards. November 8, Mazarin imparts to M. de Longueville a proposition of marriage from the emperor with Mademoiselle. (See the *Memoirs* of Mademoiselle; also chapter i. of this work.) December 22, Mazarin to M. de Longueville: The Spaniards do not desire peace. Try to have it proclaimed that if peace is not established, it is Spain that has prevented it.

Year 1648.—January 6, M. de Longueville to Mazarin: It was the fault of the Imperialists and the Spaniards alone that peace was not concluded; all the others desired it. January 16, M. de Longueville is not of the opinion that Nancy should be given up without demolishing it. January 17, Mazarin imparts to M. de Longueville a proposition of marriage between his daughter, Mademoiselle de Longueville, and the Duke de

by the policy of its chief, M. the Prince. It is much easier to believe that it was the latter who gave the embassy of Munster to his son-in-law. Mazarin had not chosen him for his capacity, although he was not deficient in it, but to aid d'Avaux and Servien, who stood in need of him, and to give éclat to the French legation. He remained master of the negotiations, and the Condés must have been flattered to be at the head of the most important diplomatic affair, having already command of the fleet in the Mediterranean, and of the army upon the Rhine.

M. de Longueville had to pursue the great object at which the French cabinet had aimed from the time of Henry IV.,—the enfeebling of the empire to

---

Mantua. January 28, Confidential letter from Lyonne to Servien: There is much dissatisfaction with M. d'Avaux; he would have been recalled if he had not engaged M. de Longueville in his opinion. February 8, M. de Longueville announces his departure. February 23, having arrived at Trie, he writes to Mazarin a letter of compliments. March 23, d'Avaux, being found too favorable to M. de Lorraine, and too eager to make peace at any price, prepares to depart. April 27, Mazarin informs Servien that he is named minister, and charged with completing the negotiations. In the correspondence of July, frequent mention is made of the troubles of the parliament. Mazarin begs Servien to manage something in Alsace for M. de Turenne, in order to secure him. August 14, Servien gives to Mazarin the reasons for not pressing the treaty with Spain. August 21, dispatch of Mazarin: M. the Prince has just gained a battle against the archduke. France nevertheless wishes peace. If the Spaniards wish it, they will conclude it upon the proposed conditions; if not, it will be of no service to relax. September 17, he invites Servien to urge the peace with Germany, on account of the troubles.

the advantage of France. With this view it was that the very Christian king, the Cardinal Richelieu, and the Cardinal Mazarin united with the Protestant Gustavus Adolphus, drew him into the heart of Germany, him and after him his lieutenants, and sustained Protestant Holland against Catholic Spain. This struggle, which, for thirty years, was carried on with so much éclat, continued for more than twelve years at Osnabrück and at Munster. On the one side were Austria, Spain, and Bavaria, with the ecclesiastical electors of Mayence and of Cologne; on the other, the Protestant powers, Brandenburg, Saxony, Hesse, with their allies, Holland, Sweden, and France. The Protestant party wished to obtain the greatest concessions, and the Catholic party to make the fewest possible. They advanced and receded according to the vicissitudes of war. Richelieu had designated the man, who had all his confidence, Mazarin and the Count d'Avaux, of the powerful family of Messne, to represent France at Munster. When Mazarin succeeded Richelieu in the ministry, he named in his own place Count Abel Servien, uncle of the skilful and judicious Lyonne, who was to him what he had himself been to Richelieu. He retained d'Avaux, who had wit and penetration, uprightness and nobleness, with a degree of piety which made him acceptable to the Catholic powers, but which carried him a little too far to make him accommodating with them, and at the same time more anxious for the advantage of the Church than policy demanded. Servien alone was the depository of the thoughts of Mazarin, and Mazarin, like his predecessor, knew but one interest, that of the greatness of France. He was desirous of obtaining from the empire the whole of Alsace, with some strongholds upon the Rhine, in order to complete the legitimate development of France in that quarter. He had still another ambition, which Richelieu had bequeathed to him, and which he bequeathed to Lyonne: it was that of tearing from Spain the trade of Catalonia, where Richelieu and himself had cunningly carried the war against the Low Countries, without which France has really no northern frontier, and is exposed, after an unfortunate battle, to the passage of a hostile army even to the very walls of Paris. Such were the thoughts which occupied the mind of Mazarin, and which he pursued at once, by means of negotiations and by arms, with the mildness and constancy which characterized this great statesman.

M. de Longueville arrived at Munster on the 30th of June, 1645, at nearly the same time that his brother-in-law, the Duke d'Enghien, was going to take command of the army of the Rhine, in the place of Turenne, who had just suffered a very grave defeat at Mariendal. The victory of Nortlingen, of the 5th of August, 1645, gave the greatest strength to M. de Longueville; and the Duke of Bavaria, the second Catholic power of Germany, who had broken off negotiations after the battle of Mariendal, recommenced them eagerly after that of Nortlingen. The cession of Alsace was then almost gained; but victorious Mazarin could with difficulty renounce the hope which he had long entertained of acquiring the Low Countries from Spain in exchange for Catalonia. Therein resided all the difficulty of the negotiations, the knot which no skill could loosen, and which the sword alone could cut. It was reserved for Louis XIV., at the close of the seventeenth century, after having lost the three statesmen who, for a long time, formed his strength and his glory, Mazarin, Lyonne, and Colbert; it was reserved for him to abandon the schemes of his predecessors, and, when it was proposed that he should receive the Low Countries in return for his rights over Spain, to reject this favor of fortune, which Mazarin and Richelieu would have embraced with transports of joy; this he did for the sake of family interest, staking his own crown for the sake of placing one upon the head of his grandson, and jeopardizing the safety of France without giving to it, even for a quarter of a century, the alliance of Spain. We may remark in passing, that this incredible resolution, poorly covered with an appearance of grandeur, and the revocation of the Edict of Nantes, are the two great personal inspirations of Louis XIV.: they determine his policy, internal and external, compared with that of Mazarin, of Richelieu, and of Henri IV. It is impossible to recount all the efforts made by Mazarin, in 1648, to induce Spain to yield to him the Low Countries. He offered, with all Catalonia, the young Louis XIV. for the infanta Maria-Thérissa. At the same time he sent d'Estrades, with whom we have before become acquainted,[1] into Holland, in order to promote the arrangement which he so ardently desired: he went even so far as to propose Antwerp to the commerce of Holland. It was a powerful temptation; but Holland resisted it; she was weary of a war which must thus be prolonged; and besides, she was beginning to be less afraid of Spain, and was hoping a great advantage by acquiring a conquering neighbor instead of a feeble one. Spain, on her side, saw our horizon darkened with new troubles, and, full of hope, she broke off negotiations, made a separate treaty with Holland, and persuaded the emperor to unite with her in a last and powerful effort. One man alone was able to save France, menaced as it

[1] See preceding chapter.

was in 1643. This man was the conqueror of Rocroy. It was then that Condé, who was well acquainted with the position of affairs, engaged, upon the plains of Lens, on the 20th of August, 1648, in the memorable battle which we have described, in which he was as prudent as ever Turenne had been, and as bold as his own genius and circumstances permitted. From this moment negotiations were conducted with promptness. On the 24th of October, 1648, was signed, at Munster, the Treaty of Westphalia, which gave peace to Germany for a century, which there strengthened religious liberty, and which acknowledged all the conquests of France over the empire.[1]

Thanks to this treaty, Mazarin had now Spain alone in view, and he hoped soon to bring it to that point which could give to France a frontier on the north similar to that which it had just acquired on the south of Germany. He dreamed of obtaining, at the close of a few more fortunate campaigns, a treaty still more favorable than that of the Pyrenees, in 1660. He had in his hands the conqueror of Lens,

---

[1] The Treaty of Munster secured to France the sovereignty of the three bishoprics of Metz, Toul, and Verdun, of which it had been for a long time possessed; the sovereignty of Pignerol, which gave it the entry of Italy; the sovereignty of all Alsace, upper and lower, with that of Brissac and of Landau; in short, the right of garrison in the fortress of Philipsbourg.

whom he hoped to launch upon the Low Countries; it was in his power to send into Spain and into Italy, generals still superior to d'Harcourt and to Schomberg; he hoped to maintain or re-enkindle the insurrection of Naples: a magnificent future was before France. Who deprived her of this future? Who divided and exhausted her strength? Who made her, with a suicidal hand, shed her own best blood? Who sowed discord among the most illustrious of her captains? Who arrested Condé in his course, at the age of twenty-seven years, when he might yet have added so many victories to all those of his youth, when he might have planted the standard of France in Brussels or in Madrid?

The Fronde it was that committed the inexpiable crime of having stopped the rise of Condé and of French grandeur. And, in return, did it increase and develop our old national franchises? Far from that: by an inevitable reaction, it disgusted France, for a long time, with an anarchical liberty, incompatible with public order, with the force of the government and of the nation; it took away from royalty every species of counterpoise; it produced the despotism, at first intelligent and useful, afterwards improvident and grievous, of Louis XIV.

And now, what gave birth to the Fronde, or what sustained it? What raised up the old party of the

Importants, stifled, it would seem, under the laurels of Rocroy? What separated the princes of the blood from the crown? What turned against the throne that illustrious house of Condé, which, until then, had been its buckler and its sword? There were doubtless many general causes for all this; but it is impossible for us to conceal one, private, it is true, but which exercised a powerful and deplorable influence —the unexpected love of Madame de Longueville for one of the chiefs of the *Importants*, who had become one of the chiefs of the Fronde. Yes—I say it with regret—it was Madame de Longueville, who, joining the party of the malcontents, attracted thereto, at first, a part of her family, then her whole family, and thus precipitated it from the pinnacle of honor and glory to which so many services had elevated it.

Let us narrate, as rapidly as possible, what we know of Madame de Longueville, from the moment that we left her until the commencement of the year 1648.

No authentic documents, printed or in manuscript, authorize us to suppose that before the close of the year 1647, Madame de Longueville had ever passed the limits of fashionable gallantry. On the 4th of February, 1644, soon after the adventure of the letters, and of the tragic quarrel which followed it, she gave birth to a daughter, who received the name of her mother and of her brother, Charlotte Louise, Mademoiselle de Dunois, and who died on the 30th of April,[1] 1645. A year after, the 12th of January, 1646, she had a son, Charles d'Orleans, Count de Dunois, who was expected to succeed to the titles of his father, but who, ill-favored by nature, attempted, without success, various careers, and finally buried himself in the Church, at the close of the century, under the name of the Abbé d'Orleans. In 1647, she gave birth to a second daughter, Marie Gabrielle,

---

[1] *Gazette* of May 6, 1645. Died, April 30, about 2 o'clock in the morning, at the hôtel de Longueville, the Countess de Dunois, daughter, by the second marriage, of the Duke de Longueville, aged fourteen months. All the court having testified much regret at the death of this young princess, whose body, having been embalmed and placed in a lead coffin, was carried, on the second of this month (of May), to the great convent of the Carmelites, where the Duchess de Longueville, her mother, wished it to be interred near the tomb of the Mother Madeleine de Saint-Joseph; the pages and valets of the Duke and Duchess de Longueville, each with a flambeau of white wax, surrounding the hearse, followed by great numbers of others. It was presented at the door of the church, laid out upon white serge, with two breadths of white satin, charged with the scutcheons of Bourbon and Longueville, by the curate of Saint-Germain-l'Auxerrois to the Bishop d'Utique, coadjutor of Montauban, assisted by several ecclesiastics and fathers of the Oratoire de Saint-Magloire, who received it in the name of this monastery; and, having placed it under a canopy of silver-cloth ornamented with the same armorial bearings, covered with a pall of the same stuff bordered with ermine, and with a ducal crown of gold covered with a veil of gauze, after the usual benedictions and incensing, the nuns, to the number of sixty, came in a procession to the door of the monastery to receive the body, which was carried to the grave made in the cloister, and buried by the same bishop, with the ceremonies of the order of the Carmelites, whose garb this little princess wore.

who died in 1650. We shall presently speak of the last son, who was born during the Fronde.

Madame de Longueville was twenty-five years of age at the time of the duel between Coligny and Guise, in 1644. Each year only added to her charms. The glory of her brother fell upon her, and she responded to it somewhat by her own success at court and in the *salons*. She acquired more and more the manners of the times. Coquetry and wit formed all her occupation. Her delicate situation not permitting her to accompany M. de Longueville to Munster, in June, 1645, she remained in Paris; she enjoyed it very much, and, whether her heart had already been touched, or whether it was still entirely free, it is clear that she was not very glad, after her confinement, in 1646, to join, under the sky of Westphalia, a husband who was not, as Retz says, the most agreeable man to her in the world.[1] Imagine, in fact, this spoiled child of the hôtel de Rambouillet leaving Corneille and Voiture, all the elegances and refinements of life, to go to Munster, to listen to the German or Latin conversations of foreign diplomatists. It was to her a double exile, for her country was not only France, it was Paris, it was the court, it was the hôtel de Condé, Chantilly, the Place-

[1] *Mémoires*, vol. i., p. 182.

Royale, the Rue Saint-Thomas du Louvre. It was, however, necessary to obey, and to set off with her step-daughter, Mademoiselle de Longueville, who was already more than twenty years of age. In order to have something of Paris, she took with her several men of letters, and among others, Claude Joly, uncle of Guy Joly, author of the *Mémoires*, canon of Nôtre-Dame, who remained all his life attached to the Condés, and who made himself known by different works full of learning and of merit;[1] also the academician and oratorian Esprit, one of the frequenters of the hôtel de Rambouillet,[2] who had just been embroiled with the Chancellor Séguier, for having favored the marriage of his daughter, the Marchioness de Coislin, with the son of Madame de Sablé, the handsome and brave Marquis de Laval, who was killed some time after, by the side of Condé, at the siege of Dunkirk. A little before her departure for Munster, Esprit had introduced to Madame de Longueville one of the old favorite poets of Riche-

---

[1] We shall limit ourselves to citing the following: *Histoire de la prison et de la liberté de M. le Prince*, 1651.—*Recueil des Maximes veritables pour l'Institution du Roi contre la pernicieuse politique du Cardinal Mazarin*, 1652, burned by the hand of the executioner.—*Statuts et Reglements des petits écoles de grammaire de la ville de Paris*, 1672.—*Traité historique des Ecoles Episcopales*, 1678.—*Voyage fait à Munster en Westphalie et autres lieux voisins*, 1670.

[2] See chapter ii.

lieu, Bois-Robert, who had continued to be dazzled with the new éclat of her whom he had formerly admired amid the fêtes of Ruel. It was in the following terms that Bois-Robert relates to Esprit his visit, and describes to him Madame de Longueville. The verses are mediocre, but we must be satisfied, for they hold the place of an infinite number of other verses, which we might with propriety quote, in regard to the same person and the same epoch, and which are still worse :[1]

Almost conceal'd beneath the crystal wave,
She raised her naked arms her brow to lave.
My eyes the living marble haply spied;
To test its warmth my glowing bosom sigh'd.
The sprightly zephyrs in a merry mood
Her tresses bore along the silvery flood;
They kiss'd her neck, they kiss'd her cheeks, whose hues
Gay Nature when she paints but seldom woos—
A neck and cheeks that verily might claim
To put the fairest flowers of Spring to shame.
With fingers, rosy as Aurora plies,
The moisture dashing from her fretted eyes,
She now reveal'd, as ne'er reveal'd before,
Those two resplendent suns, which to adore
I dropp'd my eyes, because my feeble sight
Could not endure such dazzling floods of light;
And in one living form I saw combined
All ever seen of beauty most refined:

---

[1] *Les Epistres en vers et autres œuvres poétiques de M. de Bois-Robert Metel, Conseiller d'Estat ordinaire, abbé de Châtillon-sur-Seine*, Paris, 1659, in-8°, p. 11: *To Monsieur Esprit: he entertains him with the beauties of Madame the Duchess de Longueville, and with the favorable reception which he received from her on his departure.*

But how her coral lips shall I extol?
Oh how express the rapture of my soul,
When to the charms which bade me most rejoice,
She added too the music of her voice? etc.

Madame de Longueville left Paris on the 20th of June, 1646, accompanied by her step-daughter, and with a numerous escort under the command of Montigny, lieutenant of the guards of M. de Longueville. The whole journey from Paris to Munster was a continual ovation. Her course may be followed day by day, and from city to city, thanks to the detailed narrative of Claude Joly. Belgians, Hollanders, Spaniards, Imperialists, and every one strove to show their gallantry to the beautiful ambassadress. Governors went out to meet her at the heads of their garrisons. The keys of the cities through which she passed were offered to her. She had continual escorts of cavalry. The Duke de Longueville went as far as Wesel to meet her. Turenne, who then commanded upon the Rhine, exhibited to her his army drawn up in order of battle. Was it then that the great captain, well known to be sensible to beauty, received the impression which was renewed at Stenay in 1650, and which, prudently preserved by Madame de Longueville, always formed between them a tender and intimate connection?[1]

[1] *Letters and Mémoires of M. de Turenne*, by Grimoard, in-fol., 1782, vol. i., 1646, July 20: "My dear Sister—I wrote to you from the vicin-

On the 22d of July she made a triumphal entry into Munster. Holland was too near to her not to tempt her curiosity. She took a walk thither, if we may thus speak.[1] During all the autumn of 1646 and the winter of 1647, she was truly the queen of the congress of Munster. Her graces made their impression upon diplomatists as well as upon warriors. She connected herself particularly, in the French embassy, with Claude de Mesmes, Count d'Avaux, of whom we have already spoken, and who was the friend and correspondent of Voiture, of Madame de Sablé, and of Madame de Rambouillet. We have before us some manuscript letters of d'Avaux to Voiture: they are very agreeable, but not very natural; and, amid Latin quotations, then very fashionable among people who prided themselves upon their erudition, they show us what an impression was made by Madame de Longueville upon the dean of our diplomatic corps. She did not appear very melancholy to d'Avaux; but the rival

---

ity of Cologne, four or five days since, and yesterday passed the Rhine to Wesel. Madame de Longueville arrived the same day, and intends visiting the army to-day. From this place we shall travel with her a day or two. I confess to you that nothing in the world is more astonishing. M. de Longueville has come to meet her at Wesel. She is not at all changed, nor is Mademoiselle de Longueville. . . ."

[1] From the 21st of August to the 12th of September. See the *Voyage* of Claude Joly.

of Servien was perhaps better fitted to discover cabinet intrigues than to read the heart of a woman.

"It is to[1] Madame de Montausier and to Madame the Marchioness de Sablé that I am indebted for the favors which I have received from Madame de Longueville. . . . You say that commerce is dangerous with a person so well made, as if the great disproportion and the great distance between those persons and such as myself did not shelter me. You know that the eloquence of Balzac makes no impression upon the mind of a peasant. No, no, I am not afraid. It would be strange enough if in a peaceful assembly I had not sufficient public faith for my preservation, and if, with the passports of the emperor and of the king of Spain, Munster should not be a safe place for me. . . . I look however, I do not pluck out my eyes. I see beauty greater than I have ever seen before; I see all of what is graceful and charming that can be united, and a something which, it seems to me, can nowhere else be found, with so much majesty:

> Video igne micantes,
> Sideribus similes oculos, video oscula, sed quæ
> Est vidisse satis.

I admire with you that goodness, that generosity, and those amiable qualities which we shall always vie in

[1] Library of the Arsenal, Manuscripts of Conrart, in-4°, vol. x.

praising, but which we can never praise enough. The correctness of that mind, its strength and its extent, astonish me also, and sometimes displease me with myself; for there is in it so much that is extraordinary and above the age and the sex. Suppose that I was made of stuff as combustible as you,[1] who still complain of the trials of youth, how small a spark would set me in a blaze! A *précieuse*, who has travelled two hundred leagues to join an old husband, who has quitted the court for Westphalia, who is here in continual gayety, who was lately delighted to see a comedy among the Jesuits (truly, however, in good Latin), who gives constrained audiences, who converses pleasantly with M. Salvius, M. Vulteius, and M. Lampadius,[2] who is not frightened if a big Hollander kisses her twice during his regular daily visits, who receives agreeably the civility of another ambassador counselling him to learn German for his recreation, who with all this preserves her embonpoint and pleasant countenance. . . ."

". . . . I must indeed revenge myself a little now. Some complaints are made here of your taciturnity; but they are uttered by persons of no very great con-

[1] D'Avaux, born in 1595, was fifty-two years old in 1647.

[2] Jean Adler Salvius, one of the Swedish plenipotentiaries; Jean Vulteius, one of the envoys of the Landgrave of Hesse-Cassel; Jacques Lampadius, envoy of the Duke de Luneburg Grubenhagen. See Father Bougeant.

sequence: by no one in fact but Madame de Longueville, and she is hardly worth speaking of. She has paid you some very great compliments; her friends have received orders to solicit your remembrance; she has requested them several times to let her lose nothing in the friendship which you promised her; in short, she has sent you word that she was not proof against such continued indifference, and yet she receives no satisfaction. This is perhaps, as you say, because commerce is dangerous with her, and you yourself take the advice which you give me; but the poor princess cannot be consoled. . . . Although you were a perfect philosopher, and although you had lost sentiment and life, you should at least speak when Madame de Longueville looks at you, even as did the statue of Memnon when it was illumined by the rays of the sun. If you continue, I doubt not that you will be set down as a mute. Give your orders, if you please. All that I could do for you was to answer your letter to M. the Duke d'Enghien.[1] Madame, his sister, read it with great pleasure; and, M. Esprit entering the room a quarter of an hour afterwards, she was very glad to have an-

[1] In default of the subject and of the date, choice may be made between the different letters written by Voiture to the Duke d'Enghien, about this period, and which will be found in the works of Voiture, vol. ii., of the edition of 1745.

other pretext for seeing it again, and left her seat to hear it read once more. This is not all: she requested me to send it to her the next day, with the promise that she would take but a single copy to place among her papers. I will not tell you how much she thinks of it; but will content myself with simply confessing, that it is one of the most delightful things in the world, to see this mouth filled with your praises, and that your name is nowhere more magnificently entertained. . . ."

Voiture is not in arrears with his ingenious correspondent on the account of Madame de Longueville:

". . . . I am very impatient to witness the return of Madame de Longueville after the conclusion of a good peace. What you say to me of this princess is as beautiful as she is herself, and I shall keep it for her to look at some day. . . . Tell the truth, my lord: do you think it is possible to find, I do not mean in a single person, but in every thing that is beautiful and lovely throughout the world—do you think it is possible to find so much wit, grace, and charm as there is in this princess? Be on your guard. She writes to us wonderful things concerning you, and of the friendship that exists between you. Commerce is dangerous with her. I assure you besides, that she is as good as she is beautiful, and that there is no soul in the world more lofty or better than hers. . . ."

A little while after, January 9, 1647, he says:

". . . . Respect has hitherto prevented me from writing to Madame de Longueville; but you make me much more afraid of her by representing her to me as being so serious and so occupied with politics. We take great pleasure in imagining her entertaining M. Lampadius (he is said to be dressed ordinarily in violet satin), M. Vulteius, and M. Salvius, and especially that big Hollander.

> 'Dulcia barbarè
> Lædentem oscula quæ Venus
> Quinta parte sui nectaris imbuit.'

"His advice to her to study German for her amusement, has been a subject of great mirth for Madame de Sablé and Madame de Montausier. . . ."[1]

Among the monuments of the abode of Madame de Longueville at Munster, we must place the portrait which was made of her by Anselme Van Hull, and which was engraved with those of M. de Longueville, of d'Avaux, and of Servien, in the collection of portraits of all the princes and diplomatists assembled at Munster.[2] It is a bust. Even in the engraving, mediocre as it is, we perceive the charming softness of the eyes. A mass of blonde hair sur-

---

[1] Voiture, vol. i., pp. 368, 369, 371, 374.

[2] In-folio, Rotterdam, 1697. This portrait has been reduced and engraved anew by Odieuvre.

rounds her face.[1] Her bosom, partly exposed, appears in its modest beauty. A small collar of pearls adorns a fresh and delicate neck. The following lines, written perhaps by d'Avaux or Voiture, are placed beneath the portrait:

These heroes gather'd in Westphalia,
From France, the North, from Spain, Italia,
Finding so many charms in me,
Fancy, as my face they see,
That I the living form must be
Of Peace and Concord, hither sent,
War's dire misfortunes to prevent.

In the mean time, all the circles of Paris mourned the absence of Madame de Longueville. Godeau did not cease to urge her return in the name of the hôtel de Rambouillet:

"Is it not better, madame," wrote he to her, "that you should return to the hôtel de Longueville, where you are still more powerful than at Munster? Every one is wishing it this winter. My lord, your brother, has returned covered with palms; come back yourself crowned with the myrtles of peace, for it seems to me that it is not enough for you to carry olive branches alone. I dare not explain myself farther, lest I should be guilty of gallantry. This I leave to the Julies and to the Chapelains, etc."[2]

[1] Madame de Longueville seems in this somewhat fatigued. She was at this time in a delicate situation.

[2] Villefore, part 1st, p. 75.

She had enjoyed sufficiently her brilliant exile, but, with her habitual politeness and sweetness, she dissembled her weariness. In the winter of 1647, she had two reasons for returning to France. Her father, M. the Prince, died at the close of December, 1646: this was an immense loss to his family and to France, and its consequences were soon keenly felt. In addition to this, Madame de Longueville had, for the third time, found herself *enceinte* at Munster. Her mother was, for this reason, anxious to have her at home; and M. de Longueville was constrained to permit his wife to take the road to Paris.

Her return to France—first to Chantilly, then to Paris—in the month of May, 1647, was a very different triumph from that which characterized her journey upon the Rhine, and into Holland, and her abode at Munster. She found the crowd of her adorers more numerous and more eager than ever; and in the first rank was her brother, the Prince de Conti, who, fresh from college, was taking his first lessons in the world. Let us say a word in regard to this new personage, who now appears for the first time, and who will play a very conspicuous part in the life of Madame de Longueville.

Armand de Bourbon, Prince de Conti, who was born in 1629, was eighteen years of age in 1647. He had a good mind, and not an unpleasant face;

but a slight deformity and a certain feebleness of body, rendering him unfit for the army, he was early destined for the Church. He had studied among the Jesuits at the college of Clermont, with Molière, and M. the Prince, before his death, had obtained for him the richest benefices,[1] and demanded a cardinal's hat. While waiting for this hat, Armand de Bourbon was living at the hôtel de Condé, partly an ecclesiastic, partly a man of the world, all occupied with wit, and greedy of every species of success. The glory of his brother filled him with emulation, and he dreamed himself of warlike exploits. When his sister returned from Germany, he went to meet her, and, dazzled by her beauty, her grace, and her fame, he began to love her rather as a gallant than as a brother.[2] He followed her blindly in all her adventures, in which he exhibited as much courage as lightness. When he had made his peace with the court—thanks to his marriage with a niece of Maza-

---

[1] There are three very good portraits in-fol. by Daret, by Rousselet, and by M. de Lasne, all of this year, 1647. In all of them, Armand de Bourbon has a fine face, and already shows the marks of some high ecclesiastical dignitary. Daret supports his medallion by little angels, who are playing with the hat of the future cardinal—a charming composition, after the design of Lesueur. In Rousselet, Fame bears the medallion of the young prince, Religion presents him with a mitre, War carries a suit of armor, Politics a crown, and Philosophy the sun of intelligence and the mysterious serpent. This was truly the image of the uncertain destiny of the Prince de Conti.

[2] Madame de Motteville, vol. ii., p. 17.

rin, the beautiful and virtuous Anne-Marie Martinozzi—he obtained the command-in-chief of the army of Catalonia, in which capacity he acquitted himself with great honor. He was much less successful in Italy. On the whole, he was far from injuring his name, and he gave to France, in the person of his young son, a true warrior, one of the best pupils of Condé, one of the last eminent generals of the seventeenth century. Constrained, through ill-health, to betake himself again to religion, the Prince de Conti finished, where he had begun, with theology. He composed several meritorious and learned works on various religious subjects.[1] In 1647, he was entirely devoted to vanity and pleasures. He adored his sister, and she exercised over him a somewhat ridiculous empire, which continued during several years.

The court and Paris were then occupied with festivals and enjoyments, which all were eager to share with Madame de Longueville. To please the queen, Mazarin multiplied the balls and the operas. At a great expense he sent to Italy for artists, singers, male and female, who represented an opera of *Or-*

---

[1] *Les Devoirs des grands, par Monseigneur le Prince de Conti, avec son Testament*, Paris, 1667.—*Traité de la Comédie et des Spectacles selon la tradition de l'Eglise*, 1667.—*Lettres du Prince de Conti, ou l'accord du libre arbitre avec la grace de Jésus-Christ*, Cologne, 1689.

pheus, the machinery and decorations of which are said to have cost more than 400,000 livres. The queen delighted in these spectacles. France also, as if touched with its own grandeur, took pleasure in the magnificence of its government, and seconded it by redoubling its own luxury and elegance. The pleasures of wit occupied the first rank. The hôtel de Rambouillet, near its decline, was shedding its last rays. Madame de Longueville reigned there as well as in all the circles of Paris; and, it must be confessed, with her good qualities she had also the defects of the best *précieuses*. The following is the picture which Madame de Motteville has traced[1] of her person, of the turn of her mind, of her occupations, of her credit, and of that of the whole house of Condé, at this period, which may be considered as the most brilliant of her life: "This princess, who, during her absence, reigned in her family, and whose approbation was sought as if she were a true sovereign, did not fail, on her return to Paris, to appear in greater splendor than when she left it. The friendship entertained for her by the prince, her brother, authorizing her actions and her manners, the greatness of her beauty and of her mind increased so much the cabal of her family, that she was not long at

---

[1] *Mémoires*, vol. ii., pp. 14–20.

court without almost entirely engrossing it. She became the object of all desires: her clique was the centre of all intrigues, and those whom she loved became also the favorites of fortune. . . . Her intelligence, her wit, and the high opinion entertained for her discernment, won for her the admiration of all good people, who were persuaded that her esteem alone was enough to give them reputation. If, in this way, she governed souls, she was not less successful by means of her beauty; for, although she had suffered with the small-pox since the Regency, and although she had lost somewhat of the perfection of her complexion, the splendor of her charms exerted a powerful influence upon those who saw her; and she possessed especially, in the highest degree, what, in the Spanish language, is expressed by those words, *donayre*, *brio*, *y bizarrie* (gallant air). She had an admirable form, and her person possessed a charm whose power extended over our own sex. It was impossible to see her without loving her, and without desiring to please her. Her beauty consisted, however, more in the colors of her face than in the perfection of her features. Her eyes were not large, but beautiful, soft and brilliant, and their blue was admirable: it was like that of the turquoise. Poets could compare the incarnation upon her face to lilies and roses only; and the light shining hair which accompanied so many wonderful things, made her more like an angel, such as our poor nature can imagine one, than like a woman. . . . She was then too much engrossed with her own sentiments, which passed for infallible rules while they were not always so, and there was too much affectation in her manner of speaking and acting, whose greatest beauty was attributable to delicacy of thought and correctness of reasoning. She appeared constrained, and the fine raillery, exercised by herself and her courtiers, often fell upon those who, while rendering her their homage, felt, to their mortification, that honest sincerity, which ought to be observed in polite society, was apparently banished from hers. The virtues and praiseworthy qualities of the most excellent creatures are mingled with things which are opposed to them: all men partake of this clay from which they draw their origin, and God alone is perfect. . . . In fine, it may be said that at this time all greatness, all glory, and all gallantry were confined to this family of Bourbon, of which M. the Prince was the chief, and that fortune was not considered a desirable thing, if it did not come from their hands."

It was about this time that the two sonnets of Voiture and of Benserade divided the court and the city, the *salons* and the academy. Almost all the documents appertaining to this little literary contest have been preserved;[1] but we have discovered some hitherto unknown, which we cannot withhold from the reader, because they show the passion which then existed for literary matters, the ascendency of Madame de Longueville, and the peculiar delicacy of her taste.

Voiture had just died in 1648, and his friends had caught, as the last sigh of his muse, the sonnet to Uranie. At the same time another sonnet appeared, written by one of the rivals of Voiture, younger than himself, and who had not been formed at the hôtel de Rambouillet: it was the complaint of a lover who pretended to be more miserable than Job, because Job could at least groan aloud on account of his misfortune, whilst the poor lover was compelled to suffer in silence:

> Job, whom a thousand torments grieve,
> Shall to your eyes his torture prove;
> And yet with reason shall believe
> That they will not your pity move.
>
> Regard his ills in every light,
> Feel every word as he explains:
> You grow accustomed to the sight
> Of one who suffers and complains.
>
> Although his anguish was extreme,
> Yet human patience you will deem
> To have e'en his by far outdone.

---

[1] *Mémoires de Littérature*, vol. i., pp. 116–184.

He suffer'd pangs past all belief,
Complain'd, and told them one by one,
But I have known far greater grief.[1]

All the fashionable lovers of the day, the languishing and the dying, admired this description of their martyrdom, the height of sorrow being to suffer without complaining; and it is certain that the close of the sonnet of Benserade is neither without spirit nor without charm. It created a furor. The sonnet of Voiture was of a very different character. It possessed a finished elegance, somewhat feeble it is true, but elevated and animated by a certain passionate accent, which is sweetly felt throughout it. It was of a more distinguished and more rare quality, and for this reason it had at first less success. Balzac[2] composed upon these two pieces a formal dissertation, in which he weighs in the balance of the most scrupulous criticism the merits and the defects of both. Corneille, annoyed by a quarrel which turned attention a little too much from his own works, began to make sport of the two sonnets; afterwards, the affair acquiring more and more literary interest, he engaged in it himself, and took sides with Job against Uranie, in a sonnet in which he does not hesitate to say that Voiture's is doubtless *better conceived*, *better*

[1] *Œuvres de Benserade*, 1697, vol. i., p. 174.
[2] *Œuvres de Balzac*, in-folio, vol. ii., pp. 580–594.

conducted, better finished, but that he would prefer to be the author of the other. He returns to the charge in an epigram which terminates as follows:

The one displays more art, the other much more life;
The one is more precise, the other much more *naïf;*
The one shows labor long, the other much more sprite:
In short, the one is right well made, the other pretty, quite.
    To use the fewest words I can—
    The one springs from a soul polite,
    The other from a gallant man.[1]

This was a very imposing judgment, and, to all appearance, there was little hope for Voiture, when Madame de Longueville undertook his defence. Her situation was somewhat embarrassing. Her brother, the Prince de Conti, was at the head of the Jobelins, and Esprit, who had accompanied her to Munster, and on whom she might have depended upon any occasion, Esprit, who, without ceasing to be of the Church, was occupied with the most gallant literature, as he will at a future day be occupied with sentences and maxims, had written very warmly in favor of Benserade. But Madame de Longueville was not the person to take the lucky side and to abandon her old friend Voiture. Her authority soon changed the face of the combat.

In the camp of the Jobelins was the Countess de

[1] *Œuvres diverses*, edit. de 1740, Amsterdam, pp. 162–165.

Brégy, one of the ladies of honor of Queen Anne, and wife of a famous ambassador, from whom we have a collection[1] of prose and verse, and some *questions d'amour*, to which Quinault replied by order of the young king. She was much surprised to learn that Madame de Longueville preferred to the universally applauded sonnet a piece of verse which had not produced a very great effect. She hastened to write to her, asking permission to maintain her own opinion against hers. The following is her letter, with the diplomatic reply of the ambassadress of Munster.

Madame de Brégy to Madame de Longueville.

"Job, in ages past, was scarcely less humiliated than I now am to find myself opposed to the opinion of Your Highness; for if I had not enough sense to conform myself to it, my spirit of divination ought to serve the other in this encounter, and not permit him to endure the shame of seeing himself opposed to sentiments which I have regarded as a rule by which one could never fail. But, since I have taken up the cause of Job, more unfortunate because he suffers at your hands than on account of all his first

---

[1] *Les Œuvres galantes de Madame la Comtesse de B., imprimé à Leyde et se vend à Paris*, in-18°, 1666.

[2] *Œuvres galantes*, etc., p. 17.

evils, be pleased, Madame, to allow me an opportunity on Thursday evening to defend an unhappy person, against whom the devil has cunningly excited your persecution, as the only means of divesting him of that patience which he has exhibited for so many ages, and which cannot be preserved when one is despised by you."

Madame de Longueville[1] *to Madame de Brégy.*

"Your letter has done more for the sonnet of Job than Benserade himself; and it occasions me so much regret at not entertaining sentiments conformed to those of the person who wrote it, that, if it does not make me alter, it makes me at least condemn my own, thus obtaining from me a preference for Job, which I should have always refused so long as the sonnet had spoken for itself. This, I think, is all that a generous person can do for a party to which she does not belong; and I assure you that if yours is not that of my choice, it is exalted in my esteem. I shall be glad to see you on Thursday, and to hear you advocate the cause of Job; but be admonished, at least, that I will hear you argue against my past sentiments only, consenting no longer to oppose your own, etc."

---

[1] This letter is printed among those of Madame de Brégy, with many little errors, which we correct without indicating them.

The two ladies contended, as we see, in the most courteous manner; but they contended warmly and for a long time. I conjecture that aside from literature there was some secret motive in it all. Madame de Brégy was beautiful and coquettish as well as intellectual. She could, without much difficulty, believe that the piece of Benserade was addressed to her, and that it was an indirect declaration of a somewhat plebeian love, condemned to wear out secretly in suffering. Benserade had, at least, composed for her an epistle, in which he pleads the fear of love as his excuse for flying from her.[1] Madame de Longueville could not have forgotten all the verses which Voiture had written in her praise while yet quite young; and perhaps the latter, on again beholding, in 1647, the noble beauty in all the splendor of her charms, quitting his former familiarity for an affectionate respect, was desirous of ending as he had begun, and dying, as was then said, in the service of her whom he called Uranie, a celestial beauty upon whom he dares scarcely to lift his eyes.

In love with Uranie I'll pine e'ermore;
Absence nor time to me affords a cure;
Naught can my pain the least relief procure,
Nor any thing my freedom e'er restore.

---

[1] *Œuvres de Benserade*, vol. i., p. 97, and *Œuvres de Madame de Brégy*, p. 98.

Her chains oppress me each day more and more;
But witnessing her beauty passing pure,
I willingly can any death endure,
And e'en her tyranny dare not deplore.

My reason, feebly though, sometimes essays
To urge me to revolt, its strength arrays;
But when to use it I am ever prone,

It strives in vain my shackles to remove
Then claims that worth is Uranie's alone,
And, more than all my senses, prompts to love.

Madame de Longueville thought, moreover, that her preference was supported by very good reason, and in this we are inclined to agree with her. The work of Benserade possesses undoubtedly more wit, invention, and even originality, since it is certainly something quite new to place in the mouth of Job a declaration of love: that of Voiture, to us, possesses a secret and melancholy gracefulness which touches the heart. With Corneille, we find the sonnet of Job *prettier*, though *unnatural*—a strange eulogium, and one hardly to be expected here from either party pronouncing it; but the sonnet of Uranie seems to us to proceed more from one in love, and this it is which decides us. Perhaps if Madame de Longueville had conversed with Corneille, she would have converted him in the name of their common principles; she succeeded, at least, in overcoming her brother, the Prince de Conti, who, after having made a sonnet to Benserade, at last took the part of Voiture and of his sister. She launched against him Sarrazin, whose commentary in verse we still possess —a commentary that turns into ridicule the sonnet of Benserade and the opinion of Esprit:

> Sir Esprit, of the Oratory,
> In you we piety perceive,
> Thus crowning, as you do with glory,
> "Job, whom a thousand torments grieve." etc.[1]

Madame de Longueville herself wrote to Esprit a letter, in which she evinces a fine cultivated literary taste. She acknowledges, in the sonnet of Job, a gallant air and delicacy, but nothing more. With the exception of a few lines, all the others seem to her full of faults, and she carries refinement and preciseness so far as to designate certain expressions of Benserade as disgusting, meaning by this, vulgar. On the contrary, she finds in the sonnet of Voiture, beauty and force of expression, with thoughts which, though not new, possess the sovereign merit of passion. She makes a thousand concessions to Esprit; she asks pardon for her audacity in differing with

---

1 The last line of each of the couplets of this commentary recalls successively and in their order the lines of the sonnet of Benserade. It is not in the works of Sarrazin of 1654, nor in his *Œuvres Nouvelles*; it will be found in the 1st vol. of Benserade, p. 175.

him;[1] she announces, at the same time, that she means to continue the war; she appeals to *all Rambouillet*, and jests pleasantly upon this new kind of Fronde.

Madame de Longueville to Monsieur Esprit.[2]

"It is true that I am in the utmost astonishment to find our tastes so different in this matter; and my astonishment is the greater because it seemed to me a subject upon which our sentiments should be the same. For, in short, with the exception of the seventh, eighth, and last lines of the sonnet of Job, I find it not only full of faults, but even of such as you have never been able to endure; its expression goes so far as to be disgusting; whereas, in the piece of Voiture (at least in its last six lines), the most beautiful and forcible expression in the world is united with a thought which, though not certainly new, is so passionate that it should, it seems to me, be more highly

[1] During his youth, Madame de Longueville paid much attention to Esprit, in order, probably, to please Madame de Sablé, his avowed protectress. She took him with her to Munster. Here she testified for him the greatest regard. In an unpublished letter, of October 13, 1646, she recommends him to Mazarin for a benefice. Mazarin does not seem to have been much pleased with him. He writes to Servien, March 22, 1647, with seeming discontent, that Esprit solicits from Munster "to be of the house of Monsieur." Melanges de Clérambault, vol. cxxx.

[2] Library of the Arsenal, Manuscripts of Conrart, in-4°, vol. ii., p. 13.

esteemed than the mere delicacy which characterizes that of Job. I confess that it has as gallant an air as any thing that I have even seen; also, although I find reason upon my side, I think that if there is none which authorizes the other party, there is at least the greatest cause in the world for preferring its taste; and if one may suffer himself to be seduced without dying of shame, I confess that it is upon such an occasion. This is all that my natural justice can permit me to feel for those who have not followed my sentiments. I send you what will acquaint you with the manner in which my brother has made known his own, that is, his final opinion; for the first was made in prose, and more favorable to Uranie than to Job, but with the declaration that if he should choose to send one of the two sonnets to his mistress, it would be that of Job. Neither party was satisfied with this judgment, not being able to turn it fully to its own account. A more decided one was demanded. There are some who think that even this[1] is not so; but, for my own part, I am contented that Voiture is therein pronounced admirable and grand, and Benserade only gallant and pretty. He has made another sonnet, which I send you also, together with the list of our friends and of our enemies.

---

[1] The final opinion of the Prince de Conti.

They have taken sides uninfluenced by prejudice, politics, or any other motives than the force of reason in some cases, and the gratification of taste and blindness of mind in others. But I am not going so far as to use invectives, and I think that there is as little generosity in attacking a father of the Oratoire, as there would be in assailing an unarmed man. I close therefore for the very reason which made me prefer Uranie to Job, and the celestial muse to a man infected from the crown of his head to the soles of his feet.

"I beg you to tell M. the Abbé de Croisy,[1] that I wish him to take my part. I forgot to tell you that we are writing circular letters, and that we expect the opinions of M. and Madame de Montausier, of all Rambouillet, and of M. and Madame de Liancourt. In fine, this matter will not rest here; and if the excitement about it continues, the ministers will be more apt to occupy themselves with it than with the assemblies of the nobility; and the tolerance shown for our seditious manners, is the strongest indication which we have had for a year of the humbling of

---

[1] We have no knowledge of the Abbé de Croisy. We are inclined to believe that the copy of Conrart is here defective; and we propose to read the Abbé de Cerisy, Habert, of the French Academy—a wit then of some reputation, and author of works now forgotten; among others, *Poésies Chrétiennes et diverses*, dedicated to the Prince de Conti. He died in 1654, at the age of forty-four years.

royal authority, for they are cantonments against the fundamental laws of a well-governed State.[1] In short, God wills it, and we have nothing to say.

"A word of reply in regard to persons of your own party and of mine, etc."

Madame de Longueville gained the day; all the hôtel de Rambouillet went over to her side, and Benserade, beaten after having been triumphant, thus complained to her who had robbed him of his glory:

You give me then the lowest place!
The vanquish'd in this contest I,
I, elevated once so high,
Must now conceal my blushing face.

This evil luck will soon apace
Through mem'ry's fane my name decry;

---

[1] This allusion to the assemblies of the nobility fixes the date of this letter, placing it more than a year after the epoch with which we are occupied, that is, at the close of 1649, when the nobility rose against the new brevets. But, although written at the close of 1649, this little affair shows faithfully the manner in which Madame de Longueville passed her life in 1648. It is surprising that, in the great collection of pieces relating to the two sonnets (Mélanges de Littérature, etc.), not a single date is given. Our conjecture in regard to the letter of Esprit, is confirmed by the following note, found in vol. xi., in-fol., of the papers of Conrart, p. 1118: "In the month of December, 1649, all the court was divided in regard to the two sonnets of Voiture and Benserade. Every one took sides and declared in favor of him who was most admired. Of the two parties formed upon this subject, those of the first were called *Uranins*, and Madame de Longueville was their chief; those of the second were called *Jobelins*, and M. the Prince de Conti was at their head. M. the Prince (Condé) being urged to say of which he would be, would never explain himself otherwise than by declaring both to be very fine."

And fallen, I must ever lie
O'erwhelm'd with sorrow and disgrace.

We give also this pretty quatrain of Mademoiselle de Scudéry:

'Tis but the simple truth to say,
Job's fate most strange hath been;
Tormented ever, day by day,
First by a demon, by an angel then.

Such were the frivolous pastimes, at once innocent and dangerous, of Madame de Longueville. All the prosperities and all the felicities of life surrounded her. Every thing conspired in her favor, or rather against her,—the triumphs of the mind as well as those of beauty, the continually increasing glory of her house, the intoxication of vanity, the secret desires of her heart. The trial was too strong; she yielded to it. In the enchanted circle in which she moved, more than one adorer attracted her attention; one of them succeeded in winning her, according to all appearances, at the close of 1647 or at the commencement of 1648. She was then about twenty-nine years of age.

François, first Prince de Marcillac, afterwards, upon the death of his father, Duke de La Rochefoucauld, was the eldest son of François de La Rochefoucauld, whom Louis XIII. created a duke and a peer in 1622, and of Gabrielle de Liancourt.

He was born December 15, 1613, and at an early age married Mademoiselle de Vivonne. He served honorably in Italy and in Flanders, and in 1646 he was wounded at the siege of Mardyk. As Retz says, he was not a warrior, although he was a very good soldier. Without being very handsome, he was well formed and very agreeable. What distinguished him especially was his wit. Of this he possessed an infinite fund, of the finest and most delicate. His conversation was mild, easy, insinuating; and his manners were at once the most natural and most polished. He had a lofty air. In him vanity supplied the place of ambition. At an early age he showed a fondness for distinction and for intrigues. Profoundly selfish, and having succeeded in acquiring a knowledge of himself and in reducing to theory his nature, his character, and his tastes, he set out with contrary appearances, and with those chivalrous manners affected by the *Importants*. One of his first connections was with Madame de Chevreuse, who gave him to Queen Anne. He entered so earnestly into the interests of the queen and into those of Mademoiselle d'Hautefort, that he conceived or caught the idea of carrying them away. "I was," says he,[1] "at an age when one loves to perform extraordinary

[1] Collection Petitot, vol. li., p. 353.

and brilliant things, and I thought that nothing could be more so than to carry off the queen at once from the king, her husband, and from Cardinal Richelieu, who was jealous of him, and of bearing away Mademoiselle d'Hautefort from the king, who was enamored of her." He did not execute this fine project; but Richelieu, who had some suspicion of all these intrigues, placed him for eight days in the Bastile. It seems that he was not entirely a stranger to the conspiracies of Cinq-Mars. At the death of Richelieu he hastened to Paris, and, when that of Louis XIII. had placed the supreme authority in the hands of Queen Anne, he imagined that his fortune was made. He sought successively various important offices which the queen could not grant, whatever fondness she might have entertained for him. Madame de Chevreuse exacted for her old friend the government of Havre, which was then of the highest consequence; but this government was in the family of Richelieu, and Mazarin could not take it away from the Duchess d'Aiguillon. La Rochefoucauld aspired to the command of the cavalry; he was very brave, but he was not considered capable of such an employment. He tried thus several schemes; the queen applied herself to soothing his disappointments, by manners so tender, as to retain him, as would be now said, in a moderate opposition, and keep him from taking part in the violence of Beaufort. He was not then covered with the disgrace of the *Importants*, though he shared it to a certain extent; and he did not cease to be, or to seem to be, very much attached, not to the government, but to the person of the queen. He looked continually for some great favor at her hands. These favors not arriving, he determined to procure through intimidation what his fidelity had not been able to secure.

It was during this state of his feelings that he met Madame de Longueville, on her return from Munster, surrounded by the most earnest admirers. The Count de Miossens, afterwards Marshal d'Albret—handsome, brave, full of wit and of talent, as enterprising in love as in war—was paying her a very zealous court. La Rochefoucauld persuaded Miossens, who was one of his friends, that, after all, if he should overcome the resistance of Madame de Longueville, it would only be a victory flattering to his vanity, whilst that he, La Rochefoucauld, would be able to turn it to a very good account. This was certainly a very touching and heroic reason for loving! Corneille did not think of it in the *Cid* and in *Polyeucte*. We have, however, done no more than to transfer, with the utmost exactness, a piece from La Rochefoucauld himself, which we will now quote, word for word :[1] "So much unprofitable labor and so much weariness, finally gave me other thoughts, and led me to attempt dangerous ways in order to testify my hostility to the queen and Cardinal Mazarin. The beauty of Madame de Longueville, her wit, and the charms of her person, attached to her all who could hope for her favor. Many men and women of quality strove to please her; and besides all this, Madame de Longueville was then upon such good terms with all her house, and so tenderly beloved by the Duke d'Enghien, her brother, that the esteem and friendship of this prince might be counted upon by any one in the favor of Madame his sister. Many persons vainly attempted this game, mingling other sentiments with those of ambition. Miossens, who afterwards became Marshal of France, persisted in it longest, but with similar success. I was one of his intimate friends, and he told me his designs. They soon fell to the ground of themselves. He saw this, and told me several times that he was about to renounce them; but vanity, which was the strongest of his passions, prevented him from telling me the truth, and he professed to entertain hopes which he had not, and which I knew that he could not have. Some time passed in this way; and, finally, I had reason

---

[1] Collection Petitot, vol. li., p. 398.

to believe that I could make a more considerable use than Miossens of the friendship and confidence of Madame de Longueville. I made him believe it himself. He knew my position at court; I told him my views, declaring that my consideration for him would restrain me always, and that I would not attempt to form a connection with Madame de Longueville without his permission. I will even confess that I irritated him against her in order to obtain it, without however saying any thing untrue. He delivered her entirely to me, but he repented when he saw the result of this connection. . . ."

La Rochefoucauld pleased Madame de Longueville, doubtless, by the graces of his mind and the charms of his person, and especially by that glory won for him by his conduct towards the queen, which was enough to dazzle a pupil of the hôtel de Rambouillet. He paid her homage which was, to all appearance, the most passionate in the world. In proportion as he insinuated himself into her heart, he skilfully aroused in her that desire of appearing and of producing an effect, so natural in woman. Little by little, he displayed before her eyes a new object which she had not yet perceived—an important part upon the theatre of events just opening. He transformed her natural coquetry into political ambition, or rather he inspired her with his own ambition.

When Madame de Longueville, touched by the passion shown for her by La Rochefoucauld, had determined to respond to it, she gave herself up to him entirely; she devoted herself to him whom she dared to love; she made it a point of honor, as well doubtless as a secret happiness, to share his destiny and to follow him without looking behind her, sacrificing to him all her private interests, the evident interest of her family, and the strongest sentiment of her soul, her tenderness for her brother Condé.

Oh admirable thing! do you know who it is that commits a crime against this devotion? He precisely who makes his profit in it. La Rochefoucauld expresses himself thus in regard to Madame de Longueville:[1] "This princess possessed all the advantages of mind and beauty to such a degree and with so much charm, that it seemed as if nature had taken pleasure in forming a masterpiece. . . . But these fine qualities were rendered less brilliant by a stain which was never seen upon a princess of such merit, which found no imitations on those who entertained for her a particular adoration; a stain which so transformed her in their sentiments, that she did not recognize her own. At this time the Prince de Marcillac shared her mind, and as he joined his ambition

[1] Collection Petitot, vol. li., p. 455.

to his love, he inspired her with a desire for business, to which she had a natural aversion."

Let us listen to the declared enemy of Madame de Longueville, her step-daughter, the Duchess de Nemours: "It will doubtless cause astonishment[1] that Madame de Longueville should have been one of the first (to join the party of malcontents), she who had nothing to hope from that party, and who had no reason to complain of the court. . . . M. the Prince felt an extreme tenderness for his sister. She, on her side, humored him, less from interest than from the particular esteem and tender friendship which she had for him. At this time neither she nor the whole cabal showed much wit in their designs; and although they were all possessed of enough of it, they employed it only in gay conversations, only in commenting and refining upon the delicacies of the heart and of the sentiments. They made all the wit and merit of a person to consist in making subtile distinctions and representations, sometimes unnatural enough. Those who made the most display were, in their opinion, the most creditable and most learned persons, and they treated as ridiculous and coarse whatever approached to grave conversation. . . . It was La Rochefoucauld who gave to this princess so

---

[1] *Mémoires*, p. 18, etc.

many hollow and false sentiments. As he exercised a very great power over her, and as he seldom thought of any other person than himself, he drew her into all the intrigues in which she engaged, only to be able thereby to promote his own ends."

Madame de Motteville, whom we must never grow weary of studying and citing when we wish to know and to establish the truth, after having marked the principal motive which urged La Rochefoucauld in his pursuit of Madame de Longueville, adds: "In[1] all that she has since done, it is clearly seen that ambition was not the only thing that occupied her soul, and that the interests of the Prince de Marcillac there held a prominent place. For him she became ambitious, for him she ceased to love repose; and in order to be sensible to this affection, she became too insensible to her own glory. . . . The declarations of the Prince de Marcillac, as I have already said, had not been displeasing to her; and this nobleman, who was perhaps more selfish than tender, wishing through her to promote his own interests, believed that he should inspire her with a desire of ruling the princes her brothers. . . ."

Finally Retz, who was perfectly acquainted with all the actors and all the actresses of the Fronde, and

[1] *Mémoires*, vol. ii., p. 15.

who, in regard to this epoch, merits not to be believed without reserve, but to be listened to seriously, closes the most charming eulogy upon Madame de Longueville with these words, so often repeated, and which contain the true judgment of posterity: "As her passion obliged her to make politics only a secondary matter, from the heroine of a great party, she became its adventuress."[1]

We must either renounce all historical criticism, or from these accumulated testimonies, which we could have much increased, we must draw this conclusion: 1, That before her connection with La Rochefoucauld, Madame de Longueville remained entirely unconcerned in every political intrigue; that she was occupied only with intellectual matters and gallantry, suffering herself to be guided absolutely in every thing else by her father and by her brother; 2, That it was not on her account, as has been often repeated, that La Rochefoucauld entered the Fronde; that, far from this, it was La Rochefoucauld, and La Rochefoucauld alone, who, little by little, engaged her in it, designedly and selfishly; 3, That the conduct of Madame de Longueville in the Fronde must be referred to La Rochefoucauld, who governed her, and that the only good thing in her is the character which

---

[1] *Mémoires*, vol. i., p. 219.

she exhibited when the intrigue became a tempest, when it was necessary to risk her person, to stake her happiness, her repose, her fortune, and her life, retaining still under the hand of another what she could never lose—the pride of soul and brilliant energy of the sister of the great Condé.

It is not our business here to give a history of the Fronde, to make known its peripetics, its principal personages, the true springs of their actions, their apparent patriotism, their real ambition, their unstable hopes, their perpetual changes. We wish simply to describe Madame de Longueville; it is to her, without separating her from her brother Condé, that we would confine ourselves in this labyrinth of intrigues: here even we will show her only in the first scenes of the Fronde.

As soon as La Rochefoucauld had entered the heart of Madame de Longueville, he occupied it entirely. She employed in his service all the charms of her person, the resources of her mind, the greatness of her heart. Careless of her interests, and turning her back upon the fortunes of her house, she attacked openly, or undermined by artifice, that royalty which her family had supported, and which had been still more the support of her family. Forgetful of her most just resentment, even of her honor, she entered the ranks of those who, in 1643, had endeavored to blast in the bud her fresh and unsullied fame. The daughter of the Condés went over to the Vendômes and to the Lorraines, made common cause with Beaufort and with Madame de Chevreuse, and exposed herself to the risk of encountering in this new circle her old and implacable enemy, Madame de Montbazon. If Guise had not then been at Naples, she would doubtless have testified her perfect change by shaking the hand that had slain Coligny!

In the mean time La Rochefoucauld did not forget his reason for desiring so ardently the conquest of Madame de Longueville. He had wished, as he himself tells us, to reach the brother through the sister, and to draw into the Fronde the house of Condé, which had hitherto been a rampart to the queen and to Mazarin.

M. the Prince had died at the close of 1646, and with him his family had lost its political helm. Madame the Princess remained firmly attached to the queen; but Madame de Longueville succeeded, without much difficulty, in numbering among the malcontents the Prince de Conti, who, while waiting for a cardinal's hat, was not sorry to make some noise, play some part, and acquire an importance which might make him compare favorably with his brother. She needed no great cunning to draw among the malcontents her husband, who was naturally inclined towards them. But the great difficulty was to win Condé himself.

The latter imagined that he had great cause of complaint against the cardinal. At the death of his brother-in-law, Brézé, in 1646, he asked to succeed him as High-Admiral of France. It was impossible to add this office to the number already possessed by the Condés; but, through management, the queen gave it to no one, and set it down for herself. M. the Prince, who was still living, ambitious and greedy, had warmly resented this refusal. The impetuous Condé had not concealed his anger. He was also much irritated at being sent into Catalonia to replace d'Harcourt, with the promise of every thing necessary to carry on a campaign worthy of him; and that he had been left, without the aid promised and earnestly claimed, between a strongly-fortified place, which he could not take by assault on account of the condition of his troops, and a powerful army which he could neither wait for nor reach, so that he was obliged to raise the siege of Lerida, and to retreat in good order before the emeny. He felt that he had done well, but it was the first time that he had given way; in spite of him, his glory suffered by it, and he complained with bitterness of what he called the disloyalty of the cardinal. Finally, he was sent into Flanders to take command of a very feeble army,—not an army destitute of courage, but entirely undisciplined. Besides, it must be confessed, the true genius of Condé was for war. In this, again, he is the first of his age, and equal to the greatest in antiquity and in modern times,—as ardent as Alexander, as resolute as Cæsar, as fertile in expedients as Hannibal, as capable of making precise and vast calculations as Napoleon, which may be seen by the plan of the campaign by which, in 1645, he proposed to dictate peace to the Emperor in Vienna. He possessed all the qualifications of a warrior. He knew not only how to achieve a victory by the boldness of his manœuvres, but he knew how to calculate upon one, and, as Bossuet said of a very different person, he left nothing to fortune which he could accomplish through prudence and foresight. He was as good a military manager as he was an active and enterprising general. He excelled in the art of encamping and of besieging, as well as in that of fighting, and he surpassed Vauban. By turns, he exhibited that audacity which confounded Mercy at Fribourg and at Nortlingen, and that great prudence which led him to raise the siege of Lerida, and which at a later period, in 1675, wearied Montecuculli. With the most happy instincts, he united profound study. In Catalonia he marched with a copy of Cæsar in his hand, explaining it to his lieutenants. He formed the greatest generals, commencing with Turenne, who served under him during two campaigns, and finishing with that Luxembourg who, if he were rejudged, would perhaps be found not inferior to Turenne himself. Let us add this very striking fact: Condé is the only modern captain who never suffered defeat, and who was always victorious when he commanded in chief. Turenne was beaten twice in regular battle—at Rethel and at Mariendal; Frederic commenced with reverses; Napoleon terminated his dazzling career by two frightful routes—Leipsic and Waterloo; Condé alone was ever triumphant. He had arrayed against him the three greatest generals of Europe—Mercy, Montecuculli, and William; not one of them was able to deprive him of even the shadow of an advantage. We might easily extend, without exhausting it, the eulogy of the warrior in Condé; but, we acknowledge it, he had not the qualifications of a great politician, because at bottom he had no true determined ambition. First prince of the blood in a monarchy such as was that of France in the seventeenth century, what could he desire beyond the acquisition of glory? And after Richelieu and under Mazarin, this glory could be reached by him only on the battle-field. It was for this and for this alone that his father had reared him. He was also subjected, at an early age, to that severe discipline of ambition which teaches to speak at the proper moment and to be silent, to exhibit no humor, to keep the eye fixed upon the highest object, never suffering it to be turned aside by secondary interests, or by the caprices of the imagination or of the heart. Such is the ambitious man; such were, more or less, Henri IV., Richelieu, and Mazarin; for it is just to place Mazarin in this illustrious company. All three had a great end to attain, which they pursued with constancy. Condé had no aim; he formed no great design, being by birth as high as he could become —all that he could ever dream of being, unless he acted the madman or the traitor; and he had a mind perfectly correct, with a corresponding heart. His conscience and his good sense told him then that he had nothing to gain by all the intrigues in which others wished to engage him; that his place was near the throne, in order to protect it with his sword against its enemies, whoever they might be, whether at home or abroad. If he had kept this place, he would have attained to a rank much higher than even the usurpation of royalty. Let us not hesitate to look at it, that we may the better feel the greatness of his fall: to his five years of brilliant victories in Flanders and upon the Rhine, from 1643 to 1648, he might, beyond all doubt, have added, during the war which continued between France and Spain after the treaty of Westphalia, new victories, which, in two campaigns, at most, might have forever conquered Belgium, as the preceding had added Alsace to the French territory. He would then, at the age of thirty, have gained as many battles as Alexander, Hannibal, and Cæsar; and still there would have been before him twenty years of vigor, twenty other victories, like that of Senef, for example,[1] which he gained upon the verge of old age, before laying aside his sword, as a monument of what he might have done from 1648 to 1675. Incomparable would have been his destiny had he performed his part as first prince of the blood, firm defender of the crown yet loyal interpreter of the nation; bearing to the queen without frightening her, and to Mazarin, while sustaining him, the legitimate complaints of the nobility, of the parliament, and of the people.

There was, in fact, a cause for the Fronde; Mazarin, almost equal to Richelieu as a diplomatist, had not, in the smallest degree, the genius of his master for the administration of State affairs. Incessantly occupied with increasing the territory and strengthening the royal authority, he attended to little else,

---

[1] Condé gained the battle of Senef, in 1674, with 45,000 men against 65,000, commanded by the Prince of Orange. Had it not been for the cowardice of the Swiss infantry, who refused to fight, he would have destroyed the entire army of the enemy.

and suffered abuses and disorders to creep in everywhere. The great wars which he undertook, the four or five armies which he was obliged to support, had exhausted France, which did not always find in glory a consolation for its misery. It had been necessary to increase the taxes, even to sell the public offices, in order to have means for paying the troops. The authority of the parliament had often been eluded or disarmed. The blood of the nobility had flowed in torrents. The people groaned under the heaviest burdens; and if the sentiment of national grandeur abandoned them even for a moment, the greatness of the evil caused them to utter complaints, and drove them to revolt. I do not accuse the people: they are seldom wrong; they move only when they suffer; they agitate only to improve their condition, or at least to make it less unhappy. It is parties that are culpable, when, instead of striving to afford relief to the evils of the people, they apply themselves to rendering these evils more poignant and more bitter, by inflammatory declamations, thus driving the people beyond all bounds. I pity, in 1648, the people, naturally irritated by the increase of taxes, and by the disorders of the administration; I condemn the Fronde, which, in its chiefs, with few exceptions, was deceitful and corrupt, violent and mad; and I am in favor of Mazarin, without loving him or without being deceived in regard to his defects and his faults, because, after all, he served France well, conducting with great ability its affairs abroad, and diminishing, by the peace with Germany, its misery at home. I admire Condé in this first Fronde, for having resisted his own injuries, the antipathy which he felt for Mazarin, the solicitations of his own family, and of his sister. I shall blame him in the strongest terms when, unfaithful to his fortune and to his glory, sacrificing the part of a principal to that of an accessory, putting temper in the place of policy, he shall engage in the intrigues which he had spurned, and shall allow himself at first to humor, then to serve the Fronde.

He commenced very differently. In the beginning of the troubles, Condé, without having enough of the statesman to crush the sedition in its bud, preserved at least a lofty bearing towards the malcontents; he lent a careless ear to the proposals of his sister, and having no taste for popular agitations, and not more for the tumultuous and often ridiculous deliberations of the parliament, occupied only with the coalition of Spain and of the empire, he went, in the spring of 1648, to take command of the army of Flanders, resolved to strike a blow and to repeat the victory of Rocroy. Not being able to secure him, the malcontents wished at least to profit by his absence. While

Mazarin, for the best interests of the country, was demanding its utmost resources, and turning every thing into money, in order to raise additional troops, the Frondeurs, that is, a few of the great lords, supported by a part of the nobility, aroused the people and the parliament, who had not the least idea of the true situation of affairs; for the parliament was not a political assembly, and the people were simply aware that they were suffering. Mazarin, entirely occupied with the peril of the frontier, did not give enough attention to domestic dangers. He had kept very few troops near him, and one fine morning it happened that the Frondeurs took possession of Paris. The battle of the barricades followed close upon that of Lens. On his return, Condé found royalty humiliated, the parliament triumphing and dictating laws to the crown, the Duke de Beaufort, with whom he once thought of measuring swords in defence of the honor of his sister, freed from his prison of Vincennes, and master of Paris by aid of the populace who idolized him; the fickle and vain Abbé de Retz transformed into a tribune of the people; the Prince de Conti into a captain; M. de Longueville under the guidance of his wife and La Rochefoucauld; and the feeble Duke d'Orleans fancying himself almost a king, because he saw the queen humiliated, and because the Frondeurs, cunningly flattering his self-love, were treating him like a sovereign. Condé, at a glance, saw the situation of affairs and his duty also; and, without any hesitation, he offered his sword to the queen.

He had a stormy explanation with his sister.

It is pretended, that for some time their reciprocal tenderness had suffered more than one interruption; that, in 1645, Madame de Longueville had crossed the loves of her brother and Mademoiselle Du Vigean; that, in 1646, Condé, seeing her too intimate with La Rochefoucauld, had caused her to be called to Munster by her husband: but for this we have only the authority of the Duchess de Nemours,[1] and nothing is less probable. The passion of Condé for Mademoiselle Du Vigean extinguished itself, as we have seen, and as all contemporaries affirm. The attentions of La Rochefoucauld to Madame de Longueville may have preceded the embassy of Münster, but they were not observed until 1647, and it is at the close of this year that Madame de Motteville places them, while attributing them especially to the desire of La Rochefoucauld to share the credit of the sister with the brother. But it is very certain, that as soon as the latter remarked this connection, he disapproved of it entirely; and not succeeding in

[1] *Mémoires*, p. 19, etc. Villefore has followed Madame de Nemours.

his effort to rouse his sister from the intoxication of a first love, he passed from the most ardent affection to a bitter discontent. In the autumn of 1648, on his return from Lens, this connection had acquired its greatest strength, and become almost notorious. Madame de Longueville, directed by La Rochefoucauld, did then every thing in the world to gain her brother: she brought to bear upon him all her allurements, all her fondlings; she put into operation every thing which she thought might influence this passionate and fickle heart; she failed. He did not succeed in gaining over her his accustomed ascendency. They quarrelled and separated openly. Madame de Longueville plunged more deeply into the Fronde, and Condé applied himself to giving the new *Importants* a harsh lesson.

It is not my intention to enter into details. I wish simply to show that the brother and sister, in their opposite conduct, exhibited the same blood and the same audacity.

The queen had retired to Saint-Germain with the young king and all the government. Paris was under the absolute control of the Fronde. In spite of the first president, Molé, the l'Hôpital of the seventeenth century, it stirred up the parliament, by the aid of a few ambitious councillors and by seditious and mischievous inquests. It disposed of a great part of the Parisian clergy, through the coadjutor of the archbishop, Retz, who possessed and exercised all the authority of his uncle. It had continually at its head the two great houses of Vendôme and Lorraine, with two princes of the blood, the Prince de Conti and the Duke de Longueville, followed by a very great number of illustrious families. It gave law in the *salons*, thanks to a brilliant troupe of pretty women, who drew after them the flower of the young nobility. In short, the army itself was divided. Turenne, with his troops, who were stationed upon the borders of the Rhine until the perfect conclusion of the treaty of Westphalia, obedient to the suggestions of his eldest brother, the Duke de Bouillon, who wished to gain his principality of Sedan, had just raised the standard of revolt, and was threatening to place the court between his own army and that of Paris. Add that the parliament of the capital had sent deputies to all the parliaments of the kingdom, and that it was thus forming a sort of formidable parliamentary league in the face of monarchy. Condé took command of all the troops that remained faithful, and everywhere opposed the insurrection. He wrote himself to the army of the Rhine, which knew him, and which, after the route sustained by Turenne at Mariendal, had been led back by him to victory: these letters, supported by the proceedings of the government, succeeded in arresting the revolt; and Turenne, abandoned by his own soldiers, was obliged to fly to Holland.[1] At ease upon this subject, Condé marched upon Paris, and placed it in siege. Instead of disputing the ground, as he might have done, foot by foot, with the sedition, he allowed it the freest course, sure that the spectacle of licentiousness, which could not fail to appear, would, little by little, restore to loyalty those who had for a moment gone astray. He began by calling, in the name of the queen and through his mother, all his family to Saint-Germain. The Prince de Conti and M. de Longueville did not dare to disobey; but La Rochefoucauld saw that the Fronde was in the greatest peril; he hastened after these two princes; he brought them back to Paris, made the Prince de Conti generalissimo, placing under him the Dukes d'Elbeuf and de Bouillon, who shared authority with the Marshal de La Mothe Houdancourt, governor of Paris.[2] As to Madame de Longueville, she excused herself to the queen and to her mother on the grounds of her delicate situation, which would not permit her

---

[1] History of Turenne, by Ramsay, vol. ii., *Mémoires* de Turenne, p. lix., and the letters of Queen Anne, *Preuves*, p. viii., etc.

[2] Philippe de La Mothe Houdancourt, Duke de Cardonne, Viceroy of Catalonia, the husband of the beautiful De Toussy, who, upon strong suspicions, was arrested in 1647, and for whom M. de Longueville interceded from Munster.

to undertake the least fatigue. In fact, Madame de Longueville was in this condition, for the last time, in 1648, when, it must be confessed, her connection with La Rochefoucauld was well known. It was in this condition that, willing to share the perils of her friends, proud also of playing a part and of filling all the trumpets of fame, she acted the warrior as well as she was able. There is, it is said,[1] a portrait representing her as Pallas, just as, a little later, Mademoiselle was represented; her light hair covered with a helmet, and her soft eyes trying to wear a martial look. It is at least certain that she shared all the fatigues of the siege, that she was present at the reviews of the troops, at the parades of the citizen soldiery,[2] and that all the civil

---

[1] Father Lelong speaks of this portrait, by Poilly, in-fol.; we have sought for it in vain. It is probable that Father Lelong has referred to Madame de Longueville the fine portrait by Nicolas Poilly, the more or less authentic inscription of which is: *Mademoiselle de Montpensier*, with the equivocal arms, at once of the Orleans and of the Condés. We think, however, that it is Mademoiselle much embellished.

[2] The war movement of Paris, in this first Fronde, is well depicted in these couplets of an unpublished song of the *Recueil de Maurepas*, vol. ii., p. 43: *Blocus de Paris pendant le Carnaval de* 1649:

"Que vous nous causez de tourment,
Fâcheux Parlement!
Que vos arrests
Sont ennemis de tous nos interests!
Le carnaval a perdu tous ses charmes;
Tout est en armes,
Et les amours
Sont effrayés par le bruit des tambours.

and military plans were discussed before her. The memoirs of the times are full, in regard to this, of the most curious details. The hôtel de Longueville was continually filled with officers and generals; nothing was seen there but plumes, helmets, and swords.

Notwithstanding all this, the democratic spirit

La guerre va chasser l'amour,
Ainsi que la cour;
Et dans Paris
La peur bannit et les jeux et les ris.
Adieu le bal, adieu les promenades,
Les sérénades
Car les amours
Sont effrayés par le bruit des tambours.

Mars est un fort mauvais galant,
Il est insolent,
Et la beauté
Perd tous ses traits auprès de sa fierté.
L'on ne peut pas accorder les trompettes
Et les fleurettes;
Car les amours
Sont effrayés par le bruit des tambours.

. . . .

L'on ne voit plus d'esprit sensé;
Tout est renversé.
Le sénateur
Tranche à présent du grand gladiateur.
Les échevins ont quitté la police
Pour la milice,
Et le bourgeois
Croit avoir droit de réformer les loix.

Place Royale, où tant d'amans
Contoient leurs tourments,
Ou leur destin
Étoit souvent flatté par Constantin;
Tu n'entends plus, au lieu de tant d'aubades,
Que mousquetades,
Et les amours
Pour leurs jouëts n'ont plus que des tambours.

which had originated the Fronde, was not satisfied: it beheld with displeasure all the forces of Paris in the hands of the brother, of the brother-in-law, and of the sister of him who commanded the siege. Believing very little, and with reason, in the patriotism of the princes, the citizens demanded some sureties from the chiefs who might at any time betray them, and make peace, at their expense, with Saint-Germain. No one seemed to know how to appease this multitude, without which nothing could be done. It was then that Madame de Longueville showed that, if she had forgotten her true duties, she had retained the energy of her race and the intrepidity of the Condés. She took her young children, and, notwithstanding her delicate condition, proceeded to the principal quarter of the insurrection, the hôtel de Ville, placing herself in the hands of the people as a hostage, with all that was most dear to her.[1] Her example was followed by the Duchess de Bouillon.[2] "Imagine," says Retz, "these two beautiful persons upon the balcony of the

---

[1] *Le premier Courrier Français traduit fidèlement en vers burlesques*, 1649, p. 11.

> ". . . Ce seigneur prudent et sage (M. de Longueville)
> Donne ses enfans en ostage
> Avec Madame leur mamam,
> Qui n'est superbe comme un paon,
> Mais dont l'humeur douce et courtoise
> Cause avec la moindre bourgeoise."

[2] Eléonore-Catherine-Fébronie de Bergues, whose merit equalled her beauty: she married in 1684, and died in 1657.

hôtel de Ville; more beautiful because they appeared neglected, although they were not. Each held in her arms one of her children, who were as beautiful as their mothers. La Grève was full of people, even to the housetops; the men all raised cries of joy, and the women wept with tenderness.[1] There, on the night of the 28th of January, 1649, Madame de Longueville gave birth to her last child, a son, who was baptized by Retz in the church Saint-Jean-de-Grève, having for its godfather the Provost, for its godmother the Duchess de Bouillon, and who received the name of Charles de Paris;[2] the child of the Fronde, handsome, talented, and brave, who during his life was the troublesome hope, the melancholy joy of his mother, and the cause of her greatest grief in 1672, when he perished, in the passage of the Rhine, by the side of his uncle.[3]

---

[1] Vol. 1st, p. 221.

[2] *Le quatrième Courrier*, etc., p. 8:

> Né, dis-je, dans l'Hôtel de Ville,
> Il fut à Saint-Jean baptisé
> Et ce jour christianisé.
> . . . .
> Or, cette duchesse (de Bouillon) et la ville
> Tinrent le jeune Longueville,
> Et le nommèrent Carolus
> De Paris, et s'il en faut plus,
> D'Orléans; s'il en faut encore,
> Comte de Saint-Paul, que j'honore,
> Pour la ville étant le Feron (Prévôt des marchands).

[3] Charles de Paris, Count de Saint-Paul, was at first destined for the

For some time, Condé limited himself to subjecting Paris to a blockade more and more rigorous, and to small attacks, the effect of which was not very encouraging to the citizen troops. The gentry alone, even during their negotiations with Mazarin, fought well. They carried on the war in two modes, by the sword and by epigrams, songs and vaudevilles. The party of Mazarin, as may be conceived, accomplished very little with Madame de Longueville.[1] Condé himself, who had loved her so much, and who, after-

---

Church. There is a charming portrait of him, by Nanteuil, after Ferdinand, which represents him, at the age of eleven years, in 1660, with an abbé's cross, and this inscription upon the border: *Messire Charles Paris d'Orléans, Count de Saint-Paul, Abbé de St.-Remi de Reims*, etc. It is impossible to find a more graceful creature.

[1] Notwithstanding her sacrifices, democratic suspicions did not spare her. The *Recueil de Maurepas*, vol. ii., p. 417, contains a song under this title: *Les Honni soit-il de ce temps-ci*, in which Madame de Longueville has also her couplet:

"Servir pour ostage à la ville,
Croire son conseil très-utile,
Tandis que son mari nous vend;
Tous les jours estre à l'audience
Et ne résoudre que du vent,
Honni soit-il qui mal y pense!"

Another couplet from a Mazarin song, same volume, p. 255:

"Si l'amour de Marsillac
Fait durer ce miquemac,
De longtemps la paix n'est faite,
Et bientôt cette amourette
Nous mettra tous au bissac."

The collection of historical songs of the Arsenal, have a few other pieces more difficult to cite.

wards, will resume for her all his early tenderness, did not hesitate to ridicule her with the accustomed license of his language. He diverted himself very much at the expense of the martial spirit of his brother, the Prince de Conti, and he lampooned his adversaries, among others the Count de Maure,[1] the youngest of the Montemarts, with so much spirit and in such a soldierlike way, that he abused the troops and the citizens, when they dared to venture a few steps from the ramparts of Paris. To enable one to judge of the Fronde, even in this first period of its short, yet too long history, it will be sufficient to say that it had from that moment recourse to the only remaining enemy of France; that these great patriots, who continually reproached Mazarin with being a stranger, applied to Spain, and that an envoy of the archduke and of the Count de Fuensaldaigne was received, and heard in full parliament. Is it astonishing, after this, that in the course of a few years, the young Louis XIV. should, without attracting attention, enter this same parliament equipped for a ride and with whip in hand! Demagoguey produces necessarily tyranny, and, what is more sad, it therewith produces universal applause, bruising the hearts of those alone who had not merited it, and had

1 See chapter ii., verses of Condé on the Count de Maure.

simply desired a moderate liberty. When the shameful proposition was made to receive the Spanish envoy, the President de Mesmes, turning towards the Prince de Conti, addressed to him these severe words :[1] "Is it possible, sir, that a prince of the blood of France proposes to give audience upon the *fleurs de lys* to a deputy of the most cruel enemy of the *fleurs de lys !*"

Condé thought that it was time to bring matters to a close. He rendered more rigorous the blockade, and multiplied the attacks. It was in one of these attacks, at Charenton, February 9, 1649, that he lost his best friend, the younger Coligny, the brave d'Andelot, then Duke de Châtillon, the husband of Isabelle de Montmorency, one of the heroes of Lens, where he served in the capacity of a lieutenant-general, from which office he was about to be elevated to that of marshal ; he was, it is true, somewhat easy in his life and manners, but he promised to make

---

[1] Retz, vol. 1st, p. 247 : "The President de Mesmes, a man of capacity, uncle of him whom you now see. . ." This certainly means Henri de Mesmes, second of the name, eldest son of Jean Jacques de Mesmes, M. de Roissy, brother of Claude de Mesmes, M. d'Avaux, the skilful diplomatist of whom we have before spoken, brother also of Jean Antoine de Mesmes, whose eldest son was Jean Jacques de Mesmes, third of the name, successively counsellor to the parliament, president, grand-master of ceremonies, one of the forty of the French Academy, who died in 1678. His uncle, Henri de Mesmes, here spoken of, was president of the parliament from 1627 until his death, in 1650. We have excellent portraits of these four De Mesmes.

for France a captain of the strength of his brother-in-law, Montmorency Boutteville, Marshal de Luxembourg. Condé flew to the spot where Châtillon had just fallen, received him in his arms, and, bathing him with tears, caused him to be transported to Vincennes, where he drew his last breath.[1] All historians

---

[1] He was thirty-nine years of age, and left but one son, born after the death of his father, and taken off quite young in 1650. The following is the manner in which *Le Courrier François* relates, in its fifth number, the death of Châtillon :

. . . .
Navarre, brave régiment,
Lascha le pied vilainement.
Le Prince, adverti de l'escarre
Quo le canon fait sur Navarre,
Pensa crever dans son pourpoint,
Mais pourtant il ne creva point
Dans l'esperance de combattre
Le bourgeois qu'on tenoit à quatre,
Qui comme un diable juroit Dieu
Qu'il vouloit secourir ce lieu ;
Il dit de Condé peste et rage.
Mais le Prince à son advantage
Attendoit messieurs de Paris,
Comme le chat fait la souris.
Assuré sur son éminence,
Il avoit grande impatience
De taster le pouls au bourgeois
Qui ne sortit pas cette fois.
Il est prudent et craint la touche,
Joint qu'il n'aime pas la cartouche
Dont si fit son canon charger.
Paris n'en voulant point ronger,
Le Prince qui faisoit fanfare
Commit pour soutenir Navarre
Chastillon avec du renfort ;
Mais il l'envoyoit à la mort,
Car aussitôt au bas du ventre
Une balle de mousquet entre
Sans respecter ce duc nouveau,
Jeune, vaillant, adroit et beau,
. . . .
Aussi ne put pas s'empescher
Condé de lui donner des larmes
Et trahir le dieu des alarmes,
Ennemi de dame pitié ;
Mais ce furent pleurs d'amitié
A cause de leur parentage . . ."

The collections of Mazarinades for the year 1649, contain an *Agreeable and true narrative of what happened before the taking of the king in the city of Paris*, where the author puts in the mouth of the dying Châtillon a discourse against Mazarin. We have again : 1st, The Regrets of Madame de Chastillon on the death of her dear husband ; 2d, The Adieux made by M. de Chastillon, before dying, to his mother and his wife ; 3d, The Apparition of the spirit of M. de Chastillon to the Prince de Condé, etc.

agree in their descriptions of the great grief into which Condé was thrown by this death; it animated him still more against the Fronde. At the same time, it showed the court the importance of terminating a war which was sweeping so many brave men from both sides, to the great joy of Spain; and by showing in this place the point of his sword, and by speaking with firmness in that, he soon brought Paris and the parliament to ask peace, and Mazarin to give one which was humiliating to neither. He did not simply obtain a general amnesty; he did more: he represented that, in order to disarm the Fronde, it was necessary to listen to its legitimate complaints, which constituted its strength; and that royalty once replaced above all factions, it was wise to make it the origin of all necessary ameliorations. Hence the royal declaration of the 12th of March, 1649,[1] which annulled all the measures taken by the parliament during the preceding six months, which expelled the envoy of Spain, placed all the civil and military forces in the hands of the king, interdicted, during the remainder of the year 1649, every general assembly of the parliament, but which promised that Paris should see the return of the king, that the parliament

[1] See Madame de Motteville, vol. iii., p. 215. She confirmed the declaration of February of the same year, and those of May and of October, 1648.

should henceforth consult him in regard to extraordinary imposts, and that, if a treaty was made with Spain, the parliament should choose one of its officers to assist in its formation. The declaration said nothing in regard to the nobility, for the very simple reason that there was among them no general cause to be satisfied, and that private interests alone demanded attention.

It is amusing to read, in Madame de Motteville,[1] a piece entitled: "*Particular demands of Messieurs the Generals and others interested.* They each had, at Saint-Germain, deputies who treated for them. For example, the Duke de Beaufort was not contented with what had been privately offered to him. He asked much, because his heart was still swollen by the pride occasioned by the remembrance of his past favor. He wished the ministry to reward him for his chains and his imprisonment; he spoke proudly; he declared loudly that he would not make terms with Mazarin; and, carrying his resentment farther than others, he rendered the adjustment of his affairs more difficult. . . . Madame de Montbazon, who was beloved by the Duke de Beaufort, gave hopes that she would at least please him, if she could have what she desired. She obtained moneys and abbeys; and

---

[1] Vol. iii., p. 282, etc.

the Duke de Beaufort, who loved her, was pleased that this lady could profit by the inclination which he had for her."

In short, every one was, or strove to be contented. The Prince de Conti was the first who left Paris to salute the queen. He was presented by Condé, who made him embrace the Cardinal Mazarin. The Prince de Conti, in his turn, presented the Duke de Bouillon, La Rochefoucauld, the Count de Maure, and many others. M. de Longueville, who had gone to Normandy to arouse that province and its parliament, did not delay to return to offer his homage, and it was quite time for the beautiful and proud duchess to show her submission. The scene is worth relating: "I was alone,"[1] says Madame de Motteville, "with the queen, and she did me the honor to speak to me of the embarrassment testified by the Duke de Longueville in saluting her. As I knew that Madame de Longueville was about to enter, I arose, for I was on my knees beside her bed, and placed myself near to the queen, resolved not to stir, but to discover whether this witty princess would be more eloquent than the prince her husband. As she was naturally timid and apt to blush, all her care could not save her from the embarrassment which she experienced

[1] Vol. iii., p. 268.

on meeting the queen. I was sufficiently near to these two illustrious persons to know what they said; but I heard nothing except *Madame*, and a few words which she pronounced so low that the queen, who listened attentively to what she would say, could not comprehend a single sentence."

This same Madame de Motteville, so veracious notwithstanding her benevolence, so difficult in every thing concerning the queen, her mistress, does not hesitate to give to Condé the honor of the peace: "We should not forget to observe here the disinterested firmness of M. the Prince, who, without considering either his family or his friends, acted always for the interests of the king."[1]

It is true, for the memorable service which he had just rendered, Condé reaped scarcely any benefit; but his noble conduct increased the splendor of his last campaign of 1648; it added to his military titles those of defender and saviour of the throne, of pacificator of the kingdom, of arbiter and enlightened conciliator of parties; it gave the climax to his credit and to his glory. Happy would it have been, if, after having thus terminated this sad war, he had quitted the court and its intrigues, to seek other battle-fields, and to finish another war somewhat more useful and

---

[1] Vol. iii., p. 209.

more glorious to France—that which still remained with Spain! Happy also had been Madame de Longueville, if, taught by her own conscience, in her last interview with the queen, and by the shameful denouement of the miserable intrigues of which she had the secret, instead of still serving as their instrument, she had shown her courage in resisting them; if, after all the proofs of devotion which she had just given to La Rochefoucauld, she had strongly represented to him that, even for his own interest, a different course was necessary; that it would be better to look for fortune and honors by making himself esteemed, than by trying to be feared; that ambition as well as duty showed his place to be by the side of Condé, in the service of the State and of the king; that it was easy for him to obtain in the army some post, where he would have simply to march forward, trusting to his courage and his merit! But even if she had been wise enough to speak thus to La Rochefoucauld, she would not have succeeded in gaining his ear. This restless spirit, this ever-discontented vanity, pursuing by turns the most dissimilar objects, because it selected none within its reach, this *indefinable something*, as Retz[1] says, which was in La Rochefoucauld, caused him to abandon the great

[1] Portrait of La Rochefoucauld in Retz. Vol. i., p. 217.

and straight roads, and led him into by-paths full of precipices. The poor woman there follows him, and aids him in his extravagant and guilty designs. Receiving the law instead of giving it, she strives to promote the passion of another by devoting to his service all her coquetry and greatness of soul, her penetration and intrepidity, her attractive sweetness and indomitable energy. She undertakes to mislead Condé, to take away from France the conqueror of Rocroy and of Lens, and to give him to Spain. But let us not anticipate these unhappy times. We have now traced the last glorious days of Condé and the first faults of Madame de Longueville. Let us stop here; let us not enter upon the civil wars about to follow, impious wars, in which the brother and the sister will treasure up long remorse, in which the one will signalize himself by exploits so deplorable, that he will some day veil himself at Chantilly, for the sake of his own glory and of France, and in which the other will display the most brilliant qualities of mind, only to weep for twenty-five years among the Carmelites and at Port-Royal!

THE END.

Standard Historical Works.

I.

THE HISTORY OF ROME.

By THOMAS ARNOLD, D. D., Late Regius Professor of Modern History in the University of Oxford, and Head Master of Rugby School. 1 large vol. 8vo. pp. 686. Price $3.

II.

HISTORY OF FRANCE,

FROM THE EARLIEST PERIOD TO THE PRESENT TIME.

By M. MICHELET, Professor à la Faculté des Lettres, Professor à l'Ecole Normale, &c. Translated by G. H. Smith, F. G. S 2 vols. 8vo. pp. 480 and 400. Price $3 50.

III.

HISTORY OF GERMANY,

FROM THE EARLIEST PERIOD TO THE PRESENT TIME.

By FREDERICK KOHLRAUSCH. Translated from the last German Edition. By James D. Haas. With a complete index prepared expressly for the American edition. 1 vol. 8vo. pp. 487. Price $1 50; or, an Illustrated Edition, neatly bound, $2 50.

IV.

HISTORY OF ENGLAND,

FROM THE PEACE OF UTRECHT TO THE PEACE OF PARIS.

By LORD MAHON. 2 large vols. 8vo. pp. 590, 609, well printed, $4.

V.

A DIGEST OF THE LAWS, CUSTOMS, MANNERS, AND INSTITUTIONS OF THE ANCIENT AND MODERN NATIONS.

By THOMAS DEW, Late President of the College of William and Mary. 1 vol. 8vo. pp. 670, well printed. Price $2.

VI.

A MANUAL OF ANCIENT AND MODERN HISTORY.

By W. C. TAYLOR, LL. D., &c. 1 large volume, 8vo. pp. 866. Price 2 25.

VII.

THE HISTORY OF CIVILIZATION, FROM THE FALL OF THE ROMAN EMPIRE TO THE FRENCH REVOLUTION.

By F. GUIZOT. Translated by W Hazlitt. 4 vols. 12mo. $3 50.

www.ingramcontent.com/pod-product-compliance
Lightning Source LLC
LaVergne TN
LVHW020107110826
845151LV00001B/91

* 9 7 8 1 4 2 5 5 4 3 6 6 2 *